LIVING IN A NEW COUNTRY

by the same author

THE ROAD TO BOTANY BAY:
An Essay in Spatial History

Paul Carter

LIVING IN A NEW COUNTRY

History, travelling and language

faber and faber
LONDON · BOSTON

First published in 1992
by Faber and Faber Limited
3 Queen Square London WC1N 3AU

Phototypeset by Intype, London
Printed in Great Britain by
Clays Ltd, St Ives Plc

A CIP record for this book is
available from the British Library

ISBN 0–571–16329–7

10 9 8 7 6 5 4 3 2 1

For Bill and Margaret
in England

Contents

List of Illustrations

Acknowledgements

In 1989 the Literature Board of the Australia Council awarded me a one-year Fellowship; in 1990–91 I held a two-year Australian Research Council Grant administered through the University of Melbourne. The essays and other writings in this book have been greatly facilitated by this support and I would like to place on record my gratitude to these bodies for the generous interest they have shown in my work.

Chapter 2 was originally published in *Island in the Stream* (Sydney: Pluto Press, 1988): my thanks to the editor of that volume, Paul Foss, for his editorial advice and to the publisher for permission to reprint my essay. My sincere thanks also to Gael Newton who let me consult the typescript of her book, *Shades of Light: Photography and Australia, 1839–1988*: without her exhaustive photographic research, and her generosity in sharing it, my impression of the absence of any photographic records of Australian exploration in the period 1839–89 could not have been confirmed.

Chapters 5 and 7 first appeared in *Meanjin*, the latter under the name of Vin Williams; Chapter 4 was originally printed in *Scripsi* and later in *Poetry Nation Review*. My thanks to the editors of those journals for bringing to bear their stylistic and bibliographical skills. I also owe a special debt of gratitude to the editorial collective of the *Yale Journal of Criticism* who, with exemplary solicitude and persistence, first licked Chapter 1 into publishable form and then published it.

My thanks to the Australian National Gallery, the Art Gallery of New South Wales, the Newcastle Region Art Gallery, the National Gallery of Victoria, the Public Record Office, Victoria and the State Library of Victoria for permission to reproduce items in their collections. I am indebted to Lady Maisie Drysdale for allowing me to reproduce the works of Russell Drysdale and to Legend Press Pty Ltd, Sydney, sole copyright owner of Albert Namatjira's works, for permission to reproduce that artist's *Palm Valley*.

Introduction

Living in a new country can mean many things depending on where you lay the stress. For English painter and writer Adrian Stokes it signified a second birth. Entering Italy via another birth canal, the Mont Cenis tunnel, he had the impression of a world born in the same instant. He saw 'bright rectangular houses free of atmosphere, of the passage of time'. All history seemed to gather in the present: 'the sun shone, the sky was a deep, deep, bold blue'. In contrast with murky London and its nameless childhood horrors, there was in the Mediterranean a clear and perfect fit between words and things, inside and outside: the *mensa* of dreary Latin classes was transformed into a piece of furniture, decisively casting shadows.[1]

Stokes laid the stress on living. But the new vitality he experienced in the south was inseparable from its novelty: the peculiar zest he attributed to certain architectural milieux sprang from the sense they gave him of astonishment, surprise, of being in a state of permanent apparition. To be fully alive meant finding one's fantasies projected outwards and stabilized in stone. The novelty of Italy was proportional to the freedom it offered him from his old self. Impressed by the outwardness of Italian life, a quality as much aesthetic as temperamental, Stokes found the strength to turn his own psychic life inside out. The new country did not erase the old one – 'Rapallo could not oust Hyde Park' – but it did supply a position from which to speak, to begin again the laying down of habits.

Stokes's experience is so momentous, both emotionally and in terms of his life's work, that it is natural to regard it as uniquely personal. It therefore comes as something of a surprise to find his contemporary, the composer William Walton, reacting to the first sight of Italy in exactly the same terms: 'the train went into the tunnel, and when it came out on the Italian side they found the most marvellous sun. He never recovered from this moment of revelation, the shock of seeing such brilliant light . . .'[2] It seems that the newness of the new country is both more subjective than Stokes imagined and more objective. The revelation of light belongs more to the mode of arriving than to the place reached. At the same time the revelation can be shared and, it may be argued, characterizes a particular social milieu – that of the Sitwells and their artistic protégés.[3]

The novelty of living in a new country refers less to a place than to the manner of arriving there. The Berkeleian solipsism of imagining a country springing into existence as one sets foot in it, as if it were not already inhabited and did not harbour psychic (and other) monsters of its own, defines the motivation of the migrant: the power of identification with his new surroundings expresses an equally powerful desire to forget, to put the past well behind. But, as Stokes realized, this is not easily done or even perhaps desirable. Any orientation to the new environment depends initially on finding resemblances between it and the home left behind. The clarity of light (and life) here may throw the muddiness of one's former existence into clear and critical relief, but the very possibility of comparison implies a conceptual vocabulary that can be transported from one place to another.

If this *mensa* is more table-like here, it is because the new country is strangely familiar. Its novelty resides not in its absolute strangeness but in its strange familiarity. To arrive in Italy at least is to come home, to realize how foreign the land of one's birth really was. But here is the rub: the well-tenanted hills, the luminous piazzas with their 'ever-bustling happy trees' harbour disappointment. It is nice to find perfection in the flesh, to discover one's deepest bodily fantasies bodied forth in prospects of stone, but the very completeness of this new world, its self-containedness, threatens to re-enclose the migrant psyche, to reduce it once more to passivity.

There are those of us, including Stokes, who have found Italy imaginatively constraining, who have wondered where the voice might find a home amid these perfectly sounding and resounding spaces, and who have yearned for an environment less pictorial, less smugly eloquent, where instead, as the Australian writer Marcus Clarke put it, one might find 'the strange scribblings of Nature learning how to write'.[4] It was the aesthetic equivalent of this – an art in which forms palpably emerged from their natural matrix – that Stokes characterized as Venetian; and he championed it against what he called 'Florentine grace'.[5] It may be that there is a connection between Venetian art, unfinished, asymmetrical, its perspectives reversed so as to confront the contingencies of life in the historical world, and life in a new country, where the novelty is abiding and habits remain improvised, provisional and superficial.

For it is possible to lend living in a new country an entirely different intonation – to pronounce it as a question. Is life possible in a new country? What is a new country? It is to these more radical questions that the essays in this book attend – and not only essays but other writings, biographical, Utopian and polemical – for it would be a mistake to think the subject, any more than the country, is settled and that a single skein of discourse wound back and forth between the twin spindles of self and space, life and place, could adequately represent the openness of existence here, the uncertainty of its outcome. The solipsism of imagining countries as new has already been commented on: new countries are autobiographical fictions.

They are also poetic devices, creating metaphorical connections where more logical ones fail. For against Stokes's sense of entering a world where names belong, where words are washed clean and restored to their original place in the world, there are new countries in which entry depends on giving up one's former name and tongue and where the light does not illuminate the countryside but specifies its emptiness, its lack of names. Here the migrant does not arrive once and for all but continues to arrive, each new situation demanding a new set of responses, almost a new identity. And, as the newcomer improvises a host of accents, affiliations and interests to mirror and flatter the expectations of those he meets, so the question arises of how to connect. Displaced, disturbed by the emptiness of resemblances – 'Mediterranean', and yet . . . – the property of selfhood falls into doubt.

To cobble together a personality it may be necessary to accept the many voices repeating in one's head, to acknowledge that outside the context of their utterance one's opinions have very little value at all. So with writing in this situation: to salvage a thesis it will be necessary to abandon the linear narrative, to embrace a variety of voices. Of course my living in a new country is not representative: bureaucrats may find it hard to see the relevance of explorer narratives to the question of access for migrant women to community services. But as much as it is possible to rationalize the movement of these essays from, say, a hermeneutical view of the past to a more performative notion of history and writing, it is also possible to lay emphasis on the intuitive passage between chapters, on the kind of travelling these spaces imply.

For the gaps invite the reader to make a translation: what is the relationship between the imaginary architecture of Vincenzo Volentieri and a discussion of colonial perceptions of the corroboree? Partly it is quixotic, purely autobiographical. Any thematic continuity is coincidental. But in a new country mere coincidence is not an indication of the superficiality of appearances and the solipsism of one's knowledge: it is also a poetic principle, a way of coming to grips with the meaninglessness of words and things. The double aspect of life in a new country, the way in which phenomena simultaneously point towards the past and the future, and, as they do so, undermine the reality of appearances – buildings becoming mere façades, names enigmatic puns – brings into question the basis of communication.

How does one get from one place to another, whether in space or in dialogue, when the terms of reference constantly bifurcate and, instead of converging on the vanishing point of one's meaning, reverse perspective and converge only in the breast of the speaker? In this situation casual coincidences may be the only means of getting on: pantomimic imitations of other people may be the best way of bridging the gap, of fitting language to situation in a country where nothing as yet has a fixed meaning. In this situation, and so long as getting from one place to another is as much a matter of language and history as it is of travelling, the explorer narratives do bear directly on questions of political and social policy. A migrant poetics, an understanding of the rules of translation, the metaphorical leaps involved in living in a new country, may contribute more to psychic health than any number of bureaucratic initiatives.

Coming from Italy to Australia (as I did ten years ago), one comes from one south to another; but one also comes to a country where the meaning of the south is simultaneously deepened and reversed. In Keats's day surgeons recommended the south as a cure for consumption: Italy was acceptable, Egypt was better but, most curative of all, was Australia – as if, in Australia, the air of the south was redoubled in potency. Yet go too far and this dream of living in a new country evaporates into the historical and psychological miasma of the great southern land – the imaginary continent whose non-existence Cook established and for which Australia may be a mis-placed substitute.

The double meaning of the south has a particular nuance in Austra-lian consciousness, but it is a parable for the much more generalized experience of living in a new country. For despite the nationalist pundits the novelty of the country is not a property of the place, but a description of how it is seen. To live in a new country is to insist on the provisional nature of appearances, on the arbitrariness of names: this might be a table but it might as easily be a *tabula rasa*. Marcus Clarke's description of the Australian bush as pre-literate occurs in the course of an essay about a painting, Louis Buvelot's *Waterpool near Coleraine*. His imaginary 'dweller' who 'becomes fami-liar with the beauty of loneliness', who 'learns the language of the barren and the uncouth, and can read the hieroglyphs of haggard gum-trees' is an aesthetic prescription[6] – the novelty of the country lying in the way it is read, in the act of decipherment.

And the act of decipherment, which the essays in this book engage in, cuts both ways: it can read the difference of the country, and hence reinforce the rhetoric of nationalism; or it can read differently, insisting that the familiar novelties of the place are less fixed than they appear, less Italianate. But to read differently, and hence to find a way into the contemporary situation of the migrant wherever he and she may find themselves, it is perhaps necessary to do more than acquire the languages of many countries and to become an expert in translation.

The decipherment of the extinct languages of ancient Egypt and Mesopotamia depended on assuming that scripts could be understood without reference to the sounds they represented. Successful decipherment depended on not listening to phonetic patterns, on treating language as a logical system of unitary signs whose meaning was fully encompassed lexically and grammatically.[7] It is no accident that these translations occurred in the same culture that was incubat-ing the telegraph and the telephone, for they visualized and mathemat-icized language in much the same way. The aim of the palaeographers

5

no less than the engineers was to exclude arbitrary noise from the system, to maximize the efficiency of information transfer.

But in a new country language has yet to settle down into lines of writing, yet to detach itself from the contingencies of speaking and hearing; even between speakers of nominally the same tongue, it is fraught with misunderstandings. The tools of dialogue – pronunciation, intonation, accompanying gestures – are fluid in signification, frequently ambiguous and eclectic in style. Communication becomes less a matter of distilling the informational essence of the situation than of entering into a dialogical contract that, however hard to translate, represents the desire to make contact. This meta-communication, the irony of communicating the difficulty of communicating, is impervious to decipherment in terms of the logic of information systems.

In a new country it is precisely the noise that constitutes the novelty of the situation; and the analysis of the pre-semiotic realm of noise means removing social phenomena from their writerly and historical contexts and replacing them in the milieu of the spoken and the spatial. To understand the novelty of the situation it is not enough to decipher the strange scribblings of nature. The wind in the trees also has to be taken into account, and the difficulty of deciding whether that sound is a word, this space already a place with a history.

To those whose new country is older than ours, who were here before us, this preoccupation with the provisional nature of things can be maddening. To draw attention to the disablement of language, to build historical edifices from factual minutiae that decent history consigns to the margins is at best to retard social and economic progress; and at worst nothing more than a solipsistic projection, another fictional fantasy licensed by the decadent condition of the indigenous intellectual culture. But these patriots who preach a unique provenance and who urge us to settle down peaceably (and quietly) misunderstand the nature of our scepticism – just as their too assertive iconoclasm represses the migratory origins of their own rhetoric and the frailty of their claims to belong.

The newcomer's scepticism is not only a response to the difficulty of naming – of finding tables that answer to their name – it is an expression of disbelief that those already here seem oblivious to the

6

arbitrariness of their linguistic, historical and environmental destiny. They speak as if they cannot imagine living anywhere else and, even though they admit (and even exult in the fact) that the country they live in remains in many ways indescribably foreign, they refuse to acknowledge the stand-in nature of the cultural grid they impose on it. The newcomer recognizes the migrant psychology of the resident population, the gap between name and thing and the nightmare of living in a world of representations that never touch down in lived experience; but when he seeks to articulate this, he is greeted with silence, with furrowed brows and a tacit order to hold his tongue, to behave as an infant.

There is a suspicion that this unease with social forms displays a lack of attachment to the country. If Stokes's sense of a natural fit between society and landscape engenders a passionate loyalty, then its antithesis presumably breeds alienation and a puzzling willingness to flit overnight to another country. But, even if this is true, we have to ask whether this lightness of touch may not be a less destructive way of inhabiting a new country. The aesthetes may have loved Italy but, as any visitor to the museums of Boston and Washington well knows, this did not prevent some of them abetting the rape of its churches and palaces. And the antipodean parallel is obvious enough: it was not the uncountried workers but their propertied masters who exploited the land.

The formal end of the Cold War obliges us to face our double historical inheritance. The period of modernity has been characterized by the massive displacement of populations. We are almost all migrants; and even if we have tried to stay at home, the conditions of life have changed so utterly in this century that we find ourselves strangers in our own house. The true novelty is to live in an old country. But despite the normality of displacement, we find the migrant vilified. For alongside the fact of ethnic integration, we also witness a recrudescent nationalism, a yearning for the purification of racial roots and the extermination of alien elements. It hardly needs a psychologist to tell us that the new Fascist scapegoats the migrant because he recognizes in him his own repressed desires, his own shame.

In this situation it becomes more than ever urgent to develop a framework of thinking that makes the migrant central, not ancillary, to historical processes. We need to disarm the genealogical rhetoric of blood, property and frontiers and to substitute for it a lateral account of social relations, one that stresses the contingency of all definitions of self and the other, and the necessity always to tread lightly. Living in a new country is not an eccentricity: it is the contemporary condition. We live as others allow us to live, creating meeting places as we go along. Such places may not be monumental, they may be nothing more than encounters, spatial events that leave behind them less litter than a campsite, yet they can form the basis of a social fabric, one that does not suppress the contingency of its community but makes its migratory haphazardness the material out of which it weaves its identity.

To elaborate such a framework is the task of another book, but the writings collected here intend to give at least some of the background to life in that new country. In an oblique and non-programmatic way they argue that the new country is never simply a geographical location and always a historical and poetic destiny. And part of its appeal is that its endless deferral of arrival, while it can induce a sense of placelessness and depression, is also a formula for life – a prolongation of the journey that cheats death. But none understood this better than Stokes who, in a poem significantly titled 'Anniversary Day, May 29th: Entrance to Santa Sophia Refused', wrote:

> The continents are ceaselessly abridged.
> No entry finishes.[8]

1   Plotting

Australia's Explorer Narratives as 'Spatial History'

Although explorers occupy a prominent place in Australia's nationalist pantheon, the significance of their narratives as distinctive forms of *historical* writing has not received serious attention. Perhaps one follows from the other. The explorer journals describe the country in its pre-mapped state: but this state is soon superseded, not only by the explorers' own draft charts, but by later travellers linking up their routes to other routes. Before long the one-sidedness of the first journey has been replaced by the ubiquitous view of the map. The explorer's heroism remains and can be annexed to the national destiny, but his experiences along the way are now historically obsolete. His day-by-day narrative, with its uncritical detailing of local conditions, survives, if at all, as an index of one man's experience – a fertile source for biographers and film-makers, but without any practical effect on people now living in the country he first traversed.

The Australian literature of exploration is extensive: in the first hundred years of European colonization government and private interests sponsored a series of expeditions designed to solve the enigma of the Australian centre. Coastal explorers like Matthew Flinders (1801–2), P. P. King (1818–22) and J. L. Stokes (1840–42) looked for promising estuaries that might indicate the existence of rivers draining from the interior. Hypothesizing inland seas and Nile-like rivers, inland explorers like Charles Sturt (1828–9, 1844–5), Sir Thomas Mitchell (1831, 1835–6, 1848), Ludwig Leichhardt (1844–5) and Edward John Eyre (1840–41) converged on the centre. And although it was left to men like the Gregory brothers (1859), J. M. Stuart (1861–5) and Ernest Giles (1871–6) to establish the uniformity of the centre with other semi-arid regions of Australia, this did not prevent the earlier travellers from producing elaborate reports of their excursions, often incorporating ethnographic and other scientific

9

material. Despite their lack of discoveries, few explorers felt able to describe their journeys in under 600 pages and two substantial volumes.

The literary merit of the journals as narratives was recognized by contemporaries. According to one reviewer, Sir George Grey's journals combined 'the interest of a romance with the permanent qualities of an historical or scientific treatise'. Eyre's journals produced in another reader 'a feeling similar to that which follows the enjoyment of a pleasant work of fiction'.[1] But to subsequent readers and historians this stress on the fictional has seemed to undermine the journals' claims to factual accuracy. As titles like *The Chipped Idol* and *The Hero as Murderer* (referring to Sturt and Eyre respectively) indicate, biographers have assumed the journals' transparently autobiographical motives and asked what their elaborate rhetoric was designed to conceal.

Although it ignored the explorers' claims to geographical accuracy, there were some grounds for this biographical reductionism. Unlike a conventional narrative history, the journal of exploration featured the historian's own achievements. The published account was a revision and elaboration of rough journals kept in the field: in some cases the rough journals were reworkings of yet earlier notes. Hence the published narrative was not based in any naïve sense on primary sources: nor were the explorer's sources available for critical scrutiny. It was easy to conclude that the writer's chief ambition was not to record history but to *make* it – to establish his own historical significance. In preparing his *Journal of an Expedition into the Interior of Tropical Australia* the Surveyor-General of New South Wales, Major Mitchell, borrowed the structure of Camoes's *Os Lusiadas* – a poem he had translated. The rationale for this lay not simply in Mitchell's desire to represent his journey as an epic of colonization, but in the recognition of a parallel between the poet's life and his own. Mitchell believed that, like Vasco da Gama, Camoes had made the voyage to India: in celebrating Christianity's advent in the east Camoes had to some extent recapitulated his own life story.[2]

But this tendency to regard Australia's explorer narratives as purely personal accounts of a journey – to treat them as no different from other travellers' tales – obscures their historical significance as narratives of a *first journey* where, as yet, no road exists (and where, by extension, the narrative itself cannot proceed confidently forward). As I want to argue here, the historical meaning of the exploration journals is inseparable from their *spatial* occasion. The fact that the way ahead forms the subject matter of the narrative not only ensures its historical value apart from its possible biographical interest; it also serves to distinguish it from other forms of narrative history.

Explorer narratives are characteristically discontinuous. They also lack 'plot'. On these two grounds alone they are of theoretical as well as historical interest: the means by which they advance the story are pertinent to understanding the mechanisms of fiction; they also suggest that the current narrative/non-narrative debate in historical circles is based on a false opposition. It may be that, under certain conditions, narrative *can* respect the discontinuity of historical action. But first it is necessary to characterize the journals in more detail.

I

Our strange language was repeated as glibly by the rocks of Australia as if they were those of our native land.

John Lort Stokes

Australian exploration literature is distinguished by the absence of two thematic devices contributing profoundly to the 'emplotment' of, say, Indian and African travel journals. First, with a few notable exceptions, Australia's indigenous population plays no determining role in structuring them. The attitude of local Aborigines may decisively influence the explorer's success or failure – in the case of Edmund Kennedy's ill-fated Cape York expedition (1847) bringing about his death – but they rarely enjoy any narrative status. They are not perceived as incipient plot-makers likely to determine the journey's ultimate results but, when they appear at all, are as motiveless as the 'natural productions' of the country. Rather than welcoming the Aborigines as a source of local information, the explorer represses their presence, cultivating instead an attitude of studied indifference. Sturt writes at one point, 'A small tribe of about sixty had collected to receive us, but we passed on without taking any notice of them.'[3] And, although Sturt's behaviour may have been determined by a recognition of his vulnerability to attack, it also embodies a narrative

11

attitude, a determination not to provoke irrelevant 'subplots'. As Grey remarks, 'No signs whatever of the natives had been again seen; this restored my confidence . . .'[4]

Second, Australian journals of exploration differ from classic accounts of colonial exploration elsewhere in that they do not culminate in major discoveries. With the exception of Sturt's Murray River, the explorers fail on the whole to locate economically, or even conceptually, profitable geographical objects. E. J. Eyre concluded a narrative of over 500 pages, published in two well-illustrated volumes, by remarking:

> I have no important rivers to enumerate, no fertile regions to point out for the future spread of colonization and civilization, or no noble ranges to describe from which are washed the debris that might form a rich and fertile district beneath them; on the contrary, all has been arid and barren in the extreme.[5]

Nor could Eyre claim to have greatly extended geographical knowledge of those regions he had traversed. Whether attempting unsuccessfully to cross the 'horseshoe' of salt lakes to the north of Adelaide or following the coastline westwards round the Great Australian Bight, Eyre had been unable 'from the circumstances under which I was placed . . . ever to deviate from my direct line of route, either to examine more satisfactorily the character of the country, or to determine whether the watercourses, some of which occasionally bore the character of rivers (though of only short course), had embouchures opening to the sea or not'.[6]

Eyre's experience was not exceptional. Sturt, Mitchell, Leichhardt and others all failed to find the longed-for change in the country that would signify water and the triumphant conclusion of their journey. And it was a frequent criticism of these and other explorers that their descriptions of places, not to mention their latitude and longitude readings, were too rough to be of much use to later travellers. Nevertheless they industriously reported their failures – or, according to the biographical myth, sought to divert attention from them by recasting their diaries in the form of a heroic or mock-heroic picaresque novel.

If this was their aim though, they singularly failed: for instead of capitalizing on such external phenomena as they did find, whether human or geological, the explorers steadfastly drew attention to their absence. Far from seeking to 'bunch' their day-to-day entries into significant (if fictional) episodes serving to advance the narrative, they dwelt on their failure to advance, the repeated experience of disappointment. Far from suppressing intervals of inactivity as uninteresting, they expatiated on their cloudy lack of definition. Signs of change, far from indicating a change, usually foretoken the opposite: an absence of change, a deferral of dramatic action. Instead of subordinating incidental details to the swelling theme of discovery, they seem to invert narrative conventions, subordinating any larger theme to the relating of details.

A passage chosen almost at random from Sturt's *Two Expeditions into the Interior of South Australia* illustrates these and other aspects of their narrative style:

> We returned to the camp, after a vain search for water, and were really at a loss what direction next to pursue. The men kept the cattle pretty well together, and, as we were not delayed by any preparations for breakfast, they were saddled and loaded at an early hour. The circumstances of there having been natives in the neighbourhood, of whom we had seen so few traces of late, assured me that water was at hand, but in what direction it was impossible to guess. As the path we had observed was leading northerly, we took up that course, and had not proceeded more than a mile upon it, when we suddenly found ourselves on the bank of a noble river. Such it might in truth be called, where water was scarcely to be found. The party drew up on a bank that was from forty to forty-five feet above the level of the stream. The channel of the river was from seventy to eighty yards broad, and enclosed an unbroken sheet of water, evidently very deep, and literally covered with pelicans and other wildfowl. Our surprise and delight may be better imagined than described.[7]

Thus far the narrative respects fictional conventions: an unforeseen obstacle (a lack of water) provokes a crisis (an immediate threat to the lives of both men and animals); the crisis precipitates a drama of search and discovery in which the human interest centres on the men's display of moral and physical courage. Our identification with their interests ensures we find the location of water cathartic.

13

But at this point the narrative conventions break down. The resolution of conflict turns out to be apparent only. For they quickly find that 'the water was so salt as to be unfit to drink'. Sturt comments:

> Whence this arose, whether from local causes, or from a communication with some inland sea, I knew not, but the discovery was certainly a blow for which I was not prepared. Our hopes were annihilated at the moment of their apparent realisation. The cup of joy was dashed out of our hands before we had time to raise it to our lips.[8]

Far from converging on a climactic discovery, the narrative works to defer conclusions, to dissipate any firmness of either narrative or spatial direction. Instead of hypotheses leading to their confirmation or denial, they simply lead to other hypotheses: the Aboriginal path leading northwards, which promises escape from a situation in which all directions are hypothetical escape routes, leads instead to another bifurcation and reversal. The 'river' not only fails to provide an eventful conclusion to this section of narrative: it stimulates another set of undecidable narrative and spatial alternatives; for perhaps the river leads to the inland sea, or perhaps not. Alluding to the anastomosing nature of Australian creeks – their tendency to distribute surface water rather than channel it into tributaries – Sturt in the same journal comments of another 'river': 'In any other country I should have followed such a water-course, in hopes of its ultimately leading to some reservoir; but here I could encourage no such favourable anticipation.'[9] The same may be said of the narrative: constructed around absences, it sails from absence to absence without ever reaching home.

This inversion of narrative expectations is not only a structural and thematic peculiarity: it has a lexical and syntactic aspect. For the explorer-writer's inability to advance the narrative smoothly is intimately connected to his inability to *name* phenomena accurately. In the above passage the 'river' turns out not to be a river in any conventional sense. Nor can it be described as a sea. Signifying its own opposite, it can only be named in terms of what it is not. Its real name remains unknown. And *this* dilemma can only be hinted at rhetorically – by way of the 'cup of joy' figure of speech. Only now it is the figure of speech that describes their situation (their disappointment) literally, while the historical action of drinking from the river turns out to be a mime, a rhetorical flourish without any basis in reality.

The open-endedness of the journals, then, is bound up with an inability to name – and hence to fix – phenomena definitively. The nightmare that threatens to engulf the explorers is not simply that of a lingering death in the desert: it results from the falseness of appearances, from the fact that, as Stokes observes, the country echoes back the explorer's words: it substitutes mimicry for dialogue, with the result that the explorer is made uncomfortably aware that the country he is describing may exist nowhere except in his conjecture. As the explorer Warburton reflected, 'It is useless to hazard opinions in this country, for there is not a single thing upon which we have formed strong conjecture and expectation that has not turned out in the end quite different from our anticipations.'[10] Since, when the country speaks, it lies, silence alone reliably describes it.

Nevertheless, if the journals have a single aim or 'plot', it is to name the country travelled comprehensively: it is the explorers' repeated inability to do this that constitutes the drama of the narrative, the desire that propels it forward. But this drama is as much a linguistic as a historical one. For in the absence of proper names the explorers were constantly obliged to resort to syntactic and lexical stratagems which, if unable to define spatial experience unequivocally, could at least allude to its unnameability. The 'places' that names corresponded to might be locations in the text as much as geographical objects.

Hence, on a later expedition, Sturt writes: 'The peak itself was nothing more than a sandy eminence on which neither tree or [sic] shrub was growing, and the whole locality was so much in unison with it, that we called it "Mount Misery".'[11] Here is a natural feature ('a sandy eminence') that becomes a place by being named for what it is not – a 'peak'. But to name this non-place with which the locality is 'so much in unison' means improvising a figure of speech, a cultural oxymoron – 'Mount Misery'. For here is a place where the normal associations of words cease to function. But where is this place outside the text itself? What Sturt effectively creates here is a place in the narrative, not so much a place-name as a name-place that serves to record the absence of a place in reality. The sentence as a whole names, as directly as it can, the absence of nameable things. In this context lexical and syntactic elements are deployed *metaphorically*, to evoke an experience that language can only falsify. Thus, at one place Eyre observes, 'As fast as we arrived at one point which had bounded our vision (and beyond which we hoped a change might occur), it was but to be met with the view of another [unbroken line of cliffs] beyond.'[12] If Sturt can only differentiate the landscape by fashioning a cultural oxymoron, Eyre has no choice but to describe it by inventing a 'point' – a rhetorical place that functions to name the *absence* of such places in spatial reality.

Even these remarks show, I think, that the explorer narratives cannot be regarded simply as retrospective fictions, self-seeking glosses of historical events. Rather they represent a 'working through' of the historical material, an attempt to constitute experience historically, to understand how the non-temporal consciousness of space – the phenomenon of space as an infinity of directions – might be an essential ingredient in the *psychic* occupation of the new country. But if the explorer journals can be classified as historical narratives, albeit of a rather special kind, it remains to ask what they narrate. What is it that gives the discontinuous aggregation of details its narrative direction? And can the narrativizing impulse be said to represent a historical experience or simply to falsify it in the interests of producing 'a feeling similar to that which follows the enjoyment of a pleasant work of fiction'?

2

At the latter part of my journey, I had, as it were, retraced the whole course of my life.

Ludwig Leichhardt

Difficulties in naming, the necessity of working through experiences that resist easy rationalization, the urge to repeat (to represent) beginnings: all these characteristics of the explorer journals irresistibly suggest psychoanalytical analogies. And since a number of critics have drawn our attention to the narrative strategies Freud himself employs, most notably in his enigmatic text *Beyond the Pleasure Principle*, in order to realize his own 'masterplot', it is possible to see how such analogies need not lead to a new form of biographical closure (the psychobiography) but may instead illuminate the way in which 'plot as a logic of narrative' operates in the explorer literature.[13]

In a loose but suggestive way the explorer-writers themselves frequently compare the process of journeying to the experience of dreaming. At a moment of great crisis, when the lives of his men depend on their leader's ability to navigate his little boat south for help, George Grey reflects, 'This unknown coast, which so many had anxiously yet vainly wished to see, passed before our eyes like a panorama or a dream, and ere many years have hurried by, it is probable that the recollection of this day will be as such to me.'[14] Here the process of repression is, as it were, caught at the moment of its formation: further, by displacing his anxiety for his landbound and beleaguered men into the antithetical image of effortless mobility – the coast sliding by – he has already inaugurated the dreamwork that, in future years, will make this experience so difficult to recover. Writing up the traumatic experience, by narrating it obliquely in this way, Grey seeks to ally it to his own life-trajectory, to avoid 'the backward path that leads to complete satisfaction' (the avoidance of all dangers). He seeks to avoid the trauma of mere repetition. But it is debatable whether he achieves this: for, calling his trauma a dream, he represses reality. Any analyst treating Grey would first have to disentangle the dream within the dream, the dream that was not dreamt!

But this may be the point: the dreamlike states that the explorers report, and which their narratives simulate when they glide effortlessly from one discontinuity to the next, from one reversal to another, are *waking* states. Their content, however unpleasurable, is not repressed. Far from seeking what Freud calls 'the backward path', their pleasure appears to lie in *deviating* as far as possible. Peter Brooks, it will be remembered, makes extensive use of this spatial metaphor in *Reading for the Plot*. In nineteenth-century novels, he writes, plot is a condition of 'deviance and abnormality'. Deviance is, he argues, 'the condition for life to be "narratable": the state of normality is devoid of interest, energy, and the possibility for narration. In between a beginning prior to plot and an end beyond plot, the middle – the plotted text – has been in a state of *error*: wandering and misinterpretation.'[15]

Characterized by suspension of the normal rules of language and logic, the explorer's world is eminently narratable in Brooks's sense.

But in another respect the explorer journals are quite unlike Victorian fiction: for, while in the novel deviation implies a trajectory, a goal beyond itself, in the exploration journals deviation is an end in itself.

Another way to express this difference is to suggest that the explorers' narratives lack an unconscious. Building on the model of psychic life intimated in *Beyond the Pleasure Principle*, Brooks shows that a narrative's dynamic depends in part on an unresolved tension between conscious and unconscious elements. In Freud, 'the narratable life of the organism is seen as a detour, a deviance from the quiescence of the inorganic which has been maintained through the dynamic interaction of Eros and the death instinct'.[16] Similarly in fiction 'the plots of repression and social advancement are threatened by a repetitive process obscurely going on underneath and beyond them'.[17] But narrative repetition is also the means whereby the plot achieves identity and direction. Only by repeating what has been repressed can the fictional life-plot unfold: 'we cannot really move ahead until we have understood that still enigmatic past'.[18] But in the explorers' journals we appear to have narratives without a plot – narratives in which repetition, far from marking a neurotic retreat from life and its pleasurable dangers, is both a source of pleasure and a means of getting on.

Avoiding as far as possible the subplot of Aboriginal encounter, and substituting minute accounts of the foreground for any maplike comprehension of the journey as a whole, the explorer sublimates his desire of arrival and finds satisfaction in the certainty of disappointment. The lack of any sign of ending provides the motive for going on. In this environment, further efforts to advance are the prelude to yet profounder retreat. There is no conflict comparable to the interaction between Eros and the death instinct: here travelling itself is the assurance of satisfaction. Significantly, 'the charm of novelty', a cliché of the explorer-writers, describes an attitude towards travelling, rather than a reaction to novelties actually discovered. The explorer travels in a permanent state of expectation; and he appears to desire nothing more than this. The principle of repetition is not a bar to the fulfilment of his goal: it becomes the goal itself.

Consequently, whatever *physical* difficulties the explorer may meet, *psychically* exploration signifies freedom from care, a return to the fantasy of immediate wish-fulfilment; in this sense, each day's entry, necessarily unclimactic and repetitive, stands in a metonymic relation to the text as a whole, one that is as open-ended as its individual parts. The *locus classicus* for this position occurs in the journals of the coastal surveyor John Lort Stokes. Describing the pleasure of expectation, he writes:

> To the production of the emotions I allude to, beauty of landscape is scarcely necessary. We strain forward incited by curiosity, as eagerly over untrodden heath, or untraversed desert, as through valleys of surpassing loveliness, and amid mountains of unexplored grandeur; or perhaps, I should say, more eagerly, for there is nothing on which the mind can repose, nothing to tempt it to linger, nothing to divert the current of its thoughts. Onward we move, with expectation at its highest, led by the irresistible charm of novelty, almost panting with excitement, even when every step seems to add certainty to the conviction that all that is beyond resembles all that has been seen.[19]

Here there is progress because there is no progress; a 'steady-state' of expectations is substituted for the prospect of eventual return. In fact, to be without lines of associative reasoning is to be freed of the need to go over old ground. In a psychoanalytical, as well as a geographical, sense, you are where you want to be because you were never there before, nor ever will be again. The repetition of appearances is a formula that overcomes the opposition between reality and pleasure, between motion and stasis, quiescence and change.

In the explorer journals it is the absence of plot-like elements – the 'important rivers' or 'noble ranges' that would have obliged (and enabled) the explorer to 'deviate' to an end – that becomes the plot of the narrative. The story to be told is replaced by the act of telling. The interest of the narrative lies in seeing how it goes on, in what happens where nothing happens. In this sense, the plot may be nothing other than the rhetorical deception practised by the narrative itself. But, if so, it is a deception that does not depend on the literary skills of the writer but is inherent in the nature of his experience. In exploring, Stokes writes, 'all are here on an equal footing; the most finished writer and the most imperfect scribbler are on the same level'.[20] In describing the absence of 'novelties' there is, it seems, no place for the larger plot that characterizes fiction. All are on the 'same footing' not least because there is no other way to go, no other route that would bring them home more quickly. 'Here', it seems, is a state of constant excitement, a steady-state of expectation.

The onward motion of such a text cannot be plotted as a parabolic curve: if the x axis represents the life process dominated by the death instincts and the y axis the deviant energy of Eros (the space of the plot), the narrator's psychic education does not resemble a parabolic curve, a birth-to-death trajectory climbing high above the horizontal before sinking back to meet it again. Rather it resembles a line drawn parallel to the x axis, but located within the realm of consciousness. This is not to deny that the explorer confronted extreme physical difficulties, but even these exerted a constant pressure on the explorer that was preferable to the chaotic resistances encountered at home. Hence Eyre may complain: 'Such, indeed, has been the sterile and desolate character of the wilderness I have traversed, and so great have been the difficulties thereby entailed upon me, that . . . I have never been able to deviate in any way from the line I was pursuing . . .'[21] But these difficulties are pleasures compared with the frustration felt in not being able to travel at all. Pent up at Fowler's Bay awaiting official instructions, Eyre 'sighed for freedom':

> Fatigue, privation, disappointment, disasters, and all the various vicissitudes, incidental to a life of active exploration had occasionally, it is true, been the source of great anxiety or annoyance, but all were preferable to that oppressive feeling of listless apathy, of discontent and dissatisfaction, which resulted from the life I was now obliged to lead.[22]

Despite resembling the vicissitudes of life – and hence belonging to the plot's deviant realm of 'machination' – the world of exploration is characterized by a return to an earlier state. Hence the 'disasters' of travelling are not in Freud's sense dangers that inhibit the maintenance of the pleasure principle, and thus launch the explorer on the road to psychic maturation. Rather they represent a way of avoiding that deviation into adult responsibility. The true danger that confronts the explorer lies in the false 'home' of social life: his psychic ambition is to come home by another route or, better, to defer homecoming as long as possible. In this sense the narrative impulse behind the explorer journals recalls the instinct of self-preservation that, says

Freud, ensures 'the living organism struggles
against events (dangers, in fact) which might help it
aim rapidly – by a kind of short-circuit'.[23] The most sig
of exploration is that it allows *no* deviation, except the d
constant repetition.

However, repetition is not simply intrinsic to the material: it
a means of structuring its telling. For, while the explorer is rele
from the angst associated with the reality principle, he does not have
his way. Rather, unpleasurable angst has been replaced by an anxiety
that is, as it were, pleasurable. Freud defines angst as 'a particular
state of expecting the danger or preparing for it, even though it may
be an unknown one'.[24] This is precisely the explorer's permanent
state: only now it yields him pleasure. And it does so because, instead
of focusing on the unknown and the dangerous, he concentrates on
the experience of its infinite deferral; so long as he continues in this
state, he knows no arrival, no return; he enjoys a kind of immortality.
Repetition, the act of putting one foot in front of the other, one day's
events after another, ensures the pleasure never ends because it is
never completed.

In this sense the explorer narrative marks a deviation back from
plot into narrative, towards a psychic place simultaneously over the
horizon of the past and the future, where it is never necessary to
rationalize loss by improvising a literary variation on the Freudian
infant's 'fort-da' game. As Major Mitchell wrote in the draft Introduction to his *Three Expeditions into the Interior of Eastern Australia*:

> In exploring I have felt my heart at peace. No angry passion rises
> to disturb the silent progress of the surveyor, to shake the hand or
> dim the brow. No irritable humours are set afloat. You have no
> absurd opinions to combat, no point to strain, no adversary to crush,
> no fool to annoy you. You are actuated by fear or favour of no man.
> There is no juggling here, no sophistry, no intrigue, no tampering
> with the evidence, no attempt to make black white, white black, but
> you may resign yourself into the hands of a greater power, that
> of Nature, with the simplicity of a child, the devotion of an
> enthusiast.[25]

Exploring clears the path of those challenges that normally bar pro-

۸ess. His submission to Nature, like the submission of the instincts to Ananke, the necessity of mortality, is accompanied by the pleasure of immediate gratification, the prospect of continuous wish-fulfilment provided by the mere fact of travelling. This narrative impulse, the conscious determination to make one's life a pure narrative, to make a virtue of repetition, is not repressed: indeed, the eschewment of temporal plot may be said to be the exploration literature's chief formal characteristic.

If the explorer narratives avoid the deviation of plot, they nevertheless cultivate every possible narrative deviation. Barthes refers to the 'dilatory space' of narrative – the complex series of reversals, postponements and errors that both retard and bring about the fulfilment of the plot.[26] In the explorer texts a dilatory space may be said to characterize the whole space of action. But it is more than a metaphor. For, as I have suggested, in the exploration literature the narrative impulse is not motivated by any expectation of temporal closure, return or denouement. Temporally, the explorer narratives are plotless. But *spatially* it is another matter. After all, these journeys, although dreamlike, did not take place in the unconscious. Nor were they elaborate fictions repressing threatening psychic material. Mitchell may have given his Fourth Expedition journal an elaborate literary structure, but this did not prevent him asserting in his preface, 'The new geographical matter is presented to the public with confidence in its accuracy.'

Rather than think of the explorer writings as disguised autobiography or failed fictions, we should recognize that their true subject is *historical space* – spatiality as a historical experience. The world they describe cannot be reduced to a succession of picturesque backdrops against which they act out their personal dramas; the explorers were not travellers visiting named and nameable regions. Their journals describe an earlier condition in which historical time has not peeled off from spatial contingency and in which spatial experience has not settled down into a network of places (and place-names). The explorers were not simply travel writers; for, unlike the purveyors of picturesque places, they travelled without roads. What they described, then, was not a succession of places, but the plotting of a track along which historical time might later flood in on a tide of names.

Hillis Miller has pointed out that one etymology for diegesis, the narration of events, gives as the word's original meaning the redrawing of a line already drawn.[27] Plotting, in this context, is the desire to bring out the meaning of that line, to endow it with form, to bend it perhaps into the ring of eternal return. But the activities of the explorers precede this: their task is to draw the line for the first time, to give space a narrative form and hence the possibility of a future history, a history that will subdivide, and even efface, their own narratives in the interest of a thousand domestic plots. In this sense, writing up their journeys, they redrew symbolically a line already drawn: they lent their spatial experience narrative form. The transformation of spatiality into a historical experience constitutes the plot of the explorer journals.

But, after all, it is not so easy to escape from the unconscious. Donald Spence has argued that the process of transference involves an enactment of the past in the service of discovering historical meaning and direction.[28] Given the relative obscurity of the explorers' journals, their lack of influence on Australian writing, their absence from educational curricula, one is tempted to wonder whether the transference they attempted was successful: their maps and place-names have been enshrined in roads and towns and railways, but what of their spatial history, their attempt to narrate the open-endedness of appearances? There is at the heart of the journals a paradox: that, in order to name the emptiness, the unnameable otherness of their experience, they must, like Sturt stooping to drink, annihilate its reality. The more elaborate their geographical parapraxes, the clearer it becomes that the country resists their efforts to bring it into symbolic circulation.

This struggle to name space, to speak it as place, constitutes at least a part of the explorers' historical interest. But it also defines their pathos – and the fragility of the cultural tradition which makes them foundational figures. For the country, of course, was not empty, but replete with languages and directions. The depressive emptiness that the explorers attributed to it, and which prevented them from achieving any kind of dialogue with the local people, condemned them to inhabit a mirror state – where often all they could see in the distance was a mirage resembling the illusion of their own presence. And, while they sought to combat this with an attention to detail (refusing to subordinate the order of space to the imperatives of

23

narrative plot), the yawning otherness they could only name by not naming was of their own making.

An attention to the spatial history contained in their writings may begin the process of dismantling the mirror. In the meantime it goes some way towards explaining the continuing obsession in Australian culture with unnameable, because mythic, places.

3

The horizon was unbroken . . .

A. C. and F. T. Gregory

Although organized into a narrative, the content of the explorers' journals does not unfold temporally: one geographical object is not succeeded by another. On the contrary, as the passage from Sturt quoted earlier suggests, a variety of phenomena are characteristically grasped simultaneously; or, better, may be said to overlap and envelop each other, creating a narrative unit that does not so much define a moment as a place in the text. Hence it is not clear from Sturt's narrative whether the men got the cattle together *after* he and his second-in-command returned from their reconnaissance or before. Sturt's reflection on the meaning of the signs of Aboriginal presence helps to give the narrative a new direction, but it does not succeed the corralling of the cattle. The Aboriginal 'path' they now take is not a new discovery, but had been located previously – and, in any case, was always present. Rather, then, than organize the narrative temporally, Sturt organizes temporal elements spatially, to characterize a location that is textually, if not geographically, distinct.

Despite the linear appearance of the text, the explorers' narratives are characterized by a non-linear narration of events. The sequence of sentences belies the discontinuity of the content – the fact that the country is constantly open to baffling change, surprising reversals. Similarly, verb tenses oscillate uncertainly between past and present, in ways that respect the spatial character of events, while leaving their temporal order chaotic. This is particularly obvious in the rough journals that have not been edited for publication. Take, for instance, this passage:

All the country from where we started this morning, is all burned, and in every direction the bush is all on fire, in one part, a little west of our course, we can see the blaze some feet above the ground. At noon we rested, for a few hours, beside some water holes where there is a few acres of grass which has escaped the fire, having come the distance of 7 miles. At 4 we started and having gone a short distance, came to a creek of fine running water which runs to the northward, the most of the afternoon we have been crossing the ends of ranges, to keep our course, some of them, are a complete mass of stones apparently as if they had been heaped up for the purpose . . . [29]

In a passage like this events, places in the text where space assumes a temporal aspect, are cast in the past tense: the midday campsite is a biographical clearing in the spatial extension, a moment where memory creeps in. But this moment of temporal closure is exceptional: in general the narrative unfolds in various present tenses, whose object is, as far as possible, to subordinate the discontinuities of spatial experience to the open-ended present continuous of the journey going on.

These remarks underline the extent to which the published journals already suppress the horizon-like nature of exploratory experience – the sense in which the way ahead never repeats itself but never changes (or, equally paradoxically, repeats itself in ways that are always different). But they also serve, perhaps, to indicate the novelty of the journals as forms of narrative history. David Carr has recently defended narrative history's claim to represent historical events accurately against 'the discontinuity view' propounded by cultural theorists like White, Mink and Barthes.[30] Criticizing their contention that 'things just happen in meaningless sequence', he asks: 'Is there not a kinship between the means-end structure of action and the beginning-middle-end structure of narrative?' Invoking Husserl's argument that 'even the most passive experience involves not only the retention of the just past but also the tacit anticipation, or what he calls the protention, of the future', he claims that narrative structure is embedded in the nature of experience itself.

But in the literature under discussion it is precisely meaningless sequence that forms the subject of narration. It is the discontinuity

25

of appearances that constitutes the structure of the narrative, and the fact of their repeated difference that gives the explorers' accounts their sometimes hypnotic readerly interest. In this sense, the journals occupy a middle ground in the narrative/non-narrative history debate. For, while they eschew the beginning-middle-end structure of narrative, they remain narratives. Equally, while undoubtedly 'verbal fictions' in White's sense, 'the contents of which are as much invented as found and the forms of which have more in common with their counterparts in literature than with those in the sciences',[31] they do not on this account forfeit their claim to historical accuracy. As I have indicated, in the context of making the first journey, verbal fictions may be an essential means of making history, as well as writing it. To find ways of narrating uniformity, of stressing the discontinuity of phenomena – their failure to link up into a linear story – may be a way of *preventing* events lapsing into mere sequence.

From this point of view the narrative history debate has been dogged by a too narrow definition of temporality. Even those who reject the plotting of connections implicit in narrative talk of 'sequence'. While acknowledging the synchronicity of historical phenomena, they have still bowed to the logic of Paul Veyne's remark that 'to explain more is to narrate better'.[32] The *shape* of temporal experience has remained linear, even if it has been allowed that the historical tapestry contains more than one thread leading from the past to the future. Temporality has continued to be conceived of in Newtonian terms, as a pure intuition independent of space. The critics of narrative history may have rejected the idea of a line drawn from 'a' to 'b', but they remain attached to the line's pure extension.

However, historical events are spatial, as well as temporal, effects. Events lack clear endings, not simply because this is the nature of temporality, but because they pass beyond the perceptual horizon of the observer. Events are not simply synchronous, they are also simultaneous: at such non-linear moments, their historical connection may only be plotted spatially. Indeed, in certain situations, a sudden awareness of the temporality of spatial perception may be what defines an experience as historical: in the context of exploration this may be the primary meaning of the act of naming – that it transfers phenomena from space to time.

According to Carr, in real life we always view our actions 'from the perspective of their having been completed'. Like storytellers and historians, how we act in real life (narrating what we are doing, selecting some facts at the expense of others) is determined by an expectation of how the future will turn out. Like historians, we conceive our individual actions as part of a larger life-plot yet to be completed.[33] But whether or not this is an adequate account of how we act in daily life, it fails to describe either the explorer's characteristic experience or his narration of it. For it is the fact that phenomena cannot be organized into an overarching narrative that engages him. Far from adopting a retrospective view, the narration (both during and after the journey) aims to prepare the *prospective* experience of travelling.

Far from projecting themselves into the future through carefully deliberated plans of action, the explorer-writers describe a steady-state of conflicting loyalties, lines of reasoning, fears and physical frailties which lead to inaction as well as action. Their narratives do not proceed smoothly towards the longed-for denouement of an inland sea or a navigable river, but consist of a multitude of fragmentary asides, speculative observations, scraps of dialogue, reminiscences which struggle inconclusively for definition and dominance. Anastomosing narratives that fan out inconclusively as they proceed, they strangely resemble the country they describe. More than this, by advancing against the tide of narrative logic, by revealing the spatial dimension of the temporal plot, a deviation that consists in recognizing the strangeness of appearances – and hence the nostalgia for a more primitive state at the heart of the civilizing process – the journals offer a fertile site of meditation. Among other things they suggest that the forgetfulness attributed to historical narratives may in part reflect the forgetfulness of their reading, the extent to which the spatial history they contain has been overlooked.

2　Invisible Journeys

Exploration and Photography in Australia,
1839–1889

... were Talbotypes taken of some of the most remarkable objects in the vicinity of the spots where water has been discovered, we should, ere long, have plans organised for a systematic exploration of Central Australia – a country which we believe to have before it the highest destiny of any English colony.

Art Union (1 July 1846)

If the nineteenth-century London magazine the *Art Union* is any guide, the camera's value to explorers was recognized early, as was its wider utility to 'travellers and tourists'. As a certain Dr Pole wrote in 1862: 'Doubtless, the idea must have occurred to almost every traveller, what an advantage it would be if he could himself take photographs, where he likes, of what he likes, when he likes, and how he likes.'[1] And thirty years later in 1891, John Thomson, instructor in photography to the Royal Geographical Society, was saying much the same thing: 'I know of no reason why photography should not find favour with the pioneer whose object is to map out a new route and to picture to the scientific world at home, in a trustworthy manner, what he himself has observed during his travels.'[2]

The advantages of being able to take away images of the country travelled were, it seems, self-evident. It was not only a means of recording space but of manipulating it. Scaling down horizons to the width of a page, it enabled one to model reality, to plan invasions. The photographic image *simulated* journeys. Boswell once remarked that he made journeys in order to keep a journal – similarly, travellers soon learnt to travel in order to bring back pictures. Photography conferred on the scientific 'pioneer' other, subtler advantages. Simplifying passage by instantaneously translating appearances into images, it enabled him to travel light. On entering image-land, originality, invisibility, otherness, became inconceivable. The camera was to the eye as bitumen is to the car: it smoothed out difference, it removed the necessity of choice associated with wet-weather tracks. You could forget where you were and become a reporter. You could save appearances and treat the whole thing as a commercial venture. Above all, you could assert a perfect fit between what you saw and the record of it.

Photography and travel went together. However, travellers were slow to avail themselves of the new technology. As late as 1891, Thomson complained that 'photography is a power placed in our hands, of which, I fear, we are too slow to avail ourselves'.[3] Among Australian explorers, resistance was even more marked: in the first fifty years of photography, *not a single expedition was photographed*. Sturt, Mitchell, Kennedy, Stuart, the Gregory brothers, Giles, Burke and Wills and other explorers continued to confine their records to maps, journals and sketches. Occasionally, the idea of taking a photographer along was mooted – on Augustus Gregory's Northern Australia Expedition of 1855–6, for instance. A photographer/artist, S. T. Gill, accompanied the Horrocks Expedition of 1846; but as an artist, not a photographer. Photographic equipment *did* accompany the Rattlesnake Expedition on its scientific voyage to Torres Strait and the New Guinea coast, though this was not strictly a voyage of *exploration*.[4]

Why, then, despite the increasingly compelling arguments of the camera lobby, did explorers persist in making invisible journeys? Why did their patrons and the public tolerate this? It was not due to ignorance. Daguerre had scarcely patented his 'singular invention . . . by means of [which] a correct view of any locality may be taken by any person in five minutes',[5] when, in August 1839, Sir John Herschel approached him, seeking one of his photographic apparatuses for the British Antarctic Expedition, shortly due to set sail for Tasmania. And, fifty years later, when William Tietkens led an expedition from Alice Springs, he was making systematic efforts to photograph the scenery, recording in his journal his frustration 'at the inadequacy of his small plate size equipment and his prior training in its use'.[6]

Perhaps the problem was a practical one. Despite Herschel's exertions, no photographic equipment was apparently taken on board; and after all, Tietkens is later describing his photographic failure, not success. But, even if Daguerreotypes were hardly a practical proposition in the interior of the 1840s and early 1850s, the development of paper photography after 1858 changed all this. Gael Newton, in her history of photography in Australia, draws attention to Bela (Julius Albert) Rochlitz, who, after trying his luck on the goldfields, became an itinerant photographer. Rochlitz, it seems, 'described tracking potential business by heading for the nearest thread of smoke on the horizon and hoping it meant people not bushfires'.[7]

Less romantically, but more permanently, a host of photographers (professional and amateur) were soon recording Australia's townscapes and landscapes. In the early 1860s, two other veterans of the goldfields, George Burnell and E. W. Cole, repeated Sturt's voyage down the Murray, taking with them a stereoscopic camera. Burnell marketed two boxed sets of sixty stereograph views from the journey, which 'seem to have been regarded as the first views of the river scenery'.[8]

Nothing so ambitious as a photographic expedition to the Grand Canyon was planned in Australia, but in principle there was nothing to prevent it. The techniques were available: by the mid-1860s, the growth of illustrated magazines ensured the taste was there. Photographers like Antoine Fauchery and Richard Daintree could make their reputation by selling views of Australia; and contemporaries like Captain Sweet in Adelaide and Charles Walter in Victoria could advertise themselves as 'specialist landscape photographers'.[9] Was it perhaps that the golden age of Australian exploration was already over by 1839? Hardly. Throughout the 1840s and 1850s, coastal and inland exploration continued apace – one of its enduring achievements, a transcontinental telegraph link, was completed in 1872. Later exploration, more local but no less fully reported in journals, flourished well into the 1880s.

Perhaps outback Australia lacked the pictorial interest to make photographic expeditions a commercial proposition. But there were overwhelming scientific arguments, too. Referring to the explorers' journals, their picturesque prose and no less picturesque illustrations, our *Art Union* critic was outspoken:

We have before us a pile of narratives of exploring expeditions into the interior of Australia, and we find that more than one-half of them are utterly worthless, from their very vague and indefinite account of the landmarks they name as directions for those who follow their route. The writers in the Australian papers complain very bitterly, and not unjustly, of this vagueness; they declare that it is of vast importance to have precise guidance to the spots where water may be found –

> 'Where'er the scorching sun is high
> And the expected fount is dry.'[10]

The remedy was obvious: let the explorers take photographs ('Talbotypes').

But despite its scientific benefits, the advice went unheeded. In 1891 Thomson was still making much the same point:

Lack of time and opportunity constrains the gifted traveller, too often, to trust to memory for detail in his sketches, and by the free play of fancy he fills in and embellishes his handiwork until it becomes a picture of his own creation. An instantaneous photograph would certainly rob his effort of romance, but the merit would remain of his carrying away a perfect mimicry of the scene presented, and an enduring evidence of work faithfully performed. He would forever banish doubt and disarm the captious critic. If his object be to write a romance of travel, a fertile imagination may supply the material without his stirring from his chair.[11]

Could it be, as Thomson hints here, that the explorer's resistance to photography was a matter of professional pride? Perhaps the heroes of geographical romance did not want the new technology, and passively resisted its encroachment on what they regarded as their own peculiar realm of activity. One can see that, while men of science might want accurate geographical data, explorers who supplied this risked writing themselves out of history; for who needs the explorer's painfully incomplete maps, provisional names and romantic sketches, when he can have 'the landmarks they name' faithfully delineated by a photograph?

But to present the explorer as a sort of visual Luddite is to misrepresent the historical situation. It is to assume, for instance, that exploration and scientific geography shared identical aims. Yet precisely this assumption was widely debated in mid-nineteenth-century geographical circles. D. R. Stoddart records as 'commonplace' the criticism that 'the [Royal Geographical] Society in its early decades . . . was concerned with exploration and travel to a degree detrimental to other more scientific or educational pursuits'.[12] Its critics, among them those scientists who broke away to form the British Association for the Advancement of Science, took the view that the explorers' narratives, 'whatever be their other merits, hardly deserve to be spoken of as scientific, and go little beyond an account of personal adventures, combined with a bare itinerary and a partial map'.[13] 'Scientific geography', the same writer contended, began where travellers' tales left off: its object was not merely to verify empirical data, but to classify them, to investigate their causes and to bring them into scientific relation one with another.

Nor was this a transitory dispute, as disagreement about exploration's scientific status persisted into the late nineteenth century. Stoddart reports the explorer Younghusband's 'embarrassment' that, during his epic overland journey from Peking to Srinagar in 1887, he had omitted to take any notice of the botany, ethnology, anthropology, etc., of the region and, as a result, was unable to satisfy the curiosity of Royal Geographical Society members eager for scientific data. 'Clearly,' Stoddart comments, 'it was no longer enough, to earn the title of geographer, simply to make dashing ride to Khiva . . .'[14] At the same time, though, Younghusband's unscientific exploring did not prevent him from being awarded the Society's much coveted gold medal.

While scientific geographers were inventing physiography, geology and geomorphology, fragmenting their discipline in pursuit of an ever greater precision, the rearguard of the Royal Geographical Society continued to defend the integrity of geography, and the necessity to base it on the work of explorers travelling 'not only under circumstances of great personal discomfort or hardship, but also of extreme peril for their very lives'.[15] This split in the geographical fraternity had its counterpart in the geographical uses to which photography was put. The travelling school may largely have ignored its possibilities as a traveller's aid, but the scientific geographers began at once to exploit it. Significantly, though, they did not take the camera into the field: they used it instead to *reproduce maps*, to facilitate the processes of enlargement and reduction.

From the beginning, the mapmakers grasped that the real value of photography to geography lay in the fact that it shared scientific geography's two-dimensional world view. Photography was not a means of reproducing landscapes, but a means of empowering scientific geography's own discourse – its claim to reduce the world accurately to a uniform projection. While this did not mean a divorce from spatial reality, it did imply the possibility of conceptualizing and controlling the earth's surface in a new way: it is no accident that one of the first uses to which the Germans put the newly developed photozincographic process was 'to provide the enormous number of copies of the various sheets of the map of France required during the war of 1870–71'.[16]

Was exploration a scientific activity? Did it produce the kind of objective knowledge which photography could validate? These questions bear directly on the character of Australian exploration. They emerge, for instance, in the rivalry between the explorers Sturt and Mitchell. Biographers have reduced this rivalry to purely personal motives. But the distinction Mitchell himself made between his method of exploring and that pursued by Sturt was based on scientific grounds. Mitchell denigrated Sturt's activities primarily because, in his view, they did not add substantially to geographical knowledge.[17] But, quite as significant as Mitchell's self-proclaimed superiority as a scientifically informed surveyor, is the fact that, unlike Sturt, unlike Eyre, Grey and Leichhardt, Mitchell's more pedestrian, more scrupulously surveyed journeys never earned him the Royal Geographical Society's gold medal.

So long as geography could be regarded as a branch of travelling, and not a science with its own methodological objects and requirements, it was perfectly possible for explorers to regard themselves first and foremost as travellers, and not as recorders of scientific fact. But, even where they did not see their role as primarily scientific, it did not follow that photography was a natural weapon in their observational artillery. The suggestion that Talbotypes of the interior should be made was, in 1846 at least, utterly impracticable: it belonged to the same realm of speculation as the idea of a trans-Australian expedition by balloon, put forward in 1858.

Besides, it is by no means clear that the *Art Union* critic was right in calling the explorers' narratives 'vague and indefinite'. They might

33

not reproduce accurately the surface of the country, or preserve precisely the relation of things. But, in *characterizing* the country, perhaps the journals and sketches were superior. The topographical detail of a nineteenth-century photograph was, literally and metaphorically, superficial. True, the mere fact the photograph had edges, was set in a rectangular or oval frame, served to distinguish *this* scene from another. But the photographic accumulation of empirical detail, the catalogue of minutiae so comprehensive as to command belief, revealed nothing about the lie of the land, its weather, its colours, its sounds.

To deduce what the photograph told about the landscape required non-photographic skills, a familiarity with the principles of physiography, zoology, architectural history and even anthropology – those very discourses which photography helped regularize and authorize. By themselves, those preternaturally still portraits of cities, harbours, forests and faces revealed nothing except the conditions of their reproduction. They could be ruins in the middle distance, or natural outcrops; there was no way of telling. By contrast, the explorers' narratives were visually sketchy, but not necessarily uninformative. There is no reason to doubt they could be read and interpreted accurately (at least by professionals). Mitchell criticized the explorer Leichhardt's published account of his overland journey to Port Essington for its topographical vagueness and lack of geographical detail. But this did not prevent another explorer, Kennedy, from taking Leichhardt's journal with him on his ill-fated journey to the tip of Cape York.

Nor must we assume that, simply because they failed to meet photographic criteria, the illustrations which the explorers appended to their narratives were necessarily fanciful. The Aboriginal portraits in Mitchell's *Three Expeditions* (1838) are strikingly classical in style, native 'Neptunes' reclining exactly like their marble, Roman counterparts in English gardens. But this does not mean they were merely ornamental: the squatter and proto-anthropologist, E. M. Curr, remarked of these portraits that they accurately captured the Murray Aborigine's distinctive stances.[18] Rather than dismiss these witnesses as irremediably Eurocentric, we should relate their observations to the broader question of the Aborigines' origins, much debated both by the explorers and, later, by etymologists like Curr.

There were, however, more fundamental reasons why explorers resisted photography's positivist ebullience. Photography made the assumption that the space of the journey could be visualized – it made no distinction between exploration and tourism. Dealing in perfect reproductions, in repeatable events, photography shared the outlook of the scientific geographer with his map: it assumed the reality of the journey lay in the facts it established, the landmarks, the track, the permanent features in their permanent, static relations. Yet exploration by its very nature occupied a pre-visual realm, one in which directions remained to be defined, journeys were one-way and lookouts (the *sine qua non* of picturesque touring) had still to be found.

Much talk of photography as a means of gaining information about remote places was informed less by a zeal for useful, practical information than by the more far-reaching upsurge in what might be called a taste for visibility. Gael Newton sets the history of nineteenth-century photography in Australia in the context of that century's desire for 'a global picture'.[19] Implicit in the *Cosmos* of Humboldt, or Darwin's evolutionary theory, was the idea of the world as a thoroughly knowable machine, a system whose workings could not only be described but modelled: one advantage of the Talbotype, according to the *Art Union* writer, was that it would enable the artist 'to delineate such scenes [the ruins of Babylon or the wilds of Australia] as faithfully as if he had visited the spot'.[20]

At a humbler, but commercially more influential level, illustrated magazines which provided picturesque evidence of faraway places were fuelling a taste for visual images and, more profoundly, reinforcing an unexamined assumption – that visual images were the real thing. People came to live in different places, even the humblest dwelling being (potentially) a scrapbook of remembered journeys, a development quaintly illustrated by the remark of an 1865 visitor to the Aboriginal Station at Corandeerk in Victoria: 'All was neat, with seats and tables of rough bush timber, and the walls decorated with pictures cut out of the *Illustrated London News*, and the illustrated papers published in Melbourne.'[21]

As a consequence of this cult of places, the process of travelling became subsidiary to the visual report of distant locales. It was in the nature of photographic expeditions that they chose certain kinds of expedition scenery, favoured certain viewpoints, certain *tableaux vivants*, and not others.

In short, it was not that the explorers' journeys were invisible – at least, not to those prepared to read and interpret their reports. Rather, their invisibility was an effect of photographic travelling, a mode of seeing the country as if it had always been there, as if it had never been conjured up for the first time by the explorer, by his choice of route, his namings, his campsites, his distress. Exploration, a process of spatial speculation, was precisely what photography could not visualize. Hence it was excluded, and with it the history of that space.

Instead of recording spatial history, photography, like the positivist science which embraced it, focused on the history of objects. But, to tell their history, objects had to be constituted as facts; they had to be reproducible in two-dimensional form, as maps, as plates, as cross-sections. Only in this form could they be manipulated and their true (scientific) relations, and hence their genealogy, be established. What 'science' left out was the moment of their first occurrence, the explorational context in which they first appeared. And it should be stressed that this scientific approach, represented by the ascendancy of photography, undermined exploration's ontological claims in other, more abstruse ways.

In the explorers' narratives, Aborigines appear *occasionally*. Their appearance is inevitably charged with narrative meaning. They are a means of getting on, a key to survival. They may spell disaster. A characteristically speculative entry in the explorer Hovell's journal reads: 'The Natives are Numerous here, but we have not seen any, only there [*sic*] Smoke, There is little doubt but they have seen us.'[22] Here is an experience photography cannot register, and which science cannot translate into 'facts'. Furthermore, here is an experience of travelling which, in the interest of the facts, has been *suppressed*. For, in the published version of Hume and Hovell's *Journal* (which a friend, W. Bland, edited seven years after the 1824 expedition), the passage just quoted appears as: 'The natives, from the appearance of their fires, seem to be numerous, though none were seen.'[23] Elsewhere, the explorer has made clear he recognizes that the native 'smokes' are 'their Signals, one to the other'.[24] Hence, in this rewriting, Bland commits a double calumny. Not only does he impose an exclusively European viewpoint on the scene, as if the Aborigines could not see the interlopers coming; he will further have it that they did not communicate between themselves either. The notion of signifying smoke is replaced by the supposition of mere fires. Against the possibility of communication is proposed the silence of animal necessity, savages keeping warm.

To explain the usefulness of photography to travellers, the *Art Union* critic drew a parallel: 'We are informed that the Aztecs of ancient Mexico possessed maps of the roads through their empire, on which the prominent natural objects or edifices which marked the chief station were rudely pictured, and that these pictorial charts afforded better guidance than the more accurate survey of the Spaniards.' Similarly, 'if the surveyors who penetrate these districts [of the forest or prairie] made sun-pictures of the points of guidance, the proper track could never slip from memory'.[25] But to take 'sun-pictures' of significant landmarks presupposes the exploring journey has *already taken place*; it assumes a succession of viewpoints which have already been 'seen'. The very idea of getting lost implies a right way missed.

Again, the intriguing suggestion that photographs could mediate between two graphic conventions – the map and the journal – ignores their complementary relationship in the context of exploring. The explorer's map is itself a picture, a series of outlines suggesting viewpoints, distances, connections, and not at all the connecting survey of, say, the bounded space of the home countries.[26] And, if the map hypothesizes future roads, possible points of guidance, then the journal describes the blank interstices of the chart: not so much filling up the blanks as establishing them, their texture and their depth of tone.

Thus the *Art Union*'s confidence in photography's usefulness merely underlines why many journeys in nineteenth-century Australia and its waters (loosely called expeditions) were not, in the full sense of the word, explorations. The essential difference between journeys of exploration and other expeditions was that, in the former case, it was the constitution of a track which was the primary objective,[27] whereas in the latter this was taken for granted: it was a road where other events and activities could occur.

How, then, did the explorer conceptualize the space of his activity? How did his description of the landscape differ from the photographer/scientist's? In the journal of his 1860 attempt to cross Australia

37

from south to north, John McDouall Stuart describes his discovery of a pillar-like rock he named Chambers Pillar. In 1901, on the basis of Stuart's description, the pioneer anthropologist (and photographer) Baldwin Spencer made a 'detour' to see the same 'remarkable natural feature'. The difference between the explorer's pre- (or non-)photographic viewpoint and that of the scientist emerges strikingly in the contrasting ways they describe what they found and saw.

Revised for publication, Stuart's journal entry for that day reads:

Friday, 6th April, Small Gum Creek in Range of Hills. – Started on the same course, 330 degrees, to a remarkable hill, which has the appearance at this distance of a locomotive engine with its funnel. For three miles the country is very good, but after that high sand hills succeeded, covered with spinifex. At six miles we got to one of the largest gum creeks I have yet seen. It is much the same as the one we saw on the 4th, and the water in it is running. Great difficulty in crossing it, its bed being quicksand. We were nearly across, when I saw a black fellow among the bushes; I pulled up, and called to him. At first he seemed at a loss to know where the sound came from. As soon, however, as he saw the other horses coming up, he took to his heels, and was off like a shot, and we saw no more of him. As far as I can judge, the creek comes from the south-west, but the sand hills are so high, and the large black shea-oak so thick, that I cannot distinguish the creek very well. These trees look so much like gums in the distance; some of them are very large, as also are the gums in the creek. Numerous tracks of blacks all about. It is the upper end of the Finke, and at this point runs through high sand hills (red), covered with spinifex, which it is very difficult to get the horses through. We passed through a few patches of good grassy country. In the sand hills the oak is getting more plentiful. We were three-quarters of an hour in crossing the creek, and obtained an observation of the sun, 116 degrees, 26' 15". We then proceeded on the same course towards the remarkable pillar, through high, heavy sand hills, covered with spinifex, and, at twelve miles from last night's camp, arrived at it. It is a pillar of sandstone, standing on a hill upwards of one hundred feet high. From the base of the pillar to its top is about one hundred and fifty feet, quite perpendicular; and it is twenty feet wide by ten feet deep, with two small peaks on the top. I have named it 'Chambers pillar', in honour of James Chambers, Esq., who, with William Finke, Esq., has been my great supporter in all my explorations. To the north and north-east of it are numerous remarkable hills, which have a very striking effect in the landscape; they resemble nothing so much as a number of old castles in ruins; they are standing in the midst of sand hills. Proceeded, still on the same course, through the sand rises, spinifex, and low sandstone hills, at the foot of which we saw some rain water, where I camped. To the south-west are some high hills, through which I think the Finke comes. I would follow it up, but the immense quantity of sand in its bed shows that it comes from a sandy country, which I wish to avoid if I can. Wind south-east. Heavy clouds; very like rain.[28]

This passage has clearly been worked up for publication. The assertion that the 'creek . . . is the upper part of the Finke' seems to be an interpolation, the fruit of later discoveries. Even the simple announcement of 'a remarkable hill' suggests editorial intervention. Stuart did not wake up, descry the pillar and, on the spur of the moment, decide to set course for it. He had, presumably, already noticed it the previous day when he observed that, 'To the north-east and east is a mass of flat-topped hills, of every size and shape, running always to the east.'[29] The relegation of the pillar's appearance to the following day suggests a desire to shape the narrative, to create, as it were, a more natural fit between the stages of the journey and the progress of the days.

Again, there is an uneasy ambiguity about the use of the present tense, which may indicate the editor's difficulty in deciding where *in time* the explorer writes from. Stuart's remark, 'For three miles the country is very good . . .', seems to resemble a statement of geographical fact. But his syntactically and grammatically similar observation, 'In the sand hills the oak is getting more plentiful', clearly refers not to the character of the country, but to the direction and history of his journey. These present tenses are like clearings in the past tense of the narrative, places where room is made to comment on the succession of objects. They can be seen as the beginnings of a second viewpoint within the narrative, one which asserts the truth of these experiences apart from the manner of their discovery.

Still, the past tense of the narrative is by no means the vehicle of mere landscape description. It is the journey, not the landscape, whose story is being told. Its motion is experienced as a succession of first appearances. The explorer does not describe the real distribution of plants, the true physiognomy of the region. He does not deduce a national character from a single native's behaviour. His object is not to regionalize the space, to unify it within a hierarchy of scientific discourses. Instead, he aims to organize the data of experience into a moving track. Quite as important as the Turneresque first impression of a hill like 'a locomotive engine with its funnel' is the fact that it has such an 'appearance at this distance' – and that, later, it appears differently.

Like the imagery, the syntax aims to preserve appearances. If the punctuation suggests the Zeno-like difficulty of preserving the experience of motion whilst cutting it up into individual, self-contained, and hence static units, the elaboration of connecting clauses – stretching forward and back, narrowing assertion to the line of progress, undermining certainty before it can take root – serves to overcome this paradox. To preserve the illusion of an advance not measured by places left behind, the explorer dissolves the appearances he announces as he goes along. New illusions of reality appear to replace those just announced.

This is not to say the explorer displays no curiosity about the country, but that his interest is oriented towards the success of the journey. In the passage quoted, the day's entry centres not on Chambers Pillar, but on the rediscovery of the Finke. The Finke is a natural track; the vegetation, the soil, even the Aborigines associated with it are clues to future directions. They do not help to regionalize the country, but they do characterize the horizon. By contrast, Chambers Pillar implies a different mode of seeing. True, from its base there is a view of the country, but this might have been obtained elsewhere. Rather, the pillar is like a natural cairn or monolith, already a monument to human (or at least, the male explorers') endeavour. What could be more natural than to commemorate here the chief patron of his journey, John Chambers? Naming is the pre-photographic way of picturing oneself at a place. If the Finke names the prospects for getting on, Chambers Pillar symbolizes the other condition of successful exploration: the necessity to translate its unparagraphed meanderings into a decisive, memorable history.

Visiting Chambers Pillar some forty years later, Baldwin Spencer acted not only as anthropologist, zoologist and geologist, he was also a tourist. He was curious to see something. He expected to bring back some souvenir, scientific or otherwise, for his trouble. Accordingly, in contrast with Stuart, Spencer is at great pains to possess the pillar, to locate it, not only geographically, but historically and visually within familiar territory. And since the difference is discursive, and not simply confined to individual tropes and turns of speech, it is again necessary to quote at some length.

We made a detour in order to see a remarkable natural feature to which the explorer Stuart had given the name of Chamber's [sic] Pillar. It was slow and monotonous travelling, because our course lay nearly at right angles to the length of the sand-hills, and in nine miles' travelling we crossed thirty-five of them until, at last, we came on to a small level stretch of country with the Pillar standing in the middle of it, and a line of hills curiously weathered so as to look like the remains of old battlements, a little to the north of it. Chamber's Pillar has the form of a tall column rising from the broad pedestal about three hundred yards in circumference and one hundred feet in height. The column itself rises about seventy feet higher and is oblong in section, one side measuring about twenty-five and the other fifteen yards in length. It is formed of friable sandstone, similar in appearance and character to the variegated sandstones at Engoordina and Crown Point. The base of the column is cream-coloured, the upper part bright red with a thin capping of darker-coloured, hard, silicified sandstone that has protected the underlying softer rock. The column is completely isolated and, standing out against the blue sky, the yellow sand-hills and dull green Mulga scrub, with a few old battered desert oaks dotted around, it forms a striking object in the otherwise dreary and monotonous landscape.

The column has naturally attracted the attention of the natives, who account for it by saying that in the far-away times that they call Alchera, there lived a very great fighting man who journeyed westwards across the country, killing all the men whom he met with his stone knife and taking all the women captive. One night, on his way back, he stopped here and, for his sins, he and the women were turned into pillars of stone . . .

In the report of the Horn Expedition, the whole of the sandstone formation as far north as the southern margin of the Central Ranges was regarded as Upper Cretaceous, the capping of all the flat-topped hills, from Mt Frank near Charlotte Waters in the south to Crown Point and Chamber's Pillar in the north, being described as Desert Sandstone . . . [30]

Here, an object is not so much discovered as 'constructed': from the successive viewpoints of traveller, geologist, artist, anthropologist and physiographer, a composite object is built up. A conceptual space is cleared around it, its nature surveyed from every angle. The directional, even linear space of the journey has yielded to the polymorphic space of scientific discourse. The pillar is no longer an event, punctuating the horizon, defining a day: it is a meeting place of different professional languages, where 'of friable sandstone', 'standing out against the blue sky', 'he and his women were turned into pillars of stone', and 'the capping of all the flat-topped hills' converge in a common sense.

This new language has a curious effect: it substitutes an image for an event. The pillar is isolated from its surroundings, compacted into a definite identity by the competing discourses beamed upon it and, by the same means, removed from the local circumstances of its first appearance. What Spencer describes is not an incident in a journey, but a working model, the historical and geographical conditions for transporting the pillar's significance elsewhere. Where Stuart's narrative lapses into the present tense, Spencer's book shifts into the past: for Spencer, narrating a journey is little more than a literary device for rendering his prodigal array of scientific findings more palatable. These differences stem in part from the authors' individual intentions; but underlying these diverging modes of description are different assumptions about the relationship between knowledge and seeing. Visibility is clearly a condition of knowing – of describing the country – for both explorer and scientist. But here the resemblance ends. For Stuart, visibility is so to speak a spatial quality, not something invested in objects, but rather a property of the explorational environment.

There is a sense in which his narrative of first appearances takes visibility for granted. As a result, Stuart – and this applies to explorer writing more generally – feels little urge to conjure up objects picturesquely, to impress them upon the reader's visual imagination. In the context of Stuart's journals as a whole, his colourful image of a locomotive is almost without parallel: it signifies the unusual nature of this particular object, that it *did* strike the author as primarily a visual experience, something interrupting the objectless scrutiny of the way ahead.

For Spencer, by contrast, visibility is invested in objects: hence his preoccupation with the delineation of outlines, his concern to mark boundaries. Spencer writes as if he has to conjure the object out of nothingness; or, better, as if his discourse is a lamp and a lense projecting the object's two-dimensional image on a screen. The existential space of the journey has been replaced by the picturesque space of science, for the various descriptions of the pillar which Spencer offers are different means of picturing the object to us, metaphorical vehicles illuminating an absent thing. Beyond estimating its bulk, Stuart and his editor seem to have felt no necessity to paint the rock further. Spencer, on the other hand, copiously fills in and layers *his* description, as if all he had before him were a black-and-white outline, as if colourful opaqueness will render it more 'real' an object of knowledge.

This discursive difference so evident in the prose of Stuart and Spencer is also evident in the illustrations of Chambers Pillar contained in their accounts. Stuart's panorama (Plate 1) might at first suggest a scientific impulse to lend his discovery coherence by placing it in the context of its surroundings; whereas Spencer's photograph (Plate 2), isolating the rock from its surroundings, seems to contradict such scientific contextualization of it. Yet, more fundamentally, these contrasting images faithfully reinforce the kinds of opposition already noted.

Stuart's description, for instance, is independent of the illustration. He does not refer to the illustration, or in any way rely on it to convey his meaning. On the contrary, the decision to include an elaborate engraving based on one of his field sketches appears to have been an editorial one. But, while the illustrator has presumably copied Stuart's stratification of the column itself (something not mentioned in the text), for the rest he appears to have interpreted Stuart's own description: there is some attempt to suggest the 'low sandstone hills' in the foreground rocks, as well as picturesque fissures at the base of Chambers Pillar (which seem hard to reconcile geologically with the hill's profile). But for the most part, the illustrator takes Stuart at his word: his distant outcrops 'resemble nothing so much as a number of old castles in ruins', the middle-distance and indeed the country generally is a vague mixture of darker, unfocused vegetation ('large black shea-oak so thick . . .') interspersed with 'a few patches of good grassy country'. The sky is treated so as to illustrate Stuart's concluding observation, 'Heavy clouds; very like rain.'

Spencer's photograph, however, is a primary means of documenting the journey. In a sense, his text is a secondary elaboration which the photograph both permits and demands – permits because it faithfully records a natural object and demands because its narrowing, black-and-white image drains the object of signification. It becomes the writer's responsibility to interpret the image. At the same time, the coherence of his narrative is now judged by its success in measuring up to the visual image. The hungry inclusiveness of the photographic image demands footnoting if it is not to dissipate into inexplicable insignificance. Hence Spencer's excursion into the 'scenic', his evocation of the pillar as 'completely isolated . . . standing out against the blue sky, the yellow sand-hills and dull green Mulga scrub, with a few old battered desert oaks dotted around . . . a striking object in the otherwise dreary and monotonous landscape'.

Such word-painting is less a description of the rock than an attempt to explain and correct the photographic impression. Thus Spencer sustains the illusion of isolation, but corrects the impression of mere dreariness. But, in any case, it is clear that the narrative's primary function is to provide comprehensive annotation of what photography has already defined as science's subject matter. So, reversing Stuart's perspective, the photograph creates an artificial enclosure or isolation which the text has to compensate for, relating the rock geographically, ethnographically, to the country outside the photograph's close-up frame.

Photography focuses on the fruit of travel; exploration writing describes travelling itself. Yet not only may this distinction seem too rigid, it seems too technologically determined. It risks suggesting the travellers were the helpless slaves of their discursive paradigms – as if an explorer could never become a photographer, and a photographer never explore. It also implies that the explorer's eye was in some sense innocent, free of the camera's desire to frame and depict. Can we really suppose explorers carried on oblivious to scientific and publishing criteria? That they felt no need to possess more completely what they saw? To bring it back? In fact, it may well be that the metamorphosis of the explorer journal (at the hands of writers like Giles and Carnegie) into romance, and its demise as a genre – to be replaced by accounts of 'expeditions', or else (to adopt Alan Marshall's phrase) 'journeys among men' – is largely due to the photographic invasion of previously invisible territory. But it should be said that, in profound ways, exploration always aspired to the photographic condition, even if these ways were not, paradoxically, consonant with the taking of photographs.

Panoramic views, formed by sticking together a frieze of photographs, illustrated the point that, even when focused on infinity, the nineteenth-century camera's gaze was narrow. Further, it longed for easily recognizable subjects – its direction and viewpoint being determined by the availability of suitable objects, ones which would compose, which could be 'read' in relation to each other. The explorer shared the photographer's close-up point of view, his narrowness of field, his concern for memorable objects. The difference was that he could only indulge this preoccupation *on the return route*; for only on returning could the first appearances of the outward track be resolved into viewpoints. Indeed, only on returning could he *recognize* viewpoints and identify the country definitely: names, tracks and compass points were the invisible preliminary to this picturesque inventory.

The photographic nature of the return journey is manifest, for example, in the following passage from Hovell's *Journal*:

I was fearful that as my Eyes were generally fixed (when approaching towards the end of our Journey, in the direction where we shall fall in with the sea) towards the front and seldom exceeding an angle of 45 degrees from the front on each side of me, that I might have misstated some part, and forgotten others, but now we are returning, and I am so well satisfied with that Country that my eyes are as much behind, as they are in front, admiring the different spots which occasionally present themselves to view.[31]

45

As Major Mitchell also commented, when he began his return journey up the Darling in 1835, he had 'a little more time for the picturesque'.[32]

But Hovell's remarks raise a question of their own. The outward journey was too single-mindedly focused on the way ahead to have time for 'spots . . . to present themselves'. This was a luxury reserved for the return route. How, then, did the explorer who did not go back the way he came describe the country he passed through? Explorers like Mitchell, Leichhardt and Eyre, all of whom made one-way expeditions, embellished their journals with elaborately picturesque descriptions. Were these mere inventions, literary goings-back over the textual ground? Or did they have an empirical basis?

The answer to these questions is hinted at by Leichhardt, again illustrating how the explorer's photographic impulse was not, strangely enough, compatible with making the first track. Leichhardt, like Mitchell and Eyre, took with him Aboriginal 'guides' and, as with all European travellers, he was impressed by the Aborigines' ability to recognize places. Referring to 'the wonderful quickness and accuracy with which Brown and Charley were able to recognize localities which they had previously seen', Leichhardt wrote:

> The impressions on their retina seem to be naturally more intense than on that of the European; and their recollections are remarkedly exact, even to the most minute details. Trees peculiarly formed or grouped, broken branches, slight elevations of the ground – in fact, a hundred things, which we should remark only when paying great attention to a place – seem to form a kind of Daguerreotype impression on their minds, every part of which is readily recollected.[33]

The complete recall of the Aborigines is here described as photographic. More precisely, in its ghostly reproduction of details which are all but invisible (and which a casual glance would certainly overlook), it is even thought to resemble the silvery completeness of a Daguerreotype. In this sense, the Aborigines are to the explorers what the camera was to later travellers – but with this difference, that the 'views' which the Aborigines recognize are not picturesque compositions, but simply signs and clues composing a recognizable path.

It is this perfect topographical recall which gives the explorers room to travel reflectively, leaving the roadmaking to the guides while they strain to characterize the country, to conceptualize it regionally. The Aboriginal guide is a travelling camera who enables the explorer to ignore what he sees and to imagine the area scenically, to anticipate the demands of the real camera and its dependence for its views on a pre-existing direction. Without the exploring memory of the Aborigine, fixing such directions memorably, this photographic luxury would have been impossible. Nor is this photographic comparison merely fanciful. However inadequate might be this Lockean model of the Aboriginal mind as a blank (photo-sensitive) sheet on which Nature imprinted itself, the suggestion that the Aborigine's spatial memory resembled the workings of a camera is at least *operationally* accurate.

In his description of Brown and Charley's pathfinding ability, Leichhardt draws attention to two quite distinct skills – that of the tracker or hunter, and that of the guide. The tracker operated in familiar territory; in any case, he was not responsible for finding his way back by the same route. On the other hand, the guide is taken along in order to make sense of the unfamiliar. Hunting animals, interpreting signs of Aboriginal occupation, he acts as a tracker; but, in addition, he is the expedition's spatial memory, connecting up the changing views into a coherent track. While the tracker might be skilled at interpreting broken branches, it is the guide who needs to be able to recognize 'Trees peculiarly formed'.

One can see how both activities conjure up the Daguerreotype effect: the glint of sunlight on bent grass, turning it into a field of scratched glass or gossamer and revealing someone's recent passage, suggests the superficial quality of this technique; the Aborigine's ability to fix uniquely in his mind even indistinct views, even doubtfully distinguished contours, shadowy banks and trees, evokes its gloomy clarity, its curious ability to record the world without any picturesque trappings. But, while tracking was a matter of interpreting signs of previous passage, how did the Aborigine go about constituting the track, ensuring the ground passed over was not lost but led ahead?

An incident in the aftermath of Kennedy's fatal expedition suggests an answer. Jackey, Kennedy's companion and guide, displayed the Aborigine's proverbial skill in guiding the search party to the area where Kennedy's body lay, but he was unable to locate precisely where he had concealed the explorer's body. Mr Simpson, master of the *Freak*, the vessel dispatched to search for the explorers, explains why: 'When we came to the edge of the scrub, Jackey was at a loss where to enter, as he said when he was carrying the corpse he did not look behind – all the objects in front being nearly alike he did not get a good mark.'[34] Jackey's preternaturally clear picture of the bush depended on *looking back*. In order to find the way ahead, he needed regularly to look over his shoulder, to keep in mind the backward view, the view towards which he would be going in the event of returning. In other words, like the photographer, Jackey's success in mapping the journey depended on regularly imagining it from the point of view of its completion. In order not to lose the way, he had to imagine the perspective of someone coming to meet them.

When the captain of the other rescue vessel, the *Ariel*, questioned Jackey's ability to identify the coast where the expedition survivors were concealed, Jackey is said to have responded: ' "Do you think I am stupid? – Mr Kennedy sent me from the camp to look out the coast, so that I might know it again when I came back in the ship, and I will tell you when we come to it, the ship must go on that way further", pointing to the south.'[35] If this was Kennedy's initiative, it still corresponded to a travelling device familiar to Jackey himself. Furthermore, its success as a means of accurately identifying the coast in question depended on Jackey's familiarity with the method involved.

It becomes evident, then, that photography and exploration were not mutually exclusive modes of seeing and knowing. Rather, photography corresponded to the explorer's backward view and return route – a discovery with profound implications for how we see the country when viewed through photographs or, indeed, when it is seen in terms of the picturesque viewpoints our paths construct for us. For the world of the photograph, like the world of the picturesque, is the world of returning: it is the world which lies invisibly behind on the outward route. To look into a country which is composed photographically is to look into a mirror revealing what lies behind the explorer's shoulder. The strangest place in this looking-glass world is where we stand looking into it but fail to see ourselves mirrored there, glimpsing instead the strangeness of our origins.

3 Culture of Coincidence

An Alternative Australian Visual Tradition

Earlier in the evening I had been lying on a sunny bank & was reflecting on the strange character of the Animals of this country as compared to the rest of the world. A Disbeliever in everything beyond his own reason, might exclaim, 'Surely two distinct Creators must have been [at] work; their object however has been the same & certainly in each case the end is complete'.

Charles Darwin, Beagle Diary

At home Darwin's reflection on Australian fauna have provoked one of two reactions: contempt or pride. Nationalist historians and, most recently, the curators of one of Australia's leading science museums have dismissed Darwin's remarks as yet another instance of English ethnocentrism masquerading as universal knowledge. Anxious to stress the difference of local culture, they have implied that, whatever his reputation overseas, in Australia Darwin fared little better than the editor of the English magazine who, without even visiting the place, pronounced that Australian birds had no songs and Australian blooms no scent. By contrast, though, others have welcomed Darwin's condescension in noticing Australia on his world tour almost with gratitude, as if the tender red thread of his route on the map bestowed on their country what it notoriously could not provide for itself, a wider intellectual genealogy, a modest, but indisputable, link with the world of ideas.

These antithetical reactions express anxieties about cultural self-definition in a colonial and post-colonial situation. In particular they reflect the ambiguous meaning of *originality* in a migrant society. To be an original in Australia is not to be a Charles Darwin, but to be 'singular, odd or eccentric'. And furthermore the significance of this strange departure from the ordinary will not be found at home, but overseas – where it may be condemned as irremediably primitive and

49

parochial or else taken up and treated as deliciously exotic, tantalizingly fresh. Small wonder artists, writers and intellectuals frequently succumb to an Oedipal impulse to murder their cultural father: except by violent means, it seems impossible to wrest authority from elsewhere.

But those who embrace the view that Salman Rushdie attributes to the migrant, that 'reality is an artifact, that it does not exist until it is made, and that, like any other artifact, it can be made well or badly',[1] may find these reactions to a patriarchal past strangely *familial*, designed to objectify a myth of descent rather than to reveal its essential unreality. The terms in which the colonizers assert their feeling of having been colonized are borrowed from the parental culture and, even as they are used to attack it, serve to reinforce its authority. To evaluate phenomena, whether human or natural, in terms of influence, on a scale that runs from the zero of utter strangeness at one extreme to the inexhaustible plenitude of tradition at the other, is already to embrace a genealogical form of self-definition, already to identify oneself with the distorting mirror of the parental gaze.

A post-colonial culture cannot escape from a dependent relationship so long as it continues to allow itself to be colonized by the vocabulary of that relationship. But what is the way out of this imprisoning mimicry? An answer might begin with Darwin's famous remarks. It is symptomatic of the polarization of Australian cultural debate that, in discussions of this passage, it is overlooked that Darwin had in mind the geologist Charles Lyell's suggestion that the enormous diversity of the world's fauna and flora could only be explained by positing a number of creations occurring independently of one another, in different parts of the world. Far from disparaging local conditions or appropriating them to a universal model, Darwin was entertaining a scheme of things that was both local and non-genealogical.

Darwin rejected Lyell's hypothesis, but it is telling that local critics and eulogists alike rarely acknowledge its existence, let alone its *cultural* application in a colonial context. Transferred from the natural to the human realm, the characterization of a culture as different from other cultures, although sharing their fundamental 'object', is a fertile one. It can be interpreted hierarchically: for instance the species of Australian painting – individual painters, their subject matter and even certain styles – may be distinct and complete in themselves, but their general morphology – their adherence to the visual conventions of Western art, its compositional and representational assumptions – remains the same. But it can also be interpreted non-hierarchically.

Authors of a recent monograph on Darwin in Australia make the point that his reflections may have been stimulated by his noticing a phenomenon that later came to be known as convergent evolution: wallabies that were quite unlike rabbits but which hopped in the same way, 'robins' that behaved like robins but whose plumage was quite different.[2] Transferred to the cultural realm this suggests an alternative way of construing local productions. A local artist who paints a scene at once different from and similar to its European counterparts may not be imitating a European model: the similarity, the convergence of appearances, may be mere coincidence – as when two people meet on the road and no one can say who was there first, although their object is clearly the same. And we can go even further and speculate that such an art may be most local when it most conceals its difference, when it least reveals its environmental origins.

What follows, then, is a sort of afternoon walk in the wood of Australian painting – not a representative catalogue and following no strict chronology – in which a non-hierarchical model of cultural self-definition is applied to some artists of this country. The consequence of this will not be an antipodean (and nationalist) Eden whence those foreigners, Tradition and Influence, are banished; but the meaning of these original transgressors will perhaps be changed. At the very least we may reach a place where, in Rudolf Arnheim's words, 'tradition and prophecy are exchangeable'.[3]

I

In 1837, while exploring Doubtful Bay on the north-west coast of Australia, George Grey came across some rock paintings quite unlike anything previously recorded in Australia. His description of his first reactions, his gradual assimilation of what he saw to familiar terms of reference, together with the later history of interpretation his descriptions provoked, provide an eloquent instance of the blindness at the heart of the rhetoric of tradition and influence.

The first painting Grey saw (Plate 3) struck him, not with its absolute strangeness, but by its enigmatic familiarity: 'on looking over some bushes, at the sandstone rocks which were above us, I suddenly saw from one of them a most extraordinary figure peering down upon me'.[4] The shift from 'us' to 'me' conveys Grey's sense that the figure on the rock answered his own gaze, looking back at him as if it recognized him. As he comments, 'I was certainly rather surprised at the moment that I first saw this gigantic head and upper part of a body bending over and staring grimly down at me.' Grey captures something of the Cyclopean terror it induced when he describes its head 'encircled by bright red rays, something like the rays which one sees proceeding from the sun, when depicted on the sign-board of a public-house' – a metaphor reinforced in the accompanying engraving where the 'rays' – which, to judge from Wandjina figures surviving in the Kimberley region, are straight and stubby – have acquired a coronal flamboyance.

Initially Grey's reaction resembles the surprise that Darwin, on the other side of the continent, felt in contemplating the local fauna. Here, as Grey's description and illustration reveal, is a figure that shows the hand of a distinct creator, whose expressive end is – if his own reaction is any guide – complete, *and* whose object appears to be 'the same'. It might have been possible to regard this as a mere coincidence, but Grey quickly sets out to translate the image into familiar terms. A second 'singular painting' in the same cave no longer evokes surprise, but the beginnings of an aesthetic interest: 'Each of the four faces was marked by a totally distinct expression of countenance, and although none of them had mouths, two, I thought, were otherwise rather good looking.'[5]

These chance discoveries spurred Grey to look for other paintings. Instead of being seen, he now desired to see, to reverse the direction of the gaze. A few days later he was rewarded by finding in a likely-looking cave a painting 'totally invisible from the outside': 'it was the figure of a man, ten feet six inches in length, clothed from the chin downwards in a red garment, which reached to the wrists and ankles; beyond this red dress the feet and hands protruded, and were badly executed' (Plate 4). The dispassionate tone of this passage not only indicates that Grey now commands the visual environment: he has introduced a critical distance between himself and the visual phenomena. This was already implicit in calling what he saw 'paintings', but now it is made explicit – the figures, Grey writes, reminded him of the prophet Ezekiel described in the Old Testament.[6] Possibly with this passage in mind, Grey later speculated that the rock paintings were Asiatic in origin.[7]

In reproduction, detached from their surroundings, it seemed natural to locate the origin of these paintings elsewhere – in the Gondwanaland of tradition and influence. Grey's willingness to seek the source of the Wandjina figures overseas was analogous to his argument that the Aboriginal tongues spoken locally around Perth and Albany had 'a common root', that 'a language radically the same, is spoken over the whole continent'.[8] In both cases attention shifted from phenomena to genealogy, from instructive dialogue to (ulti-mately) destructive monologue. And Grey's methodological assump-tions were after all conventional. The nineteenth-century past of the Wandjina figures, which he initiated, added up to a series of variations on the theme of tradition and influence.

Thus a Mr Worsnop took the view that the red lines 'were the script from the Red Sea area': the artists were traders from that region to the East Indies who had been blown off course. Translated, the 'written characters' over the head of the clothed man read 'I am a great personage . . .' A Mr Panton thought the paintings represented Sumatran or Malayan figures, the captain having his name on his turban. George Collingridge, the author of *The Secret Discovery of Australia*, thought they were Moorish and dated them to the eleventh century. A Professor Campbell had another idea: the script was archaic Japanese and, translated, read 'the number of the homeless ones is 62'. Yet others thought that the garb of the figures was consistent with a Hindu origin. Only in the 1930s did the anthropol-ogist E. P. Elkin establish that the paintings were Aboriginal and represented a group of ancestral spirits known as Wandjinas – not that this has put an end to the search for stylistic traditions and influences: another anthropologist, I. M. Crawford (who supplies the picturesque history recounted above),[9] has recently tried to relate the Wandjinas to another style of figure found in the area, known as the Bradshaw style. Somewhat reluctantly, though, he has concluded that little or no link can be found between them, either chronologically or stylistically.[10]

This little history of interpretation is not without interest. It reveals that 'tradition' and 'influence', far from going together, may be mutually exclusive terms: the search for stylistic influences on the Wandjina paintings only arose in the *absence* of a tradition to which they could be assigned. But, had they belonged to a tradition, this would have defined them as free of certain influences. Again, the fact that the learned fantasia regarding their origins arose out of examining reproductions in a book, not the works themselves, let alone their environment, underlines the technological nature of anthropological (and art historical) discourse. Tradition, as its etymology explains, is precisely what can be passed on without loss: it is what can be reproduced.

Perhaps it is not surprising that when Crawford retraced Grey's footsteps he could find no trace of Grey's prophet. After all, what he sought was not the original but a lithographic likeness. And for that he might have looked anywhere – even in the photograph of a kitchen interior in Waterville, Maine, taken at about the time he was scouring the Kimberleys. When this shot was developed, it was found to contain the image of Wandjina figures. What is more, these images obscured the picture on the kitchen wall: a print of Leonardo's already much faded *Last Supper*.[11]

And this strange coincidence points to where the real significance of the Wandjina story lies – its revelation of the way that a certain kind of cultural assimilation depends on the *absence of the object*. The head 'staring grimly down at me' made present to Grey his own foreignness in the country. It seemed to disapprove of him, to invite him to explain himself. Its eye fixed him, demanding an answer. Briefly Grey was reminded of the contingent nature of his journey, of his dependence on invisible eyes permitting him passage. Momentarily he was recalled to the dialogical nature of his exploration – to the fact that the space he mapped had a historical and social dimension, and that his translation of it into a map was only one among a number of ways forward. But the moment when a dialogue might have been opened and both parties displayed their motives passed: Grey broke eye contact, and inspecting the rest of the figure began to describe its outlines.

Putting into words what he saw, Grey cast a spell of his own against the figure's numinous aura. It was not simply that the language of art enabled the figure to be assimilated to familiar categories: the image's exorcism occurred at a deeper level, in the mere act of silently vocalizing a monologue of sounds, of renaming the place in terms not its own. Its description and reproduction – 'I ordered [the men to] proceed past the cave, so that all would have an opportunity of examining it'[12] – discharged its power to fix the eye, to define a place of dialogue, a ritual of meeting. As it is, the Aborigines whose 'numerous remains' are, both here and later, to be seen everywhere, remain 'invisible'.[13] Rapidly, Grey passes from explorer to tourist and, in doing so, progressively empties the country of its human owners. Blind to the eyes that briefly surrounded him, he refuses to imagine that the country is more than what can be seen, composed from his point of view.

> I sat in the fading light, looking at the beautiful scenery around me, which now for the first time gladdened the eyes of Europeans; and I wondered that so fair a land should only be the abode of savage men; and then I thought of the curious paintings we had this day seen, – of the timid character of the natives, – of their anomalous position in so fertile a country, – and wondered how long these things were to be.[14]

But the anomaly is of his own making and exacerbated by his tendency over the next few days to find a natural connection between the picturesqueness of the country and the paintings it houses. The cave of the prophet, he notes, 'was situated in an exceedingly picturesque position', and he reports that 'after making sketches of the paintings' they paused 'for a few minutes admiring this romantic spot'. A little further on he notes that 'the surrounding hills and cliffs . . . being overshadowed with hanging trees and climbing plants, presented as rich a painting as the eye could behold'.[15]

In the space of a few days the visual initiative has been regained. The country has ceased to be a social space of potential exchange and become a place of private reverie. Instead of signifying human presence, the paintings are interpreted in their absence. The Ngarinyin people have disappeared without even being named. The *natural, aesthetic* convergence between the country and its paintings apparently makes it possible to dispense with any human agency in their production, let alone any site-specific character. Looking with their eyes, out from under the sandstone overhang, the view was spectacular, particularly towards evening – no wonder Grey regretted that 'no

Claude of the tropics had arisen, to transfer to canvass scenes which words cannot express'. It was as if, when the white explorers looked from the Wandjinas' point of view, they saw nothing: neither themselves nor the people of the country, whose handiwork whispered at their shoulders.

As for the paintings, they could be attributed to the influence of an environment that, while local, recognizably belonged to the tradition of the picturesque.

2

In longing for a 'Claude of the tropics' Grey indicated how quickly he could flatten out and frame a historical space, how completely his cultural terms of reference enabled him to assimilate a largely invisible human environment to the visual enclosure of the picturesque. This was the blindness at the heart of his seeing: he mistook what the fixed eye saw for 'reality', and failed to perceive the remainder of space, ritually inscribed with ochre lines, beaten tracks, camping places. In the interests of representation, he drained space of its temporal dimension, the sense in which it was nothing apart from its regular travelling. It is no accident that Grey discovered his first painting 'whilst returning to [his party]'. In retracing his footsteps, Grey was already minimizing the contingency of movement; already the gaze, detached from its responsibility to navigate a route for the body, could fix on distant objects, places where no body could go. The paintings were, from the beginning, a sign that space had peeled off from time, and could be visualized apart from exploratory motion.

As soon as they were seen in this way the Wandjina figures acquired a museum-like quality: as if they were only there to be seen. As a result, instead of remarking on the convergence of interests, on the coincidence that a visible/invisible dialectic seemed to inform the lives of the local people, just as it did that of the explorers, Grey rapidly transposed the tactile evidence of presence into a powerful visual proof of absence. The mere coincidence of seeing the country as it looked back was glazed over; the eye became a mirror again, a pair of field glasses, coated inside to minimize the dazzle of the sun and sealed outside to keep out foreign objects.

At other times, though, the mere coincidence of the space of travelling with a particular mode of seeing could be a means of getting on, a way of occupying the country in a way that did not necessarily appropriate its otherness. Like Grey, the explorer Major Mitchell had 'a little more time for the picturesque' as he retraced his route up the Darling River in 1835. On 9 August he camped in view of a river prospect that especially appealed to him: he wrote a lengthy description of it in his field journal – which was replaced in his published journal by an elegant engraving of the same scene (Plate 5). Mitchell's description, couched very much in the style of 'instructions for painters', makes it clear that he was attracted to the view by its picturesque character, its harmonious composition of Claudean elements: river, overhanging trees, early evening light and expedition men, for all the world like Arcadian shepherds, leading the stock down to water. It was natural, then, particularly in a publication designed to promote the idea of settlement, that Mitchell should choose to represent the scene.

But the scene was not *representative*. As Mitchell observed, '[the twisted branches of an enormous gum tree] checquered a foreground otherwise presenting precisely such patches of warm green and cool grey as painters have usually to invent and add to landscapes, and especially to those no longer bearing the impress of "nature's native taste" '.[16] Here, in other words, was a scene that happened to coincide with the artist's interests: it might not have been typical of the scenery along the Darling River, but it was representable, containing, naturally as it were, those conditions of representation that elsewhere the artist normally had to invent. Such a scene, where nature coincided with art, did not one-sidedly translate an alien landscape into a familiar visual language. It simply took advantage of a visual pun, recording a moment *in time* where the view was equal to the explorer's eye.

Mitchell was as fond of the picturesque in writing as in painting. His place-names were no less allusive than his engravings in the manner of Claude and Salvator Rosa. And he recognized that names, like picturesque frames, might have only a punning connection with reality. On his 1846 expedition into south-west Queensland, he named a river 'Parachute' by analogy with the native word for the water, a word that sounded like 'balloon'.[17] Similarly he was amused to discover that the Aboriginal word for 'a slight elevation' they passed was, in his transliteration, 'too lowly'.[18] There was no question here of attempting to represent an Aboriginal significance: Mitchell mimicked the manner, not the matter, of what they said, the sound not the sense. Such aural and visual coincidences resembled moments of convergent evolution: no common tradition underlay them. If the landscape and its people occasionally spoke in terms the European could understand, it was a mere coincidence.

It would be a mistake to attribute to these punning strategies a suppressed desire of dialogue. Nevertheless, if only by insisting on the unbridgeable distance between how the colonizers and the colonized represented the place where they lived, Mitchell's punning asides were, albeit unintentionally, less one-sided than Grey's resort to tradition. At the very least they recognized that beyond what could be heard and seen lay much more that remained invisible and inaudible; and, further, that this deprivation of the senses was one of the conditions of invasion, and, if it belonged anywhere, belonged not to the country but to the conditions of a knowledge that depended for its reliability on never looking back.

3

Such coincidences could be laughed off, treated as meaningless, but inevitably they reinforced the newcomers' sense of the provisional nature of their passage, the difficulty in escaping from a conceptual and cultural enclosure that cut them off emotionally and intellectually from any chance of seeing and hearing the country differently. It made sense perhaps in these solipsistic circumstances, to seek to make a virtue of coincidence, to see it, not as a sign of the arbitrariness of European names and views, but as the necessary basis of *cultural* occupation, of a form of settlement that did not take for granted the pre-existence of a European-style visual enclosure, but recognized that this had to be constructed – that the first task of imaginative occupation was not to translate Aboriginal tracks into sheep tracks, but to create coincidences, to represent horizons in such a way that they seemed to converge on the eye, to confirm its rightful occupancy of the land, the coincidence of spatial and visual experience.

Such places of convergence might have the same status as retinal after-images, being produced by closing one's eyes to the outside world, but they had the same morphology as the world they excluded. Although a subjective artefact, the image could, in theory at least, be laid over objective reality and, except for certain chromatic differences, pass for the real thing. Although appearing to represent the landscape, their significance might lie in inventing an image, a memorable point of view that brought the landscape into existence, constituting it as an arena subject to exclusively visual control. More even than Major Mitchell, Australia's leading nineteenth-century landscapist Eugen von Guerard seems to exemplify this process, but again the art-historical rhetoric of tradition and influence has obscured the spatial context in which the artist painted, and which his paintings did not merely reflect but helped to create.

In a sense critics have been blinded by von Guerard's verisimilitude – by the habit which a contemporary reviewer attributed to him of providing 'a minutely laborious description of almost every leaf upon the gum trees, and of every vein and crevice in the rocks, which would make them delightful illustrations of a treatise on the botanical and geological features of the colony'.[19] Art historian Daniel Thomas recognizes that von Guerard's paintings 'are not simply topographical', but proceeds to impose on them an alternative determinism of his own: 'from his arrival in Melbourne in 1852 until after his departure thirty years later, [they] should be seen as a late survival of European Romanticism, and more particularly German Romanticism'. Formerly susceptible to influences, von Guerard's eye was, it appears, instantaneously frozen on arrival in Victoria. His extensive sketching tours through three states signified nothing, for wherever he went he was condemned to reproduce the style of his putative masters in Rome and Dusseldorf – even though, according to art historian Candice Bruce, von Guerard may never have seen 'any of Friedrich's paintings . . .'[20]

Von Guerard was kept in the saddle by a *lack* of late Romantic subjects; it was his indifference to the peculiar qualities of the Australian landscape that kept him on the move. One can but marvel at his persistence in keeping going . . . Thomas's argument reveals art-historical discourse at its most self-serving. Although he describes the paintings in complete isolation from the occasions that produced them, he makes the same mistaken assumption as the earlier critic. The latter may have thought von Guerard too realistic, Thomas may find him 'consciously romantic', but both assume that von Guerard's aim was naïve: to reproduce the Australian landscape, to select places self-evidently pleasing to the eye. Neither allows him a constructive role or entertains the possibility that he was not simply a tourist photographing, albeit imperfectly, Australia's picturesque beauty spots, but that his activities preceded this kind of seeing; that his travelling was not supplementary – a passive return to what others had already seen – but the indispensable means of bringing places into being, of rendering what was invisible and mobile visible and statuesque.

Even more than Mitchell, von Guerard sought out the picturesque. Reviewing his South Australian sketchbooks, Alison Carroll remarks, 'He would always have been looking for views while travelling, preferring a high point from which to obtain the best panorama.'[21] And John Tregenza, in the same publication, writes of a sketch made on Mount Lofty, 'He probably spent a little time walking about, looking for an ideal viewpoint, before happening on the precise spot from which it is possible to glimpse a thin sliver of shining sea . . .'[22] Here and elsewhere von Guerard was gathering material for *Australian Landscapes*, a series of lithographs published in 1866–8, 'illustrative of the most striking and picturesque features of the Landscape Scenery of Victoria, New South Wales, South Australia and Tasmania', and the conclusion seems obvious: von Guerard's travels were a pragmatic preliminary to making his talents acceptable to a colonial public.

Von Guerard was hard up and the picturesque paid – particularly when it flattered colonists that their country contained 'mountain ranges as wildly romantic as the European Pyrenees, lakes as picturesque as those of Killarney and waterfalls that may vie with Westmorland'.[23] But this explanation in terms of external influences is no more satisfactory than the art-historical appeal to that internal influence, tradition. Undoubtedly von Guerard's tours and his choice of subject matter were of their time: as Gael Newton has shown, by the 1860s not only commercial artists but also photographers were making expeditions 'in search of picturesque views for commercial sale',[24] and such was the new taste that studios whose chief business had formerly been portraiture were now able to make a living from the sale of sets of stereographs representing picturesque views. But this merely invites the trivial conclusion that von Guerard's landscapes were, however meticulous and artful, typical – historically determined artefacts which, but for the society that purchased them, would probably never have come into existence.

Left out of these accounts is any recognition of the fact that von Guerard did not simply reproduce views, but created them; and the views he created were not the mechanical result of laying a picturesque or sublime template over the countryside, but represented a novel act of seeing, a conscious attempt to construct spaces that could be visualized. The object of his panoramas – which, the art historians have observed, frequently assume an ideal viewpoint – is indeed to sublimate the landscape. Just as Freudian sublimation enables what cannot be spoken to be expressed obliquely by other means, so von Guerard's stereoscopic perspectives, with their interminable horizons and diminutive middle-distance features, admit what the eye cannot admit – a space that precedes vision, uncomposed, infinitely extensive.

The function of these views could be quite as practical as any turned out by the photographic fraternity. In painting the properties of squatters in the Western District of Victoria, for instance, von Guerard did not reproduce a place, *he found it*. In the early days the squatters' runs were not well-defined estates carefully landscaped and perspectived according to the English fashions. Their boundaries were hazy, sometimes nothing more than a visual coincidence of horizon and blue haze. Located at the junction of tracks that were coeval with the first hut, and which expressed no prior direction or location in the landscape itself, the squatter's house often had little topographical authority: adjacent to creeks that were dry or to a lake in the middle of a plain, such buildings floated off the ground, lacking a tradition of sightlines to fix them memorably in place.

Mary Shaw Turner, a descendant of one of von Guerard's Western District patrons, writes of her home at Woorwyrite on Mount Emu Creek:

> To a child who grew up in that house, 'east' always meant seeing from a bedroom window the winter sun rising over the level rim of the world between Mount Meeningoort and the Cloven Hills, 'north' was to look from the front landing up the creek towards Mount Elephant, and 'south' was from the night nursery down-stream to Mackinnon's Hill . . . [25]

But this was later, when time had composed the windows into a view and the house seemed to have a centre, to be a crossing place where the horizon met. To begin with, such landmarks did not exist, the place was featureless. There was no recognizable point of view. It was as if the property were nameless. In this context the fact that the homesteads in what Bruce calls von Guerard's 'homestead landscapes' are dwarfed by their landscapes begins to make sense.

Writing of the Western District landscape *Basin Banks* – also known as *Lake Gnotuk, near Camperdown* (Plate 6) – Bruce remarks, 'The plains stretch without limit and Mount Elephant appears as a mere blip on the horizon. Von Guerard was fond of using the panoramic viewpoint as a means of aggrandising the scene, of increasing the sense of the sublime, the noble, the profound in landscape'. And accordingly she designates this painting a 'sacred landscape'.[26] But Mount Elephant is not merely a 'blip on the horizon': it is a pivotal point or horizon feature in a number of von Guerard's Western District paintings. It is a point of reference, like a surveyor's trig. point, and serves amongst other things to relate his landscapes *to each other*, so that, quite apart from their individual picturesqueness, the paintings from these tours have a proto-cinematic quality, suggesting successive viewpoints or takes.

The 'cut' von Guerard's frame makes in the horizon is not determined visually but spatially: his wide panoramas do not correspond to a fixed point of view. On the contrary, they represent an eye ranging along the horizon until it finds a familiar shape that will enable it to locate itself. For such a point to fix the artist's position, it is necessary for it to be brought into relationship with a third object – it may be a middle-distance homestead or another horizon 'blip'. In this way, triangulating the landscape exactly like an explorer, von Guerard does not merely represent a visual field: he lends it a spatial history, establishing its visual identity in terms of a network of intersecting sightlines – lines that not only document the artist's journey as intimately as a journal, but which also enabled the squatter-patron to *see*, perhaps for the first time, where he belonged.

But what the squatter saw was not his house but the views his house released. The diminutive verandahed building at the centre of the painting was not the picture's focal point. Quite the reverse: it was the vanishing point, a mirror to the eye's own ambition to establish a local perspective without recourse to picturesque stage props. It is no accident that, whether they are 'sublime' or merely 'Australian genre', von Guerard's paintings employ a characteristically stereoscopic perspective. Any attempt to project a curvilinear reality on to a two-dimensional surface obliges the artist to improvise a perspective scheme that saves appearances. Von Guerard's stereoscopy not only preserves the curvilinear depth of the landscape, but exaggerates it, pulling the edges of the view round towards the viewer and pushing the centre away, diminishing it, endowing it with a bowl-like depth. The effect of this may be numinous, but it is also human. It suggests a landscape that has not yet been flattened out and rendered statuesque, a pre-visual realm, still spatially contingent, charged with directions, propelling the traveller forward, opening up ahead and wrapping itself round behind.

Against this background it becomes possible to see a painting like *From the Verandah of Purrumbete* (1858; Plate 7) somewhat differently. Stylistically and thematically it is no doubt not 'typical' of von Guerard's Western District paintings. Considered as spatial history, though, and not in terms of tradition and influence, it may be one of the artist's most personal works. For here, for once at least, there is what might be called a convergent evolution between von Guerard's eye and the eye of the house. It was his practice in a number of his squatter commissions to *fix* the patron's property by painting it from two, often diametrically opposite, points of view. This was the case at Purrumbete where, from the small headland across the lake, he also painted a view looking towards the house (Plate 8). In this sense his verandah view does not so much depict a view as a point of view: in focusing on the headland, it looks back to its origins across the water, to the place whence it was first seen and located.

Bruce draws attention to the linking device of a sailing boat, which appears in both paintings.[27] But more significant in tying them together are their horizons: from the verandah, it is the small hill at the righthand edge that, in conjunction with the headland, fixes the house's location; while, looking back across the water, it is the outline of Mount Elephant that dominates the horizon and, making another triangle between headlands, horizon and house, ensures the view is underwritten by a prior spatial history. As a result the true subject of *From the Verandah* is not a landscape, whether domestic or pastoral, but a visual coincidence, a time and place where a spatial historical event – the active process of visualizing a place – coincided with a place that already had a view of its own.

There was no necessary identity between von Guerard's view and the view from the verandah. It was just that here, fortuitously, a picturesque view punningly mimicked his own spatial history. It was in this sense appropriate that the author of its picturesqueness, the artist who saw and painted it, should not be visible from the verandah, but should be represented, if at all, by a horizon.

4

Genealogies are an invitation to ingenuity. On the face of it nothing could resemble von Guerard's fertile panoramas less than Russell Drysdale's outback towns, their bare telegraph poles and verandahs reduced to a Giacometti-like thinness expressive of a drought as much psychic as physical. Compare the fairground animation of von Guerard's *Ballarat in the Early Times*, with its sense of a tent town subtly transforming itself into a permanent settlement, with the terrible abandonment of the main street in *Sofala* (Plate 9) or *Hill End*, where a whitish gable end suggests nothing so much as the ghost of a tent and the pallor of its promise. Even more obviously, contrast the outcast human giants who brood over Drysdale's foregrounds with the serene emptiness of most of von Guerard's views where, apart from the occasional, picturesquely located Aborigine, the country appears wholly unoccupied.

But these contrasts, although they make art-historical sense, conceal as much as they reveal. For all their differences, and despite the apparent lack of influence of one on the other, the two artists share an obsession with perspective or, more exactly, with the precise location of things. Framed in sharply receding verandahs or sometimes nailed to the background with orthogonal shadows, Drysdale's figures find their place, cease to be mere outcasts, in the fateful, if momentary, construction of a point of view. But implicit in their photographic arrest beside a gate or between verandah posts is the slow motion of the observer, the regular parallax of verticals opening and closing, framing a figure, cutting it in half, eclipsing it. Different as their subject matter may be, von Guerard and Drysdale belong to a common culture of seeing; they take it for granted that 'reality', if it is to have any representative power, is the construction of a point of view.

To unearth what has not been seen before and to reveal its invisibility, its spatial contingency, its relationship to the finder: this is the paradoxical quality to be found in the work of both artists. But is it mere coincidence? The idea of something no sooner found than concealed, seen only in order to be hidden, irresistibly suggests that perennial object of Australian desire: gold. Is it fanciful, ingenious, to propose this symbolic metal as the underground connection linking these two artists? Von Guerard left the Ballarat field when it failed to fulfil its promise and commenced his topographical career – his *Ballarat in the Early Times* was painted some thirty years after the event; Drysdale drove across to paint Hill End (another gold-rush town) when its promise had long been exhausted. Both confronted the paradox of an emptiness that could be seen, the physical layout of a fantasy whose spur was the invisibility of the thing to be found.

This paradox, the invisible secret at the heart of the gold-rush spectacle, need not have influenced either artist consciously. It belonged to, and continues to exemplify, a paradox characteristic of the Australian tradition of seeing. Historians have made the point that Beaufroy Merlin's now famous collection of photographs depicting life on the goldfields of New South Wales in the early 1870s would never have been made without the generous patronage of Bernard Holtermann, one of the wealthiest of Hill End's gold-rich citizens. But while the camera might aim to represent something of the atmosphere of the times, 'the off-beat cacophony of the stamper batteries; the winter snow whispering through the trees; the muffled clink of the dolly pot and pestle reducing stolen ore . . . the bowyanged miners, blue-grimed from the slate dust of the drives . . .',[28] it could not capture the moment of discovery, of coincidence between desire and reality. At the heart of its seeing was a blindness, a secret that could not be revealed.

The visual elusiveness of gold belonged less to a metal than to the cast of eye so narrowly devoted to finding it. The itinerant digger, bent on extracting the amber of the earth, did not have an ecological vision. He was prepared to destroy the landscape, literally turning the ground upside-down, in order to find what he wanted to see. As even that connoisseur of natural beauty, W. Howitt, had to admit, 'We diggers are horribly destructive of the picturesque.'[29] But this exploitative view (both literally and metaphorically) of one's surroundings was not exclusively tied to gold: it was characteristic more generally of a culture that assessed its visual and cultural capital increasingly in photographic terms. The camera shutter was a little guillotine: whatever it represented, whether it was a view, an Aboriginal profile or a flower, the photographic image signified the death of historical time and space. However clearly it mimicked the eye, its seeing was a form of blindness – not because it did not see clearly, but because to see everything was to risk focusing on nothing.

This traditional, and perhaps distinctively local, tension between seeing and non-seeing throws light on the relationship between Drysdale's travel slides – recently turned into large colour prints and exhibited in Melbourne – and his outback paintings. In 1944 newspaper magnate Warwick Fairfax commissioned Drysdale to tour the New South Wales outback in order to record the effects of the drought. In 1951 the artist visited Cape York Peninsula. In 1956, with his family, he motored through the Northern Territory and, a year or so later, he returned to this region with scientists, Jock Marshall and Dom Serventy. These were the trips that furnished Drysdale with the great themes of his paintings, and on the latter two into Australia's north-west he also took a camera with him.

Some of the images Drysdale brought back strikingly resembled scenes he had previously painted. In other cases, the photographs were purely 'scientific', recording rock paintings, wild flowers, desert animals. Like von Guerard, Drysdale had a scientific interest in the country: in recording wild flowers, desert animals, and even Aboriginal art, his camera served the same function as von Guerard's sketchbook, enabling him to record geological and botanical details that were visually interesting, even if they had no obvious aesthetic value. But the camera's view was also palpably different from that of the eye. It was not merely that it arrested time: it drained the view of meaning. Filling up the frame with details, it made a cult of coincidence. It suggested that the whole of reality could be represented to the eye, even if only in a fragmentary manner.

At the same time, the very arbitrariness of its visual arrangements suggested that something was left out – the point of view perhaps, the one-sidedness of the insight. There is a sunlit sidewalk, with

distant figures (one with umbrella) framed in a light tunnel of verandahs (Plate 10). The baker's casts its own crazy perspective across a
corrugated fence. A girl gets off (on to?) her bike; another girl with
her baby carriage caught in a tramtrack of post shadows. This in the
two-thirds of the frame to the left of the telegraph post; and to the
right, a tawny road wide as a paddock, wakes of trucks, the dark
trickle of a tree's shadow, a distant hotel. Beyond, negative objects,
objects without shadow, cirrus clouds on the town's edge.

What exactly is *seen* here? It is *Cloncurry, July 1956* – Drysdale's
record of a place passed through on his first outback trip. But what
is this? The artful composition of the photograph is obvious. De
Chirico would have approved the space's laconic punctuation, the
spindly galleries, the blatant chiaroscuro. But something more (and
less) gets into the picture: the clouds' entropic tendency to dissipate
the significance of events, the pure ambiguity of reality when it is
treated purely as a visual artefact. What do these metonymic fragments
add up to? Not a community, but an emptiness, a falling apart, disguised by the brightness of the colours.

Against this the meaning of Drysdale's oil and gouache outback
main streets becomes clearer; they aim to prevent the emptiness
from falling apart into mere picturesqueness. Resisting the all-seeing
pretensions of the travelling eye, they seek to preserve an invisibility,
a historical space whose broken mould is visible in the burnt tree, the
sheet of iron, a factory-high wall, but whose body remains enigmati-
cally invisible.

5

At the heart of the colonial culture of seeing was the invisibility of
the Aborigines. A way of seeing, foreshadowed in Grey's attention
to the Wandjinas' aesthetic rather than political meaning, rapidly
increased the distance between the two cultures. Aborigines became
figures in a landscape and, as their viewpoints were taken over, dissolved into thin air and disappeared. Their absence from places of
white settlement soon became normal. Soon it was their exceptional
and alarming *appearance* that exercised the pens of explorers and
settlers. By the latter part of the nineteenth century they had become
in the popular imagination as dreamlike and enigmatic as the interior;

expeditions were sent out to discover and study them. Before long anthropologists reincarnated Aborigines in forms that coincided with the means of their representation – the demonstration of native customs, no less than ethnographical theories, depending on the willingness of the people being studied to stand still, to pose in unnatural poses, to submit to having their photographs taken.

Perhaps this helps explain the fascination of Drysdale's strangely theatrical, yet deaf-mute figures. His solitary men and women, the huddled groups and the children, who face the painter so stoically, courageously, uncomprehendingly occupy the same place in his work as the Aborigines in the explorer literature. In Giles, in Mitchell, in Grey, the Aborigines invariably step forward, perceptibly overcoming their nervousness. Barbarically scarified and skeletoned with white paint, they are both ugly and dignified. They confront the intruder courageously; then, just as someone was about to speak or perhaps take a lightning sketch, they back away, leaving the foreground emptier than before. Drysdale's common folk, scrutinizing imminent destruction, inexplicably staying on, are noble savages in a comparable way. It seems that Drysdale views his own people as an anthropologist would, fascinated by their way of life but indifferent to the politics of it.

But if rural Australians were Aboriginalized, what about Drysdale's Aborigines (Plate 11)? Paradoxically, his now unfashionable voyeurism, his apparent willingness to view young black women through a glass stained with ebony and crimson, to stress their exotic physicality, may have had something to do with the sophistication of his own visual technology: by the late 1950s the advent of colour film was making it possible to break down the old black-and-white distinctions, to see the exotic in its true colours. This visual coincidence was technological not spiritual, but it presented the artist with a challenge comparable to that his nineteenth-century predecessors confronted with the invention of photography. If painting was now to retain its expressive authority, its emphasis must turn from the representation of colours to the act of colouring.

Drysdale's visual dilemma has a close literary parallel in Douglas Lockwood's *I, the Aboriginal*, published in 1962. This ghosted autobiography, based on more than one hundred hours of interviews with Phillip Waipuldanya, an Alawa man from the Northern Territory, purports to offer an accurate account of an Aboriginal point of view.

It seems likely that the fullness of Lockwood's account results, at least in part, from access to the latest sound technology: the wire recorder transformed voice recording, replacing the formerly cumbersome business of recording on wax with a machine that was economical, capable of running at length and usable in the most informal of settings. But the accuracy of transcription the new technology made possible did not lead Lockwood to write a more 'scientific' account. Instead he represented Waipuldanya's *voice* by inventing a hybrid argot all his own: 'It was one walkabout time at Mount Saint Vidgeon in the Never-Never Land south of the Roper River that the Medicine Man, the Doctor Blackfellow, tried to kill me . . .'[30]

The motive behind this style may have been the same as the primitivizing impulse in some of Drysdale's Aboriginal paintings: not to represent 'the Aborigine', but to represent the difficulty of representation, the blindness at the heart of seeing. In a sense Drysdale's paintings ask us to reflect on the voyeuristic assumptions of our seeing, to see that what we see is not 'reality', but an exotic artefact created by the way we look. Our images, the way we name the world, may double up with how others see it, but can never represent their point of view. Any likeness will be coincidental, one-sided and, unless we see the coincidence for what it is, it will blind us to the contingency of our historical space, our culture of seeing. It is just this doubleness that Lockwood tries to capture in phrases like 'in the Never-Never Land south of Mount Roper' or 'the Medicine Man, the Doctor Blackfellow'.

Such duplications represent the difficulty of finding a common language in which to represent ourselves to each other. It is as if Lockwood's Aboriginal I internalizes both sides of an imaginary Aboriginal–European dialogue. He glosses his own words in terms his white interviewer can understand. But the terms he uses are not translations from one language to another. They are equivalent phrases that run in parallel. At no point do they touch down in a common reality, capturing the difference between two spoken languages. If Waipuldanya's double-tongue represents anything, it is the fact that dialogue need not converge on a third, synthetic reality, a common place of agreed meaning, but can remain a game of mere coincidences, in which equivalent phrases are traded back and forth without any access of mutual understanding.

These are not theoretical issues. They bear directly, for example, on the life and work of Albert Namatjira. Most accounts of Namatjira present the awkward in-between position he came to occupy in the European and Aranda communities of Hermannsburg and Alice Springs as an indictment of race relations in Australia, whose tragic consequences could have been avoided had white Australians not continued to apply a double standard to their black countrymen – applying pressure on them to conform to white ways and ostracizing them when they did so. All of this is true, but it implies that Namatjira's art, the great series of central Australian landscapes he produced between 1936, when he first learnt watercolour techniques from white artist Rex Battarbee, and his death in 1959, was produced despite circumstances; as if, in his art, Namatjira put personal problems behind him. What could be more serene or mystically calm than his unpeopled landscapes with their glowing rust and mauve ridges, their anthropomorphic ghost gums, their delicate braid of burnt branches and rock shadows?

Those who tried to explain his rapid emergence as an artist of exquisite sensibility employed a contradictory vocabulary. On the one hand the transformation of a visually illiterate Aranda tribesman into an outstanding painter in the European manner was little short of miraculous; on the other, Namatjira was a natural.[31] Such terms recall Grey's confused reaction to the Wandjina figures and reflect the inadequacy, not to say self-contradiction, of art-historical rhetoric's appeal to the twin idols of tradition and influence. Here was a person who, though ignorant of a Western tradition of representation, proved supremely susceptible to its influence – but instead of reflecting that this paradox might be of their own making, the consequence of importing a theory of creativity that had little or no local application, Namatjira's apologists twisted his activity to suit their own habits of thinking.

In a curious way Namatjira's supposed lack of visual education, combined with an apparently miraculous ability to mimic European ways, allied him to a long, if ironic, Australian tradition. From the earliest days of colonization Europeans had been impressed by the Aborigines' mimetic skills. When Battarbee asserted that in the early weeks of Namatjira's apprenticeship 'no ordinary white man could have done what Albert did in such a short time',[32] he implicitly identified the artist's talent with his Aboriginality. Even as he stressed his non-European spontaneity, Battarbee affiliated Namatjira to another, local tradition. Namatjira's extreme susceptibility to European influences proved him to be at heart a good nationalist, a dinkum Australian capable of making something out of nothing. What could be more Australian than Namatjira's wartime resourcefulness? When paper became unavailable, 'He made "canvases" from the timber of the beanwood trees by cutting sections measuring 10 by 16 inches and sandpapering them to a satin-smooth finish.'[33]

But in the end this genealogical ingenuity of the white patrons and commentators only showed that Namatjira was an 'artist', a freak of nature who had blossomed on Australian soil, proof that here, as well as anywhere else, a creator could flourish, whose style was distinct, whose object was clear and, ultimately, no different from that of other artists. As one white observer, Andrew Schubert, remarked:

> I looked at his painting and it was a faithful reproduction of the scene in front of him. Towering walls of weathered sandstone, varying in colour from deep vermilion to shaded ochre rose sheer from the ancient river bed. Softly fronded palm trees were reflected in the crystal clear waters of rock pools, a solitary ghost gum's pure white trunk a striking contrast to the massive red boulders. I watched as Albert put the finishing touches to his painting with sure, deft strokes of his brush. He was a born artist and, as his interpretation of the scene before him proved, a great artist.[34]

Missing was any suggestion that Namatjira's paintings might conceal as much as they revealed; that, rather than represent a shared visual reality, they might mimic a European point of view and, by visualizing the country in picturesque ways, perpetuate the white viewer's blindness to its spatial history. His was not simply a 'faithful reproduction' of nature, but perhaps a perfect imitation of a way of seeing. Any resemblance to the world he or his patrons lived in was purely coincidental.

An impressive roll-call of anthropologists and art historians have quite properly rejected the simplistic assimilation of Namatjira to the Western category of genius. But, while they have pointed out how the promotion of the man and his art suppressed its social and political context, they have not entertained the possibility that the paintings themselves were strategic – that *in purely visual terms* they exploited the ambiguities at the heart of a culture of coincidence and, situated between two cultures, offered, not a unilateral view of the country but a double vision, a mirror to our unseeing, not insight.

T. G. H. Strehlow, who made the Aranda his life's study, noted that 'By learning its [watercolours's] techniques a full-blooded aboriginal could win respect and social standing in the new but inescapable world of European ways and ideas.'[35] Ian Burn and others have observed that inside Aboriginal society, too, there were significant benefits: Namatjira's art, and the money it brought in, was a way of establishing his authority among his own people – his sharing of his art with his children and relatives was a means of giving substance and meaning to traditional kinship ties.[36] Another art historian, Daniel Thomas, agreeing with John Brackenreg (who painted with Namatjira and considered that the artist 'was showing us, the newcomers, the lineage and the mythology of his people'), has recently interpreted the paintings symbolically, politically: 'Are those blackened stumps intended to remind us of human mutilation?'[37]

But, in different ways, these corrective perspectives still remain blind to the act of seeing these paintings represent – a coincidence of perception that, far more profoundly than any semiotic or social meaning attributed to the paintings, expresses Namatjira's in-between status and, more generally, the provisional nature of seeing in a country that has been colonized. At the climactic moment of his little monograph on Namatjira, the anthropologist, Charles Mountford, describes how – like Andrew Schubert – he came upon the artist painting in Palm Valley (see Plate 12), a few miles from his own 'dreaming-place'. At Mountford's request, Namatjira put aside his watercolour and began to explain, with the help of a drawing, 'the legend and geography of the surrounding country':

> Then happened something which I never expected to see, even in my most fantastic visions. It was surely an experience without parallel to watch a man depicting, in the most primitive of all arts, beliefs that stretched back to the dawn of his creation, while lying beside him, the product of the same hand, were beautiful water-colours in the art of today. It scarcely seemed possible that any man could have bridged that immense gap in artistic expression.[38]

But had Namatjira 'bridged that immense gap'? Could it not be that the watercolour *concealed* the meaning of the place – but concealed it in such a way that, to white eyes, it looked like the clearest representation of it?

In this sense Namatjira's visually appealing landscapes commemorate the invisibility of his people. They represent in the only way possible in a culture of coincidence a doubling up of vision that at once penetrates the country and renders it nameless, mute and without eyes of its own. The more clearly and passively Namatjira represents his tribal land, the more he strips it of picturesque interest – eschewing clouds, times of day, figures and natural details – the more he opens it to the eye. At the same time though, he taunts the eye with its enigma; as if, however much it is stripped back to essentials and simplified for white consumption, something remains invisible, untranslatable. But this sense of visual taboo is not to be attributed to the artist's 'genius'. It reflects the fragile nature of the historical space to which he has been relegated, the provisional character assigned to his ownership of the land. It embodies the tragedy of a visual culture where the Aborigine could survive only by disappearing, by clothing himself in white clothes and white ways so as not to darken the landscape.

6

Strolling in the groves of Australian art we come across a number of native views where a kind of convergent evolution seems to have occurred. In the paintings of von Guerard, Drysdale or Namatjira scenes are represented in which the point of view of the artist briefly appears to coincide with a view inherent in the country, in which the artist's spatial history – the contingency of his relationship to the country where he finds himself – is answered by the arrangement of objects. The harmony of the composition that results does not reflect a natural community of interest between the human eye and the landscape; it is not a pledge of arrival and occupation. On the contrary, it is artefactual and, at the heart of the balancing act whereby it orders objects in an arrangement pleasing to the eye, is a recognition of the blindness acts of visual representation entail: the forms uniquely composed here are typically invisible.

Recognizing the paintings' historical significance as acts of seeing, as translations of space into albeit brief meeting places, it becomes perhaps less important to describe them in art-historical terms. Now that the aim is democratic – not to establish the artist's genius in terms of his cultural sources and antecedent masters, but to affiliate him to a history of colonization, whose success depends on improvising contextually persuasive rhetorics (visual as well as verbal) capable of lending the strange at least a veneer of familiarity – it also becomes possible to substitute for the metropolitan myth of common origins and shared standards a *colonial* model for the transmission of ideas, styles and motifs.

When Rushdie speaks of 'imagining and re-imagining the world', he does not mean to imply a retreat from 'reality'. Rather, 'A writer who understands the artificial nature of reality is more or less obliged to enter the process of making it.'[39] Similarly, to throw off the incubus of a too narrowly conceived idea of cultural dependence is not to retreat into narcissism: it simply means acknowledging the historical resonance of our own fleeting, everyday perceptions. Whatever the origins of the terms we use, it is we who improvise out of them a world of meanings. And, even if the forms we create resemble remarkably those evolved elsewhere, it does not follow that they express the same meanings or are the outcome of identical historical processes.

These Australian paintings understand 'the artificial nature of reality'. It is not that they respect the conventions governing any transference of three-dimensional reality on to a two-dimensional surface; or that they betray the signature of style. It is the sense they convey that their verisimilitude, their attempt to document landscape elements with an almost photographic objectivity, is not a natural reaction to the character of the country, but represents an attempt to overcome the inertia of its ordinary invisibility. Despite stylistic appearances, these paintings do not naïvely represent reality. Rather they mimic what we can see, revealing how little of our surroundings we are able to visualize. Instead of converging on the landscape, these images converge on the seeing eye. The convergent evolution of eye and image mimics the mechanism of the planetarium where we see the stars constellated most memorably by roofing over the night sky.

Why should this schizophrenic cultural vision have emerged? Why should clear seeing (and painting) seem to depend on *not* seeing the country, or the points of view it already contains? And why, equally puzzling, should this migrant condition continue to go unrecognized? Despite his Blue Mountains musings on the possibility of two creators, Darwin was a biological monotheist. *The Origin of Species* stresses divergences within species – quite naturally, as without these natural selection could hardly occur. Only once does Darwin refer to convergences between unrelated species, and then it is to imply that the phenomenon is rare and in any case explicable in evolutionary terms. Still, and albeit negatively, in another of his publications, *The Expression of the Emotions in Man and Animals* (1873), Darwin does deal with the phenomenon of convergence in terms that relate directly to the historical context in which von Guerard, Drysdale and many other local painters have worked.

In *The Expression of the Emotions* Darwin tried to show that the physical manifestations of emotions – low spirits, joy, anger, disdain, shame – were broadly the same in all human races, and even had analogies among the higher animals. The argument rested heavily on the results of a questionnaire Darwin had circulated worldwide to acquaintances of his in close contact with 'savage races' and in which he had asked them to describe the native physical expressions associated with the different emotional states. The claim to racial representativeness was exaggerated: over a third of Darwin's respondents came from Australia, and the majority of these were based in Victoria. But the local bias of Darwin's sample did not prevent him from concluding that the remarkable coincidence between the emotional expressions of civilized and savage races could not be due to, say, mere convergent evolution. It clearly implied 'the several races being descended from a single parent stock'.[40]

Darwin's aim was to prove that our basic expressions of emotion *were not learned by imitation, but were instinctive.* Hence he largely excludes from his reckoning the social context of emotions and their expression. He does not entertain the possibility that emotional expressions might be a form of communication. He treats as equivalent involuntary expressions of pain and (one would have thought) rather more self-conscious manifestations such as pouting, smiling and blushing. This determination to isolate the emotions from their human context has its counterpart in the photographs Darwin assembles: in interpreting his photographs of little children laughing and crying, he never comments on the strangeness of the photographic artefact – on the double misery the little person suffers, first denied comfort and now cut off a second time by the camera's shutter. Such is his positivist bias that, although the data are nothing apart from his ability to recognize their meaning (their projection of feelings familiar to him) Darwin, the observer, never acknowledges the observer's role in stimulating the expressions he observes.

However, in interpreting emotional expressions the observer's expectations and experience are central. Darwin himself notes how in reading a photograph of a young man, prepared by the French psychologist Duchenne to demonstrate 'aggressive hardness', 'knowing what was intended, my imagination added, as I believe, what was necessary, namely a frowning brow; and consequently the expression appeared to me true and extremely morose'.[41] He further remarks that when the photograph was shown to eleven persons unacquainted with Duchenne's purpose only one of them guessed correctly the emotional expression intended.

Nor is it simply that emotional expressions may be meaningless unless they happen to coincide with the observer's expectations: the very form they take may be precipitated by the observer. Writing to Darwin in 1869, his old *Beagle* shipmate, P. G. King, asked, 'Did you ever get any answers to your queries about the habits and manners of our blackfellows? I tried to make some answers but found myself unable to distinguish the aboriginal manner from the acquired habit. All blacks I have been associated with have been more or less civilised.'[42] In other words, when Darwin's savage races expressed their emotions in ways recognizably similar to those of civilized man, it was by no means proof of a common heritage. Quite the opposite: it might reflect nothing more than an imitative faculty, one brought into play by the mere presence of the whites, and modelled on white behaviour.

The point of this little excursus into *The Expression of the Emotions* is that it illuminates those methodological assumptions that have made it possible for historians and ethnographers to overlook the phenomenon of cultural convergence. In cross-cultural situations where there is no common 'reality', sign languages, expressions of all kinds are improvised around mere coincidences. These coincidences may be verbal, taking the form of puns, or visual, taking the form of paintings that exploit nature's parodic mimicry of art's picturesque conventions; or they may be physical, a repertoire of emotional expressions borrowed from the other side and imitated – not to communicate an emotion, but to communicate a desire to communicate. But whatever form they take, they arise in the absence of a common heritage and they express the migrant perception that reality is an artefact and can be made well or badly. But it seems clear that, so long as we continue to evoke the genealogical rhetoric of tradition and influence, this alternative expressive tradition will remain unrecognized.

4 Towards a Sound Photography

A Lake Eyre Notebook

5 August 1989

Driving between the Murray, Australia's largest river, and the south-western catchment of Lake Frome, between powdery veils of rain falling always between us and the hills: how little our memory is visual. The retracing of roads or, better, the tracing of roads that are already re-tracings resembles the old gramophone needle tracking the record. The journeying does not represent something else – an inventory of views. It embodies a particular history, precisely enacting an original movement. Why do we not subject our roads to preservation? In the Otway Ranges on the south coast they have allowed enormous switchback highways to bypass or cover over the old zigzag tracks winding up and down the hills. Don't they see that this changed rate of passage, this aerial fantasy of immediate arrival – from which any gradient, any memorable interference with the pure pneumatic melody, has been cleansed – desecrates the bodies of the dead as effectively as the *remastering* of a cemetery, its smooth resurfacing as a *memorial park?*

Not that these old roads are filled with memories if by memories we mean biographical associations. From this point of view they are wholly unmemorable: the filmic succession of stills created by the rhythm of passing telegraph poles is the only sign of a subliminal structuring of the flow of time, its arrest into movement-images. Here the memory is the physical trace of a particular intention and the technology that realized it – the tracks bear witness to the character of the travellers' horizons, their origins, interests. Only in our passage it has all been speeded up: our country speaks with a Walt Disney voice.

This speed is in any case a form of forgetfulness. Even the embodiment of the country in these tracks was a form of photography – a visualizing of space – that was foreign to the vocal trace that marked, say, the Aborigines' recital of the country, *their* circulation of it in song. The old roads were photographic plates you carried around on your back; the later ones went on until the spool was empty . . .

We get out of the car near Craddock: the dark wind, babblers in the middle-distance thorn bushes; we inspect the 'roundhouse' at Peterborough, where the clap of pigeons' wings seems to play back the breaking of the building's long-broken windows; we look at a collection of anthropomorphic rocks in a window in Hawker, coruscated mouths, hard, twinkling eyes; everywhere, listening in vain for the word, the more than historical echo, the non-imitative *sound* that would give us legitimate access to the land, that would persuade us we had woken up and were not talking to ourselves . . . Behind the steering wheel the roar is utterly silent. A spectacular 'coronet of mountains' swings into view, like a lost Eden.

6 August

A dream in which a book has been written about my book. Much socializing in large Georgian houses. Bryce is promoting a photographic exhibition based on my book – 'my best work yet'. And I meet the young critic – an east-coast American by the sound of his voice – who says, 'I was drawn to your work by an interest that probably has nothing to do with what you intended, an interest in "sound photography" . . .' In my dream this seemed perfectly reasonable but, except perhaps as a description of a vocal spectrograph, what can the phrase mean?

Alexander Bell's father wrote a book called *Visible Speech* but I had the feeling the dream man meant something else: a kind of writing that respected the laws of sound, that did not exclude the environment of the sound source but, with the same respect for circumstantial detail as a photograph, let back in the inland sea of noise that plays along the littoral of our ears, day in, day out, and connects us to the world.

These thoughts follow with Freudian predictability from yesterday's meditation. They precede my return to the mythic site where *The Road to Botany Bay* began: St Mary's Peak in the Flinders Range north of Adelaide where ten years ago I saw the country laid out like a museum of natural forms and wondered what lexicon could possibly connect them, where it occurred to me that the 'ABC Range' named this difficulty (or so I said afterwards when I was asked how I had the idea for the book).

The day dawns frosty, brilliant. Sun dazzle from a roadside pool burns its image on my retina: I see a fading blue lagoon on the page where I write. Going over the dream again I recall something different: my sense of being both a guest in someone else's house and a host in my own, of penetrating private apartments and being treated as a lover or brother . . . the book as a social passport, a key to a formerly hidden country. But I felt no less displaced – like an anthropologist who, after months of painful study, gets the people he's studying to understand what he says, only to feel a stranger to himself.

Climbing the saddle between the inside and outside of Wilpena Pound – Tanderra Saddle – and throughout the stormy descent inside as far as Cooinda Camp, eyes on the ground, picking a way forward through a mosaicked relief of small rocks, pebbles – series of sandstones (white through iron red), quartzites near the top briefly. These different rocks are interspersed with plants in flower – various blues, a mauve lilac, etc. While the plants have names, the comparably individual rocks have none – or so I thought. Because they break in different ways, have different cross-sections of colours, varying combinations of elements, to describe them as, say, 'fractured sandstone' fails to capture their local distinction – their spatial distribution, their relationship to each other, here before one's feet.

In this environment, growing at discreet intervals from one another, plants can be conceived of in detachment from their surroundings. Here, over there, and five minutes on, one species of plant remains the same, attaining the same height, foliage and colouration. But rocks lack this crystalline predictability. Despite their hardness, they are vulnerable to wind and rain. Mandelstam was right: stone is concreted meteorology. But the abstraction of geological language disguises this; its insistence on deep processes which rocks *represent* suppresses the fact that these hillsides of coloured stones *are* the history of the region. They are the outcome of a long process of deposition, concretion, uplift, weathering. But they do not represent these processes: they *are* the literal, physical trace of them. The forces that created them are written in their shapes, colours, textures and sounds. They are coeval with the watersounds they orchestrate, with the waterfalls' stopped flutes. To think of these patterned surfaces as illustrations of processes that occur in any case is wrong. They are, like the weather, unrepresentative: their distribution can no more be predicted than the exact edge of the rain.

A perfect rainbow framed the way home, as we threaded the flooded paths through the Callitris plains, and E., who is six years old, wondered why we could not seem to pass underneath it. Similarly the bluffs and gorges do not represent visual effects: they are musical instruments. The play of wind across their surfaces, the *pointillisme* of scattered boulders, are both sounds, though recorded in different registers. No wonder the drift of pebbles is unmemorable: even the choral gathering of stones in the bed of the running creek leaves no distinct impression. One remembers instead the play of light, the pluvial recital. Stones mark journeys, not places; processes, not ideas.

Perhaps E. intuited their true nature best when, up and down the paths – while we turned our glasses on the exquisite plumage of a Mallee ring-neck, momentarily steady on the branch ahead – he sang out the sounds of a car changing gear or a steam engine, puff-puffing out of the station. Roads are for transport, they are places to remember journeys, reveries of other kinds of movement, including the slow motion that, over millions of years, turns shoals of tropical fish into a field of stone shells.

7 August

Rain at night on the caravan roof. Wind in the casuarinas and Callitris. Pre-dawn magpies, magpie-larks, galahs, ring-necks ... at dawn walked down the Kangaroo Gap in the Ulowdna Range (a small offshoot of the main Flinders Range) – a name suggesting amplification – and set up the microphone by the creek. Wind in the red gums, later an aircraft, the thin 'cher-cher-cher' of a red-capped robin ... the sense of shaping this into a sound event, an enclosure.

The stream sound began to acquire form: a periodicity of microsounds repeating themselves or subtly modulated by local variations in water-flow or wind-pressure. It began to be woven into my biography through its association with other sounds – the harsh calls of galahs and corellas, like outlines of hillsides, cut across its steady progress, threatening to arrest or accelerate its sound gradient. And besides this, the mere fact of recording it, of composing it into a sound photograph, a representative picture of an acoustic place.

My recording is not simply a trace; it retains a nostalgia for visual enclosure. This is evident even in the simple consideration that the microphone must be kept out of the wind and free from moisture. And there's the necessity to foreground one sound at the expense of others, to create with the direction of the microphone and the volume control an acoustic space quite unlike the natural one. Implicit in this insulation from the environment is the point of view of the eighteenth-century observer, imagining that he views nature in relative security, through a window.

What does it mean to record voices under studio conditions? When we listen to the 'dry' studio sound of BBC radio, we do not listen to people speaking: it is as if they conduct an inner monologue with themselves, one impervious to the background noise that accompanies live speech. They speak as we speak when we read silently words on a page. The one element that this style of radio consistently suppresses is the *sound* of things – voices, places.

The approach to the 'rock paintings' at Arkaroo is appropriately enough picturesque. Which is to say that the course of the track as it winds across the creek and up towards the base of the bluff creates in the visitor a sense of expectation. The hollow rock, an enormous egg broken open, comes into view only over the last rise: so, after shuffling past Perugino, Pinturicchio and the rest, one is ushered in half a dozen languages into the *silence* of the Sistine Chapel – a silence, one is always glad to note, persistently broken by the venomous hissing of many voices and feet.

But the paintings and the environment contradict these pictorial effects. An ochre line fading into the 'natural' line of a rain-rouged standstone stratum indicates a different relationship, one not of enclosure, but of what anthropologist Catherine Ellis, discussing the aesthetics of Aboriginal music, calls 'incorporation'.

The rock is a sound broken open to reveal its inner structure; at the confluence of two chattering streams, it relays their vibrations stereophonically: emu tracks, double lines, radiant circles. It is a mouth ridged like the human mouth; one imagines the sub-vocalic hum that accompanied the drawing of these lines, the historical rumour. The abstraction of parallel lines immediately suggests musical notes or intervals; the repetition of sinuous and straight lines embodies the rhythm of movement, of gestures that still retain a connection with the physical gesture needed to paint them, and whose other natural surface is found in the contours of the human body, ceremonially masked.

Not pictorial, but pictographic, these are designs to be *read* . . . that much is by now conventional white wisdom. Less heeded is the silencing that 'reading' itself involves. These are gestures to be *sounded*, enacted: their semiotic reduction to various kinds of map represents the distance of the gaze from what is seen – a division that is symbolically and physically commemorated here by the prison-camp wire grid protecting the paintings from graffitists. The grid – the anthropologist's friend when he tries to copy these painted concavities on to the flat surface of a book – disembodies us from the world of these lines. It is we, not they, who become flat and, lacking the concavity of this natural mouth and ear, acutely conscious of the banality of anything we are likely to say.

By Leigh Creek the ladders of rain had withdrawn into the sky. Dissected tablelands of cloud shadowing the northern horizon foreshadowed what lay beyond. About here the explorer Eyre noticed the ringing quality of the stones in the creek bed, metallic like bells. Has anyone paid attention to the sounds of exploration? Another explorer, Sturt, described a butcher-bird at Flood Creek that learnt a tune from one of his men. He named another bird that had 'the power of throwing its voice to a distance' and, even when it sang overhead, 'fell on our ears as if it had been some large bird upon the plain', the 'Ventriloquist'. And what of the report of cannons and the impression of castles collapsing that assailed their ears?

The geologist, J. W. Gregory, refers to 'the well-known "desert sound", when the stillness of the night is often broken by a deep booming, which appears to rise from below the surface of the ground'. He attributes this to earth movements along fault lines, but I am unconvinced. For sounds like these have been heard elsewhere. Settlers in the early days of Sydney, Melbourne and Adelaide all report inexplicable tremors and rumblings, thunderclaps out of a clear sky, distant guns. After a while the country settled down and fell silent, but to begin with it was filled with tortured voices. The desert sound is no longer heard: it was the sound of our arrival, the echo of our dread.

Gregory found little to delay him at Hergott's Springs in 1902. With the closing of the railway in 1981, there is even less reason to stay. The effect was dramatic: 'overnight', they assured us, Marree's population fell from 800 to eighty. Marree: after the theatre of the absurd the theatre of absence:

– Sleep all right last night, Den?
– Yeah, when I wasn't awake.
– Like that, was it?
– (*after a pause*) Still you couldn't complain about the noise.

At the 'Tourist Park', 8 August

But the noise was there, even if it was inaudible: the Tourist Park people said that 'Hergott's Springs' had been changed to 'Marree' at the height of anti-German feeling during the First World War. However we bought *Marree: A History of the Birdsville Track* from them and learnt that the town was already officially called Marree as early as 1883. In any case 'Hergott' had been a misspelling, the discoverer of the artesian waters being a Mr Herrgott and not, as Gregory explains, 'a profane German'. As for Marree, it is a sound signifying nothing, a word without a meaning. Our book thoughtfully refutes the claim that the word might be Kujani for Brushtail Possum: 'the arid country around the springs would not have been its natural habitat' and in any case the Kujani word for possum was 'bilda' . . . But the word was always *our* word, our Aboriginal sound.

Any etymology attributed to its echoes our history of settlement, a retrospective rationalization of what the place turned out to be like. 'Oodnadatta', the tourist brochure explains, 'is probably an adaptation of an Aboriginal word "utnadata" meaning "blossom of the mulga".' And then it adds, 'This is the more pleasing of two possible meanings for the Aboriginal place name, the other being, "careful rotten ground there!" ' But neither derivation brings us to an Aboriginal *place*-name. The place we hear in it represents our own desire, our own translation in a double sense. Such names are like signs of the zodiac wherein we superstitiously read our futures. We hear what it suits us to hear: the echo of a river – 'the native calls it Murree with the accent on the end of the word . . .'; or *la mer*, the sea inland.

9 *August*

Flying away from Marree's threadbare grid, you can take it in at a glance: its dry water channels, its broken fence lines, its bare paddocks and unfinished edges. Less a town than an archaeological site. But outlines of roads and habitations imply burial and resurrection: deep-set foundations recovered and brought to the surface – only to begin again the long process of decay. Nothing here though has put down roots: with the exception of the hotel, the town consists of galvanized iron sheds and shacks and pre-fab houses. These temporary, mobile constructions sit on the town's grid like trucks on sidings, containers of travel. Like the vandalized railway carriages, they seem set to depart: to be left behind is to be dismantled and to disappear. To settle here is to be ruined from the beginning. You imagine that, had it been possible, people here would not have lived in houses at all but in moving trains, caravans. Their thoughts would have drifted cloud-like, their voices telephonic.

The mail-cart to Cooper's Creek carried its road with it – sheets of galvanized iron that could be laid over the sand, preventing the wheels from sinking in. But the sheets of iron were heavy and on the good sections of road slowed the animals down. In the end they were jettisoned – and the mail-service presumably stopped. This might be a parable of life here, where the people lived wrapped up in roads, unable either to stay or to get away and knowing that the price of communication was disembodiment, a willingness to fly above the ground or over sleepers.

In the afternoon we drove up the Birdsville Track. The unsealed road is criss-crossed with tyre tracks. You constantly swap one set of parallels for another in an effort to avoid damaging the front axle. Like a train changing lines at a complex junction: only the lines are swimming underneath you, sinuous and unpredictable. Bitumen makes you wonder what it was like in the old days. But an unsealed road preserves first impressions. Apart from the trace of travelling, it does not make room for history.

85

This may justify a diary – that here my first impressions might coincide with those of the oldest inhabitant. Marree's temporary build-ings *may* be abandoned. But they might just as easily have been put up yesterday: in their unfinished state, they are permanently new. Looking at them, you do not think of the past they commemorate: you wonder what they were intended for. They strike you as stand-ins for buildings yet to come. You have the illusion of seeing the beginnings of settlement, not its ending. In such places where the flow of time is, like the tyre tracks, constantly fanning out and growing confused, there is no obvious narrative. The diary, written and written up, with its succession of beginnings and endings, its temporary camp-sites, may be the fictional form that maps this world most closely – a world that, rather than represent itself as a place, preserves the trace of passage, of first impressions.

Sketched Illusion Plains (see Plate 14). By late afternoon the cloud rafts had evaporated, then towards 9 p.m. mother-of-pearl fleets came in, covering the sky.

Forgot to mention: two men in the caravan park this morning played *bocce*. In the barely demarcated expanse of the park, contiguous with plains that stretched in all directions to a flat horizon, they had created an (invisible) enclosure, where they were completely at home. Taking aim, slowly rocking back and forth, knees bent, one foot slightly raised, they let the ball go, its just flight depending on their perfect balance. It was not paying for a 'site' for the night that gave these men their momentary sense of belonging, but a game. Taking control of the ball's flight, they rooted themselves to the spot: this was the condition of occupying the ground. Their slow dance was a spatial charm, designed to ward off the immensity. Above the generator engine you could hear them talking.

10 August

Temperate night, recorded pre-dawn chorus in Frome Creek bed. Dominant songster: crested bellbird. Thought I was miles from anyone until, around 6.45, there was the sound of a tent being unzipped and a car door slammed: about fifty metres from where I was recording, behind some bushes, there must have been half a dozen tents and four-wheel drives! So much for splendid isolation.

Drove to South Lake Eyre, which I had photographed yesterday from the air.

Arrival in this country, it occurs to me, has three phases. First there is the Edenic moment, the illusion of being what Major Mitchell calls 'the only Adam', the first person ever to have entered this land. Then follows the expulsion: the discovery that other people have stood here – and shared perhaps the sensation of being in Eden. Lastly comes reflection on these two contrary moments, the sadder and wiser recognition that one's pleasures are historically mediated, products of a complex technological and cultural tradition – and the conclusion perhaps that our nostalgia for the wilderness is a cultural dream, the desire to preserve it a desire to preserve ourselves.

Examples of Edenic moments: Charles Sturt describing the Cooper's Creek Aborigines as 'the finest of any I had seen on the Australian continent' – because the remotest from 'civilization'; a pioneer calling the Willouran Range south-west of Marree 'Paradise'; J. W. Gregory's claim that the 'sky-country' of Arunta and Dieri myth 'resembles the Eden of the Aryans'; our interest in etymology, the belief that an original name has been lost in the babble of voices.

But why go to the local literature? My own notebook furnishes examples: '9/8 Clayton River bed. Exquisite clarity of the senses . . . Pure air, scented with last night's stars, historied with rainfall . . .' or: '10/8 the delicious smell of the sea . . . whiskered terns stalking the offing, like a frieze of white butterflies . . . red-necked avocets, sandpipers, swans, stilts . . . intimate lap of shallow waves before a light nor'-westerly. These first appearances do not deceive: this, as it is, *is* an inland sea . . .'

I put these diary entries inside quotation marks, not because their naïve lyricism embarrasses me, but to indicate the larger meditation that was not written down. Even as I wrote them I knew the words did not express what I felt: I wrote them in the absence of any more satisfactory means of expression. Their monologue – to produce which I had momentarily to absent myself from the natural sea of my surroundings – was an attempt to ward off the silence that floods in whenever we submit time to the 'little death' of writing. You could say that they mourned the death of natural dialogue and the advent of *signs*, the burden of representation. But this is not only a dilemma as old as the history of mimesis itself: it is a political issue.

It is no accident that the Edenic moment in Australia – the illusion of a place so *natural* that as in Eden each and everything has its own name which it speaks and no metaphorical uncertainty has entered in – is associated with its Aboriginality. To invoke Eden here is to acknowledge, not the fullness of arrival, but speechlessness. The otherness of the place invites dialogue, the dialogue of lovers that escapes the mirror-condition of science's one-sided naming. This longing the Europeans project on to the Aborigines, making them the human other with whom alone a dialogue might be opened that does not suppress the 'noise' of the country, its reluctance to be represented. But the dialogue was never opened, the Aborigines were silenced, assimilated to a figure of speech instead, a figure that marked their absence from the language. To preserve themselves from their own anger, the Europeans turned their frustration outwards. Hence the second phase of arrival: disillusionment, with its characteristic trope of deception.

Dreamt last night that Lake Eyre had advanced on the camp. Water rose trickling around us, the tent poles sank deep into the mud. Tried to pull them up, the bottom sections were sucked out of my grip and disappeared. Tried to rouse L., but she would not stir. Fragments of yesterday lie scattered across the dream's ground: Lake Eyre's wind-induced tides described by the pilot in the morning, John Morrison's story 'North Wind' (which L. is reading) and Jim's vain struggle to save Lil from the bush fire . . . But the dream's origins in the everyday hardly explain its dynamism. It is impossible to *imagine* the world as dead, says Coleridge. So with dreams: their world is one of living process, of plastic transformation. To dream *is* to change the world, to endow it with new forms. We cannot live inside dreams, but we cannot live outside them either.

Imagine that our dreams exactly reproduced our waking experiences, that we could not imagine ourselves other than we were. To exist wholly in the realm of waking would be to experience the nightmare of a world that could not change itself, that was dead. It would be to inhabit a photographic world, one in which appearances never lied. But to *imagine* such a world is impossible: how, then, could I avoid dreaming of another lake than the one that all night remained placidly within itself a few feet from us? Dreaming that it flowed, endowing it with dangerous deceptive movement, I drew it into my life. The deceptiveness of things is inseparable from our identification with them: to imagine their power, we cannot help transforming them into instruments of life and death. The solution of the ground beneath my feet did not alarm me: I greeted it as a preliminary to amphibious life.

Last night, listening to the contact calls of small birds rising and falling over the plain – they turned out to be red-capped dotterel, their calls the sound of marbles ricocheting in a bag – I thought about Sturt's hypothesis that the inland sea would be found where two lines of migrating birds intersected. Observing parrots flying north up Spencer Gulf and north-west from the Darling River, he reasoned that they could not be flying into a desert. Most likely they were flying to country similar to that they had left behind, a coastal region located inland . . . Where did Sturt's ideas come from: his mechanistic assumption that birds flew with the same unerring straightness as railway lines, and that their movements were motivated by a principle of conservation – a desire to remain in one kind of territory – rather than a nomadic opportunism, an impulse to travel wherever there was occasion?

The probable answer is the Hampshire parish of Selborne. Gilbert White's classic natural history inaugurated modern migration studies. White defined migration in a rather narrow way. Scornful of the kind of parochialism that had swallows hibernating in the mud at the bottom of the village pond, he imagined warblers, thrushes and snipe travelling from the highest latitudes of Sweden to the African tropics. And noting the extreme regularity with which they appeared and disappeared each year, he hypothesized a migratory instinct independent of local variables like the weather. The paradigmatic migrant was the swallow that returned to the same barn on the same day each year.

This discovery of a machine-like instinct ruling the lives of birds raised a baffling question: how were the other appearances and disappearances to be explained – the sudden 'irruption' of a single species, the 'irregular visitor' and, more irregular still, the 'vagrant' wandering far outside its normal range, the 'rarity'? Too unpredictable to be classed as true migrants, they could only be regarded as exceptions to the rule. Sturt seems to have accepted this view of nature: he could not explain the flights of *Psittacus novae hollandiae* and Shell Parroquet except as part of the 'regular and systematic migration of the feathered races'. The birds were treated as *signs*. The possibility that they inhabited a country *without horizons*, that flying was a process, the very trace of their being and not ancillary to arrival elsewhere, seems to have eluded him.

White's overseas thoughts from home have another local nuance. His *Natural History and Antiquities of Selborne* was published in 1789; the letters it was based on went back to 1770. In the eighteen years between Cook's *Endeavour* voyage and the arrival of the First Fleet, White transformed his first impressions, his unfolding calendar of natural events, into a plan of action – a scientific hypothesis that could be tested: so Cook's open-ended journal passed into the hands of civil servants, becoming retrospectively a sketch of the future, a plan for invasion. Under the bureaucratic dispensation how could the errant habits of the Gwiyagal and the 'break-outs' of the convicts fail to defy reason? After all they were migrants who did not come back.

This is a story about *diaries* – about the totalitarian instincts of a genre that, in Boswell's words, records a 'series of uniformity'. The regularity of diaries prevents them from being truly open-ended: they stress repetition, the even flow of time, characterizing any departure from regularity as exceptional. The contingency of being in history, the experience of flying, is suppressed. Even that continuously evolving, non-repetitive theme, the weather, is constrained to repeat itself, differences over time being 'averaged out'. The possibility that life is experienced as a series of discontinuities is excluded. But days go missing even in the explorers' journals. One thing does not follow from another: sand blows across the road.

A diary may not have a plot but it retains a narrative interest, a minimal expectation of pattern. A notebook though eschews such symmetries. It focuses on the discontinuities between things. You could say it narrates the spaces between diary entries, the places where events remain unpredictable: the hawk that suddenly drops on its prey and missing its mark describes a five minute arc before landing elsewhere; the 'sedentary' yellow-chat everywhere last night and nowhere to be seen or heard this morning; the pelicans, invariably associated with Lake Eyre's flooding, that are not here.

A notebook, unlike a diary, can record absences. In deviating from one flight of fancy to another, it can emulate the local unpredictability of birds flying over. It can draw attention to the contingent nature of experience, the impossibility of deducing anything from one's first impressions. It dwells on the gaps in reason, savouring those intervals of errant reflection in which casual connections break down and one sails from absence to absence. 'In any other country,' wrote Sturt, 'I should have followed such a watercourse, in hopes of its ultimately leading to some reservoir; but here I could encourage no such favourable anticipation.' So with a notebook: its writing anticipates nothing.

09.05 4 Blue-bonnets flying due west
09.15 5 Gull-billed terns leave lake flying s. west
10.00 2 Rainbow birds heard to the s. west
10.30 1 Caspian tern on foreshore, 2 Hoary-headed grebes fly in from the north
10.32 2 Banded stilts arrive the foreshore
11.00 9 Cockatiels fly due west

I show you figures crouched on a beach, flamboyant columns, Taj Mahals and lines of camels. In oval bubbles lifting off the sea I cameo images of arrival, stands of ti-trees: what am I? . . . The mirage is to suppose you just reach 'Lake Eyre' – I'm not only thinking of the four-wheel drivers and their passengers, up to their knees in mud trying to reach the water, only to find it saline and (wonderful deception) too shallow to swim in: at intervals throughout the day a *tableau vivant* is silhouetted against the lake's glitter – a foot raised, arms flailing in an effort to balance, a row of bottoms rolling up trouser legs, and always someone a few steps behind them taking a photograph for the family album. It's not the physical vagaries of the place that strike me, but its metaphysical evasiveness – the extent to which we let it film our historical miasma.

Temporary water – water that has no connection with the 'place', but carries the place (the place-name) with it – is a reflex of our culture, the lightness of its attachments, its difficulties in alighting from the sky and settling. We get here as much by reading as travelling, as much by dreaming as by seeing. Its liquid plane, too late to fulfil a hypothesis, is a site of reverie, a place to contemplate a historical dream. Its childish collage of gibber stone, cut-out clouds and cotton-wool terns, stuck on to the sea in a white frieze, is a mirror to the collage of video clips, newspaper reports and telephone conversations that helped us plan our equipment and our itinerary.

The lightness of the surface, its insouciant dissolution of the horizon, that occidental distinction, creating a single sky-sea (it is as if we walk upside-down), its brief civilization of birds and miraculous fish, is not a convenient allegory, another Utopian metaphor. Its Mandevillean wonders cannot be assimilated to a Western tradition of exotic places. It is not the furthest rim of a *mappa mundi*, furnishing us with lubricious cynocephali, the pictures of our instincts. To treat it as a *representation* of our concerns is only to perpetuate our metaphysical imprisonment, to defer our arrival in this country, to remain steadfastly asleep. 'I've got some beautiful bird books at home, but do you think I thought to bring them . . . ?' the woman says and we, treating this space as a treasury of images, are the same. By making it a mirror of our interests (our names), we submit it to our constitutional forgetfulness. We commemorate our inability to remember its name-lessness, to hear the names that belong here.

Just east of our campsite there opens out what in North Africa would be called a *wadi*. It is treeless and littered with *glass* or with fragments of something looking like glass. Catching the sun these shards wink at me from near and far. It's as if the way ahead is marked with little lighthouses, only it is my motion that turns them on and off. Mirroring our condition here, my points of reference travel with me, reflexes of my reflexes. Let's call the semi-transparent material they are made from 'mirror stone' (not knowing its scientific name), and the place where they lie in such abundance the Valley of Mirrors.

They do not come to see Lake Eyre, but to see what others have seen in Lake Eyre. They come to be seen, not to see. They look forward to being able to say Yes, we went there. Someone is undressing: he steps into the water. But he is stepping out again: it's too muddy, he is explaining, too shallow. And the girl with him is exclaiming (in a broad Lancashire accent), 'Is that it! Is that all? 'Ave we driven a thousand miles for this? You've been talking about it for weeks . . .' And *this* will become the story, the parodic baptism – and the tacit understanding that it was not in any sense a consummation. It's not him she ridicules but the mock-heroic gesture he feels obliged to make. Making fun of his bathos, she is saying in effect: heroic self-representations are for the birds (and film directors); I'll have you as you are . . . They stand there for a few minutes, talking loudly, taking photographs. Then they drive away, leaving behind their tracks.

Here and there sheets of mirror stone embedded at a 45° angle to the horizontal form circles one or two metres across – like the vitrified rims of buried volcanoes. Shattered acres elsewhere suggest nothing so much as a brewery midden, the amber fragments bleached to ice by thousands of years in the sun. These tiny ramparts of glass remind me of Robert Smithson's Yucatan emplacements, his installations of glass along the road, that simultaneously defined a place and defined it as the reflection of another place: places you could never reach, that always reflected the place you came from obliquely.

The Europeans gave the Aborigines looking glasses. The explorer, Ernest Giles, for example, traded mirrors with the people north of here. But what did mirrors mean to men and women familiar with mirror stone? Reflective surfaces were no novelty to them. Perhaps it was the abstraction of European glass that was most impressive, its watery flatness. What could be stranger than one's own face, abstracted from its surroundings, flatly peering back from a country that no one could occupy? And if this was the country the Whites occupied, why were they giving pieces of it away? What kind of country was it anyway? To judge from these honed fragments, its surface must be like a lake, perfectly reflecting the sky. But except for reflections, who or what could dwell there? Perhaps they had no homes of their own and carried their countries with them.

Beginning to grasp the micro-topography of this gently sloping region arterial to the 'dead heart' – this means walking up the dry creek beds or climbing the tiny stone-littered headlands jutting towards the sea. The pure flat extension is gradually differentiated with tracks of memory, local occurrences (or even diary entries), and sounds. The sounds foreshadow the tracks: drawing me this way and that in pursuit of invisible birds. The visual field yields to a spatial memory and both are overlaid by an acoustic environment, whose sounds behave like flags flailing in the wind, now banners proclaiming their nearness, now rolled up and far away.

To explore is not to clear away uncertainties but to add to them.

It is a sedimentary process analogous to the laying down of rocks. Crystalline first impressions yield to cloudy complexities. The shapes of things conceal the vibrations of other events. And these vibrations are not the aura of events deep in the fossilized past: they belong to the future, being one side of a dialogue that might be opened if we began to listen to the sounds of our own voices.

The choice is as much aesthetic as historical. To imagine the country's sound history is to abandon the picturesque point of view – and the climactic narration that goes with it. It is to substitute movement for stasis, submitting to the *process* of experience (and history). In diary-like fashion we can celebrate 'a fine day' as the culmination of a long process, treating it as the longed-for clarification of a vision; or it can be regarded as a phase of transition during which clouds will begin to group, new lineages form and new breezes begin to play the water from a new direction. Today, as yesterday, a breeze springs up in the forenoon, turning water into waves, light into sound. One is not the cessation of the other, but its continuation by other means.

It occurs to me that depth may be construed in two ways, as a visual illusion or as a physical trace. Perhaps this illuminates the meaning of a 'sound photography'. I notice as if for the first time the attraction of dark vegetation-lined gullies and the artificial horizons of low hills. They create an illusion of depth: I am drawn towards them. They promise me relief in a double sense. The faint chiaroscuro they contain is similar to the light–dark backgrounds of nineteenth-century photographs: which is to say, it is superficial. For on closer inspection I find the horizon is illusory, the darkness an artefact of distance . . . A sound photography would have to convey amongst other things a depth that was not illusory . . . the undulating valley of the record groove, say, or the minuscule pits inscribed at varying depths in a compact disc.

But there is a depth within that depth that would also have to be sounded. For the depth itself might have a meaning apart from the sound that makes it. Take the conventional *signs* of Papunya-Tula painting: the boomerang shape, we are told, may represent a recumbent form, or a shelter, or a billabong – or even a boomerang. The context will determine which meaning is meant. But is it not possible that these gestures represent different *levels* of meanings? Papunya-Tula art has its origins in sand-paintings, low reliefs inscribed in the earth. The circling finger deepens the groove in the sand: what is the equivalent gesture in paint? It is not simply a question of acknowledging the secret knowledge that such paintings are designed to conceal rather than disclose but of recalling the ritual process of inscribing itself.

The visual composition represents a story. That much is easily understood. But is it not possible that it contains a literal trace of speech, its punctuated surface notating the musical utterances repeated sub-vocally during its execution? The 'depth' of a gesture would not, then, depend on its polysemic fertility, but on its physical expression of a beat, a root syllable or significant ellipsis. The chromatic range might be acoustic as well as visual. The country itself would not then be a place which ancestral figures created, a representation of their stories: it would be their physical trace. The heights and depths would, quite literally, sound their own beginnings and we could do away with picturesque gods. We could also do away with the idea that the paintings stood in for something else, like mirrors.

11 August

A strong southerly breeze all night belling out the flysheet. The morning overcast. We struck camp and late in the morning began driving back. Thinking more about the historical relationship between sound and place. To recover the sound of a place is not simplistically to give back to it its proper name. It is not that there is 'an original (natural) language' that we can reconstruct. This was the mistake of those nineteenth-century savants who believed they could deduce the lineaments of the first Aryan language. Freely associating phonetically and semantically, they imagined they had discovered the divine afflatus concealed within everyday speech. But the sound of a place is not represented: it is the place considered as a hearing zone that, like the bell of a trumpet, has its own timbre.

There remains the driving air or the falling arm – the modes of vibration and percussion that animate these zones. What do these intentional actions – the shaping of sounds into language, the beating out of a rhythm – have to do with the place? The place is not a geographical object, it is a hearing place, where certain sounds resound and begin to discover a latent harmonics. Thinking of 'Mirror States', my radio and sound installation history of Melbourne's Yarra River, the root word 'yarra' is a stand-in word for the river's real name; the history of its adoption and usage illustrates the complex verbal and behavioural mirrorings that characterized early Aboriginal–European relations in Melbourne. But these facts do not touch the *sound* of the word; they remain at the level of local history (albeit of an unusual kind).

To recover the meaning of the sound – the reasons why this sound came to fill (to create) a navigable basin and to mark a moment of coincidence and transfer between cultures – means understanding its *sound* history. It is not mere coincidence that the vibrating exhaust stack of a semi-trailer growls a sort of 'ya-a-rr-a-a' as it changes down gear. The appeal of the word-sound's rolling guttural in 1836, when the word 'yarra' was adopted as the name of the new settlement's river, may have been connected to the new prestige of the steam engine, its repetition of phonemes, its vibration, resembling the forceful thud and shudder of pistons. The sounds of contemporary transport have their beginnings in the early nineteenth century; they develop and refine the percussive regularities ushered in by James Watt. Is this far-fetched? Is not the mechanization of time the key to Beethoven's symphonic output?

But it will be said that this ignores the fact that Australia was at the time of European arrival 'a continent already filled with articulate sound'. Not at all. The transcription of Aboriginal languages is no substitute for imagining the conditions of their production, the human traditions of utterance that still might make this a place of dialogue. But to imagine that may mean modifying our too-exclusive preoccupation with writing things down – with representing voices – and entertaining the possibility that places are not blank pages but compositions, literally scored with sounds and the histories they led to.

12 August

As dawn rises orange on the serrated crests of Parachilna Gorge, I notice scrawled on a rock near the tape recorder: 'Sharon McEwen was here', plus the date . . . Other traces become visible: a pseudo-antique stone-circle, roughly stacked branches, a circle of ashes and axe gashes in the side of a fallen tree.

I record with two microphones set at right angles to each other. Pointing one towards the falls upstream, I catch in the other the gurgle of water adjacent to where I stand. The physical sources of these sounds can only be experienced temporally. I look at one, then the other, walk from one to the other. But acoustically they exist simultaneously, occupying the same space. Where though does that space exist except in the act of listening?

A rufous song-lark sings overhead, the 'bo-hoo-hoo' of doves, the 'fee-euu, fee-euu' of Horsfield's bronze cuckoo and then, around 7.45 a.m., a distant generator kicking into life.

So we come back to Parachilna Gorge in the Flinders Ranges, to almost the first place I visited in this country, a place that had such an influence on me that I remember nothing about it; those parts of it I do remember (the billing corellas, the red gum by the track) being only the external shards, the anecdotal shields protecting an unspoken, because living, experience. A body site rather than a place; a sequence of light and shade dappling face and hands; a sky built of bird-calls; a dry creek bed, forgetfulness of history.

In the afternoon I record E. singing 'yarra, yarra, yarra . . .' along the creek terrace. Apocalyptic corellas screech their disapproval from the red gum. If the levels are right (if the creek's not too loud), this is going to make the perfect opening to 'Mirror States' . . .

13 August

Our last night. We drive over to Blinman where they've done up the pub, even adding an indoor swimming pool. We buy some wine. 'You want it in a bag?' he says. 'No, it doesn't matter.' 'You want to watch out,' he says, 'an Abo will be after you.'

As we drive away I start to play back the sound.

5 Living in a New Country

Reflections on Travelling Theory

If words and objects ever coincide, it is because at certain propitious times both converge into what the prevailing polity can readily identify as an event, which does not necessarily involve exchange or communication.

Edward Said, 'Swift's Tory Anarchy' in
The World, the Text, and the Critic

A simple question: how does life in a new country acquire meaning? How do migrants find names for natural and human phenomena whose character and causes are as yet largely a matter of conjecture? How do they overcome that first giddy sense of being at sea, surrounded by sights and sounds that bear no relation to what they have been used to? What happens when, as the mid-nineteenth-century Australian settler G. F. Moore puts it in the preface to his *Descriptive Vocabulary . . . of the Aborigines of Western Australia*, 'two individuals are suddenly and unexpectedly brought into collision, neither of whom is acquainted with one word of the language of the other'?[1] Perhaps these are false questions. Perhaps such people are travellers by nature and exercise Keats's 'negative capability', resting easy with appearances without irritably seeking to get behind them to the truth. But in any case it is striking how little attention is paid to the inner dynamics of migration, to the means by which people voluntarily relocate themselves psychically as well as physically.

I

Two antithetical assumptions are commonly made about persons who remove themselves from one place to another: either that they bring with them intact the culture of their home country and, as far as they are able, impose it on their new surroundings – one recent writer, for

98

example, claims that Australia 'is becoming a depository of interesting cultural expressions which have lost ground to the point of extinction in their countries of origin';[2] or else that newcomers experience arrival in the new land as a form of rebirth and, with a minimum of regret, shrug off their former identity, swiftly assimilating to the ways of the new host culture. The same G. F. Moore recommends that 'no emigrant can be contented and happy here' unless he endeavours 'to lose the recollection of [his] former home, and if possible, of [his] former friends and feelings.'[3]

Similarly antithetical postures are said to characterize intellectual behaviour. Either the newcomers insist on rigidly transporting their intellectual interests with them, and refuse to study in any depth the productions of the local culture; or, like born-again Christians, they instantly abandon their former studies and, with a zeal somewhat embarrassing to those who have lived there longer, immerse themselves in the local culture as if it were their very own discovery. Erich Auerbach, writing his great history of representation in Western literature while living in Istanbul, is an instance of the former position; the steady flow of his philological studies, in Turkey and later in the United States, seems quite uncoloured by the vicissitudes of life as a displaced person. A contrasting attitude seems to be exemplified by the anthropologist Bronislaw Malinowski, who, in studying the culture of the Trobriand Islanders, determined to immerse himself as far as possible in the 'savage's' everyday life and as a result declared that the islands, although not discovered by him, were 'for the first time experienced artistically and mastered intellectually'.[4]

But both these reactions have an air of the manic about them and suggest a conflict suppressed rather than resolved. The displaced person who consciously identifies himself with the culture of his country of origin is a person doubly displaced. In *Crime and Custom in Savage Society*, Malinowski makes the point that the culture of a society cannot be observed directly from within: 'no native, however intelligent, can formulate this state of affairs in a general abstract manner, or present it as a sociological theory'.[5] Similarly, a migrant community that builds its identity on the conscious preservation of cultural forms stands outside the culture that produced them. The very act of conceptualizing culture distances the migrant community psychically from the continuum of social life that has been physically left behind.

In any case, the migrant's conscious decision to submit to the 'elaborate working of a system, in which every act has its own place and must be performed without fail' may satisfy a desire to belong, but the resulting sense of place is illusory. The appearance of commanding one's own destiny depends on internalizing a sociological description of human behaviour, but this, as Malinowski himself pointed out, is no more a description of society in its totality than that available to the native.[6] In effect, condemned to behave typically, the self-styled custodian of ethnic culture stands in relation to the living (both here and there) as a ghost: the forms of social life he acts out may be extinct in the country of origin, but he is condemned to repeat them endlessly. In effect, he suppresses a desire of exorcism, afraid to confront the necessity that he must be decently buried before he can be reborn.

Resurrection, however, is not achieved by an act of will alone: newcomers who set about aping the manners of the host culture may be tolerated by those around them, but they will never be accepted as 'locals'. Mirroring the host culture's languages, gestures and manners back to them, migrants will be treated at best with condescension, at worst with suspicion. Their skills as actors may enable them to get by, to avoid confrontation, but, trapped in the mirror of others' expectations, they will not construct a space where they can speak for themselves: they may *act* the eccentric, but they will be incapable of embracing a fate of their own. The newcomer's exaggerated bonhomie and almost clinical tendency to break into inconsequential laughter conceal a sense of unreality quite as frightening as that which assails the migrant who refuses to grow away from the parent country.

Whether reacting violently or dutifully to the incubus of the parent culture, the migrant fails to come to terms with the past, to integrate it into present surroundings. Both emotionally and intellectually, migrants lack a *tertium quid*, a third position that avoids the arbitrary wilfulness of the other two stances. But what form would such a third position take, and how would it be achieved? We can guess that it would not try to reduce the local to a variation of life elsewhere, nor treat the local as exotically strange, as a world apart from the world.

But this, although diplomatic, is hardly the basis for a migrant theory of meaning.

An authentically migrant perspective would, perhaps, be based on an intuition that the opposition between here and there is itself a cultural construction, a consequence of thinking in terms of fixed entities and defining them oppositionally. It might begin by regarding movement, not as an awkward interval between fixed points of departure and arrival, but as a mode of being in the world. The question would be, then, not how to arrive, but how to move, how to identify convergent and divergent movements; and the challenge would be how to notate such events, how to give them a historical and social value.

2

In *The World, the Text, and the Critic* Edward Said elaborates a point made by Auerbach himself – that his great work, *Mimesis*, might never have been written had the Nazis not forced him to seek refuge in a country where he was deprived of access to libraries equipped for European studies and where his contacts with the world of European scholarship were severely circumscribed. Said draws attention to the double historical pathos of Auerbach's position: a Jewish refugee from Nazi Germany, who fled to a traditionally hostile country, lodging in Istanbul, 'the great Oriental apostasy incarnate', he took it as his mission to preserve his own culture, which was in imminent danger of extinction in its land of origin. *Mimesis* was a work 'whose conditions and circumstances of existence are not immediately derived from the culture it describes . . . but built rather on an agonizing distance from it.'[7]

Auerbach is not simply forced to migrate physically but to confront psychic exile. For, in Said's view, 'It is in culture that we can seek out the range of meanings and ideas conveyed by the phrases *belonging to* or *in a* place, being *at home in a place*.' The question for Auerbach was how to convert exile 'into a positive mission, whose success would be a cultural act of great importance'. And, interpreting autobiographically a much later reference of Auerbach's to Hugo of St Victor, Said argues that the transformation of exile into a positive experience depended on the chance it gave Auerbach to transcend his culture, to view it from outside, as something foreign.[8]

This is true as far as it goes, but it leaves unexplained the mechanism whereby Auerbach made sense of that distance, whereby he succeeded in making his study of representation itself a representative work of Western culture. Hugo of St Victor describes a man *free* of nostalgia for his homeland – 'he is perfect to whom the entire world is as a foreign land' – and rehearses a familiar Christian equation of spiritual enlightenment with a renunciation of earthly attachments. But Auerbach's situation is different: like Aeneas bearing his father from the flames of Ilium, Auerbach wants to carry away his culture with him. The question is, how to package and label it, how to make it portable?

Said accepts Auerbach's own assertion that *Mimesis* was a reaction to circumstance, that the audacity of its ambition was a direct result of Auerbach's lack of access to books. But this biographical explanation will hardly suffice. *Mimesis* and the philological studies that led up to and succeeded it were a product of their historical times, of what Auerbach called 'the European crisis'. Introducing the essays collected in *Literary Language and its Public in Late Antiquity and in the Middle Ages*, Auerbach asserts that 'At an early date' (presumably when he was still teaching at Marburg), he came to regard 'the European possibilities of Romance philology . . . as a task specific to our time – a task which could not have been envisaged yesterday and will no longer be conceivable tomorrow.' The urgent task – which he defined as a need to demonstrate the dialectical unity of the Western tradition – arose because, particularly from Auerbach's new vantage point across the Atlantic at Yale, 'European civilization is approaching the term of its existence; its history as a distinct unity would seem to be at an end.'[9]

In investigating certain key literary movements in the great drama of European literature, Auerbach was from the beginning preparing an oration to be delivered at the graveside of European culture. His exile in Istanbul and, after the war, in the United States had, in a certain sense, been foreseen. His method of philological research – which he defined as a decision 'to select, develop and correlate strictly limited and readily accessible problems'[10] – was a technique designed for travelling lightly, for making his cultural chattels transportable. It was a translation in the double sense of facilitating their physical removal and their accessibility to readers unimplicated in Europe's fate.

The point is that Auerbach's writings were not simply a reaction to exile: they were a premonition of it. The idea that Auerbach's writing is backward looking simply because it resuscitated the past is false. No doubt his work can be said to be 'the salvaging, in the midst of sudden German betrayal and brutishness, of some vestiges of a Western tradition or precious survival of the past',[11] but this was exterior to his inner purpose, a retrospective historical rationalization of an impulse that anticipated events and to a certain extent prefigured their consequences.

He was not like the migrant who turns his back on the future, stubbornly importing his household lares and worshipping at their altar in earshot of the call to prayer. Wishing to avoid the double psychical displacement of identifying with a culture that, by virtue of the unity he now ascribed to it, could no longer be regarded as a living, developing reality, he positioned himself in advance as a pilgrim, not only a student of Dante but his latter-day follower, literally treading in his footsteps. In any case he passionately espoused the view, which he derived from one of his intellectual heroes, Giambattista Vico, that 'even the earliest and most remote forms of human thought and action must be present in the potentialities of our own human mind, and this is what enables us to understand those early forms'.[12]

3

Like Auerbach, Bronislaw Malinowski had a peripatetic career that brought him finally to Yale. But here, it appears, the parallel begins and ends. Malinowski's statements of anthropological method emphasize that he was at pains not to let his theory – his cultural baggage – travel with him. As Terence Langendoen puts it, Malinowski insisted that 'A person's behaviour in society cannot be understood by the ethnographer until he has made a very full observational record of the actual behaviour of many people.' Langendoen also quotes Malinowski's reflection on his attempt to enter into the everyday life of the Trobriand Islanders: 'Out of such plunges into the life of the natives . . . I have carried away a distinct feeling that their behaviour, their manner of being . . . became more transparent and easily understandable than it had ever been before.'[13]

This might seem a statement of the merest common sense but,

for Malinowski, a young émigré intellectual from Poland, anxious to consolidate a professional reputation in London, it also expressed a positive methodological insight. The first task of the student of primitive societies is to evacuate his mind of cultural preconceptions, to immerse himself in appearances, however contradictory or meaningless they might seem to be. Any generalizations about social structure, any theory of social organization, should be developed empirically, as a direct result of collating observations in the field.

By the time Malinowski publishes his ethnographical studies, this empirical approach has become somewhat disguised: the raw data have suffered an organization comparable to the order he wants to demonstrate in the society under study. However, the empirical basis of his method is described – and in a remarkably candid way – in the intimate journal that Malinowski kept during his first Trobriand sojourn.

In his *Diary in the Strict Sense of the Term*, Malinowski confesses, for example, to a profound boredom, composed in more or less equal parts of sexual frustration, intellectual self-dissatisfaction and a gloomy recognition that the ethnographer's lot is not a happy one – for there is, frankly, nothing to observe. He is forced to admit that the empirical data, the significant indices of native behaviour, are invisible, if they exist at all. Equally, *any* observations he makes will be *theoretical*; his 'facts' will be photographic stills, behavioural artefacts that lend themselves to study precisely because they are foreign to the lived life of the society they depict. In this context it is evident that any pattern he discovers in native life is not inherent, but is an addition of meaning that he brings to it. The deep social structures he looks for will be nothing more or less than a mirror to the meaning he seeks to find in his own life.

Hence, while Malinowski reminds himself that 'One should look at the emptiness of the surface without illusion',[14] he candidly acknowledges that 'the purpose of keeping a diary and trying to control one's life and thoughts at every moment must be to consolidate life, to integrate one's thinking, to avoid fragmentary themes'.[15] It is evident that 'the force that compels [him] to plunge [his] spirit into reality'[16] is not methodological but psychological. He describes the work of pure observation as 'a kind of opiate rather than a creative expression', and comments, 'I am not trying to link it to deeper sources. To organize it.'[17] Nevertheless, if his observations are to make sense, they will have to be subjected to creative synthesis. Malinowski's blankness of mind, his intellectual submission to appearances, is a necessary preliminary, not so much to a better understanding of the 'savage', but to the foundation of his own personality on a firmer, deeper footing.

By plunging into the savage mind, he imagines he will integrate his own intellectual, emotional and instinctual urges. He will overcome his existential desire to 'fuck them all';[18] he will justify himself historically, appeasing the guilt he feels in voluntarily absenting himself from the First World War – a conflict that prefigures that of the Second World War and lends Malinowski's studies, like the later ones of Auerbach, a double pathos: in studying the life of savages Malinowski was unearthing the unconscious foundations not only of his own personality, but of his culture. In view of the apocalypse engulfing Europe, it might be that the true lineaments of the European character could be fully plumbed only in the life of the Trobriand Islanders. But, if the future of civilization lay in New Guinea, in the recovery of its primitive roots, then there was a further irony: that this future – this Edenic existence – was put in jeopardy by Malinowski's own studies, by his wish to impose on it a sociological unity.

In short, Malinowski's descent into the primitive was self-reflexive. It was a means of integrating his own past: by shrugging off his cultural baggage, he hoped to learn to bear its burden better. The meaning he discovered in native life was the meaning he would give his own life; and, what is more, it would license his going back, his return to the centre of European culture. The anti-intellectualism of his determination to submit himself, suspending judgement, to the supple and subtle river of phenomena as they passed before his eyes, to whatever came into his mind, was itself a signature of his European culture and the historical and aesthetic crises associated with Modernism. It had precise analogies in the privileged place that Freud gave to dreams, that Picasso and Braque gave to primitive sculpture, that Ezra Pound gave to 'absolute rhythm'.

4

On closer inspection, the dramatic contrast between the backward-looking nostalgia of Auerbach and the forward-looking opportunism of Malinowski turns out to be overdrawn. It appears that Auerbach had a premonition of exile, that Malinowski had an ambition to return, and that both to some extent shaped their studies with these futures in mind. It remains to see *how* they anticipated events and sought to make displacement central to their cultural theorizing. But first perhaps it is worth inquiring why their prospective outlook – what one might call a migrational predisposition – eludes recognition.

Very crudely, the speculative and poetic cast of their thought goes unnoticed because it is subjected to historical rationalization. So we are told (and Auerbach himself authorizes the view) that the cause of his audacious plan to write a history of representation in Western literature was his involuntary exile in Istanbul. But the fact is that the thesis that Auerbach elaborates in *Mimesis* – and the high moments in Western culture that he will use to illustrate it – are already fully adumbrated in his Marburg book, *Dante: The Secular Poet*. What does this mean? Interpreted historically, it reinforces the argument outlined above, that Auerbach suppressed the fact of displacement, and carried on with his work as if exile had never occurred. Considered *poetically*, though, the continuity between *Dante: The Secular Poet* and *Mimesis* assumes quite a different significance.

Aristotle, it will be remembered, described history as the telling of that which had happened, poetry as the narrative of that which *could* happen. From a historical point of view *Mimesis* was the consequence of an earlier event. From a poetic perspective, though, *Dante: The Secular Poet* was a literary study whose themes and central thesis looked forward to what could happen; it offered a pattern, a strategy for thinking about things in the future. More than this, its shoring up of fragments – high moments in early Western literature – provided a way in which, if the occasion arose, Auerbach could carry out his own poetic purpose – his ambition, not simply to write a literary history, but to summon up the past poetically by way of an inner exploration of the potentialities of his own mind, through what Husserl calls 'a concomitant mode of production'.[19]

A comparable point can be made about Malinowski. His best-known and most contentious thesis about the societies he had studied was that they were ignorant of the biological role of the father. Australian Aborigines, Trobriand Islanders and, presumably, other comparable societies, believed that the mother was impregnated by the spirit of a person formerly living. Birth was a form of reincarnation or spiritual rebirth. The new child had, as it were, been prefigured and its appearance was unconnected with sexual intercourse. In contrast with European society, where the father's authority rested on his biological function, the place of the father in primitive societies was purely social. Lacking biological authority, his offspring had to be bound to him by other means. This, Malinowski argued, was the function of the complex kinship rules that characterized primitive society.

This thesis, set out in detail in Malinowski's little book *The Father in Primitive Psychology*, is so surprising that it is natural to attribute it to Malinowski's experience in the field – and indeed Malinowski does draw extensively on Trobriand Islands material. However, the idea that the savage is ignorant of 'physiological consanguinity as regards the father'[20] first makes it appearance much earlier in *The Family among the Australian Aborigines*, a book that Malinowski wrote in London before he ever visited Australia or New Guinea, and whose conclusions were based wholly on an extensive review of the ethnographic literature.

As with Auerbach, so with Malinowski: the relationship between his earlier and later work can be interpreted historically or poetically. Historically, much of Malinowski's work in the late 1920s and early 1930s can be seen as an attempt to vindicate empirically his view that kinship structures were independent of biologically founded social institutions such as marriage, family and clanship. The fact that, despite repeatedly announcing his intention to publish a book called *The Psychology of Kinship*, Malinowski eventually failed to do so, 'because of incompatibility between hypothesis and empirical fact'[21] merely seems to illustrate the integrity of Malinowski's adherence to empirical methods. In this case it is the *non-appearance* of a later book that is the consequence of an earlier one.

But, although the facts forced Malinowski to shelve his kinship theory, they did not force him to abandon ethnography as a science. Nor did they diminish in any way his tendency to view modern ethnography, like the Trobriand Islands, as his very own intellectual discovery. Viewed poetically, Malinowski's pre-emptive relegation of the father to the sidelines of social life was a way of creating a place for himself. The enigmatic dysfunction that he had identified in primitive society suggested that the unity of savage life could only be restored by his intervention. By removing the biological father, Malinowski could, as it were, insert himself into primitive society as a spiritual father, the person who was needed if it was to be restored to a functional unity.

Although it is perhaps unwise to indulge in psychological speculation without biographical information beyond the fact that 'in his teens [he] travelled extensively in the Mediterranean region with his mother, who was by then widowed',[22] one cannot help wondering how far Malinowski's insistence on the father's purely nominal function in the family rationalized an unresolved sense of personal guilt. Be that as it may, there is no doubt that it also freed him, psychically as well as physically, to travel lightly and become the father of a spiritual kin of his own.

5

Not long after coming to Australia on a semi-permanent basis, I wrote an article called 'Letter from Stickney'. These current reflections on travelling theory can hardly be said to stem from that article, but there is a connection in another, poetic sense. The ostensible subject of the letter was the curious, perhaps meaningless fact that an obscure Lincolnshire village had figured significantly in the lives and private mythologies of two men – the explorer Matthew Flinders and the poet Paul Verlaine – who otherwise (that is to say, historically) had nothing in common. But the broader question raised there, the field opened for inquiry, was that of how meaning is constructed in the migrant situation.

Stickney was one of a constellation of Lincolnshire names that Flinders applied to geographical features in Spencer Gulf, South Australia, in 1802. Spencer Gulf was the only significant Australian discovery Flinders could claim to have made, and he sought to identify himself with it by commemorating there 'his native province'. The importance of these names was not only biographical but political. Flinders had the misfortune to call in at Mauritius on his homeward voyage, only to be promptly arrested and imprisoned for seven years: unbeknown to the navigator, war had broken out between England and France while he had been far away in the Southern Ocean. In laying a template of Lincolnshire names over his discovery, Flinders was not only allying his fate to the past: he was prefiguring his future. His poetic arrangement of names was a means of countering any French attempts to usurp his historical claims; it named his place in a future where he would escape from exile and win an important place for himself in the annals of British exploration.

For Verlaine, too, Stickney came to signify freedom. It was not simply that, on release from Mons prison (where he had been incarcerated for his attempt on Rimbaud's life), the poet found the wide skies and monotonous views of the Lincolnshire fens emotionally cathartic, or that his post at the local grammar school as French and drawing master offered him an orderly existence that he found inwardly liberating: at Stickney Verlaine wrote more calmly and richly than ever before. Flinders in Mauritius had worked on his monumental personal geography, *A Voyage to Terra Australis*, and taken French lessons: Verlaine, seventy-five years later, also in exile, had found the peace of mind to write some of his best poems (later collected in *Sagesse*) and a chance to learn English.

Other biographical parallels or symmetries could be found, and even certain stylistic similarities. For instance, part of the charm of Verlaine's poem 'L'échelonnement des haies', a lyrical evocation of the Stickney countryside, is the subtle way it keeps in play the sea–land metaphor; and this is not simply a response to the poet's physical impression that, say, the hedgerows of foaming may blossom were like breaking waves: it expresses Verlaine's sense of liberation, a feeling he always associates with coastlines and ocean views. But the sea–land metaphor is also the *theme* of Flinders' great exploration journal: it is his responsibility day after day to distinguish the land from the sea, to penetrate a haze that, like Verlaine, he finds endlessly suggestive, a veil over inland seas or perhaps only a false horizon.

And so on. Sufficiently contextualized, the mere coincidence that Stickney had an important imaginative place in the lives of both men could be shown to be not a coincidence at all: it could be seen to rest on a convergence of biographical and psychological interests. But what was the status of this convergence? It was not historical, for there is not the slightest evidence to suggest that Verlaine knew of Flinders; besides, the poet came to Stickney by pure chance. Was it poetic, then – simply a consequence of my ingenuity in creating a significant context, and analogous to the connections made in historical fiction? But the creation of a 'significant context' is the skill of the historian. It is the historian who seeks to trace the resemblance between facts, and to order them into a narrative. A truly poetic account of 'Stickney' might begin and end with the fact that, after all, it was a historical and geographical pun, a moment of meaningless intertextuality: it implied no community of interest, no shared intentions or world view. Any attempt to give it meaning was a refusal to accept Malinowski's advice 'to look at the emptiness of the surface without illusion'.

The significance attributed to Stickney depended on not questioning two assumptions. The first of these was that a 'spirit of place' characterized Stickney. The second was that the place of the writer making these connections was without significance. The first of these assumptions formed the story of 'Letter from Stickney'. The article was, among other things, a send-up of the literary pilgrimage, that hybrid genre of topographical biography, with its confident assumption that the great writer's mind is faithfully represented in the tiles and mortar of his address. I did not expect Stickney to have an identity out of the ordinary, a historical personality sufficiently strong to exercise a determining influence on either Flinders or Verlaine.

When I visited the village, I was not disappointed. Historically speaking, 'Stickney' turned out not to be a place at all: the open, frequently inundated marshes of Flinders's day (which presumably accounted for Stickney's etymology: 'isle of trees') had been drained and enclosed by 1875 (hence Verlaine's 'échelonnement des haies'), and by the time I visited in 1983 it had all changed again. The hedges had gone, the poplar trees that reminded the poet of Shakespeare's *A Midsummer Night's Dream*, even the school and the schoolhouse had disappeared. As I implied at the time, any spirit of place discerned here was a rhetorical sleight of hand, a metaphorical tradition owing nothing to the locality: 'Since the war the . . . chestnuts leading to the Grange, the pear orchard, the hedgers who plied their trade along these coasts – they have all been laid low. Woods and hedges survive. But they survive only in writing.'

But left out of this meditation was my own place, my need to give a meaningless biographical pun historical meaning. Stickney *represented* nothing: it nominated no geographical likeness – Flinders described Stickney Island in Spencer Gulf as a place singularly devoid of trees or 'sticks'. It signified no historical connection. It was a casual pun, nothing more. If it converged on anything, named anything, it was my own migrant point of view – my sense of being thrust into a world in which cultural forms facilitated the functioning of society parodically, mimetically, without any sense of inner necessity. Words circulated, were repeated and returned. They even led to actions. But at no point was one convinced that one had made one's presence felt, that any 'exchange or communication' had been involved.

This was why Stickney, the name and the mere coincidence of its repetition in different places and contexts, struck me as historically significant. In an entirely unbiographical way its vicissitudes named my fate. It illustrated Said's insight that 'If words and objects ever coincide, it is because at certain propitious times both converge into what the prevailing polity can readily identify as an event.'[23] Only there was this important difference: here the prevailing polity did not recognize mere coincidences as events leading to other events, as moments in which a third, authentically migrant perception of historical patterns surfaced. And, being new to the country and thoroughly imbued with historical assumptions brought from elsewhere, I was in no position to demur.

6

The authority of Stickney, the name, represented nothing. More generally the translation of names from one place to another, one time to another, has rarely embodied a principle of representation. Rather, familiar names are applied in new contexts for want of better names. They are used *figuratively*, in the absence of the proper names. In this sense the naming of new things with terms borrowed from elsewhere does not represent an object but a question: the name has the same function as a scientific hypothesis, and implicit in it is the question 'Why?' Not, why does this resemble its namesake elsewhere, but why is it not the same? One recalls Roland Barthes's reflection on why we ask why: 'the ancient Greek's question, the question of meaning: What does that mean? The fact must be transformed at all costs into idea, into description, into interpretation, in short, there must be formed for it *a name other than its own*.'[24]

So long as we think of names as representing something exterior and anterior to language, as referring backwards rather than forwards, their transfer to new contexts will inevitably seem to weaken them. But in another respect the exile of language from its cultural matrix *adds* to its meaning. It also reveals the falseness of supposing that its discursive value derives solely from its power of external reference. In applying the name of a Lincolnshire village to a barren island on the world's other side, Flinders clearly attacks the idea that the name contains any representational core. He stresses its mobility, the arbitrariness of the relationship between the signifier and the signified. But this is not to reduce our names for things to nonsense; the possibility of mere coincidence reveals the provisional nature of the language we use, the fact that the terms we use are always figures of speech, and never apply literally.

Instead of being weakened by travelling abroad, names may discover a new lightness of touch; if they represent anything, it may be a new attitude towards language, a disconcerting principle that meanings are not fixed referentially but contextually, according to principles that are often phonetic rather than semantic. The revelation of the figurative nature of language is also a disclosure about its relation to time. Ricoeur has argued that the language of metaphor literally opens up a new world to us.[25] The same is more generally true of language when it is grasped figuratively (as it is in ordinary dialogue) as pointing towards a future as much as a past situation. Figurative language is the means of delineating a common space, the antithesis of the singular possession of places by name that is so dear to local historians.

But the question arises: how to describe mere coincidences in such a way that they acquire a historical as well as a poetic value? How, in the absence of a representational core, are names carried over from one place and time to another? How do they acquire a 'deeper meaning in reference to future things'? This last phrase is taken from Erich Auerbach's germinal essay, 'Figura', where he defines a textual hermeneutics called 'figural interpretation', which 'establishes a connection between two events or persons, the first of which signifies not only itself but also the second, while the second encompasses or fulfils the first'.[26] Although Auerbach is elucidating a peculiarly Christian view of history, one not necessarily shared by the modern migrant, his recognition that historical events lose none of their historicity when viewed poetically – or, as he says, 'spiritually' – makes his argument of particular interest here.

Two features of his argument are of immediate significance. The first has to do with his insistence that prefiguration – the fact that one historical event can be interpreted as prefiguring a future historical event – does not prevent *both* events from being fully historical; and the same applies to the spiritual act of interpretation – the third position from which this pattern is descried:

> The two poles of the figure are separate in time, but both, being real events or figures, are within time, within the stream of historical life. Only the understanding of the two persons or events is a spiritual act, but this spiritual act deals with concrete events whether past, present or future, and not with concepts or abstractions.[27]

The second point is that, as Auerbach clearly saw, the prefigurative historical vision that characterizes traditional biblical exegesis – and which, he believed, was essential in understanding the otherwise preposterous importance Dante accords his own life in the *Divine Comedy* – is profoundly different from 'the modern view of historical development'. History from the prefigurative point of view is always figurative, provisional, unfinished, questionable, in need of interpretation:

> In the modern view, the provisional event is treated as a step in an unbroken horizontal process; in the figural system the interpretation is always sought from above; events are considered not in their unbroken relation to one another, but torn apart, individually, each in relation to something other that is present and not yet present.[28]

Figural interpretation is, for Auerbach, the key to the European tradition of mimesis or representation; it provides the historical logic for representing reality figuratively, by a name not its own. The project was defined by the fact that historical events, like figurative language, could only name the truth provisionally; it was precisely this sense of events unfolding according to a vertical, as well as horizontal, imperative that gave European culture its sense of spiritual unity, its purpose. But, even if we subtract from Auerbach's historical model its representational burden, its value in revealing the inseparability of history from the language of history remains.

From the modern view of historical development the two places called Stickney – and all other travelling terms – *must* be considered in unbroken relation to each other. And since there is no historical connection between them, no representational core linking them horizontally, the meaning of their nominal coincidence must be sought biographically – in the psychology and circumstances of Matthew Flinders. But just as Dante meant to prefigure history when he travelled through the underworld to the antipodes, so Flinders, when he named the islands of Spencer Gulf, meant to annex his personal fate to something larger – not to reduce the new world to a reflex of the old but, on the contrary, to suggest that his personal geography had a historical destiny that remained imperfectly revealed. It is not insignificant that, according to Auerbach, figural interpretation had its origins in St Paul's ambition to colonize the known world spiritually: if the Old Testament could be shown to prefigure the world the Gentiles inhabited, then, more modestly, England's toponymy colonizing Australia could be revealed as the Aborigines' spiritual possession.

But Auerbach's argument also has a less imperialistic, migrant meaning. For figural interpretation is not only a way of unifying history, but a means of thinking about language and its figures of speech. Considered figurally, a mere coincidence of sounds is not simply a coincidence: it is a pun. But unlike the conventional pun, which obliges the listener to accommodate two (or even more) mutually exclusive meanings, the migrant pun is open-ended, a phonetic mimicry that remains to acquire a semantic value. Instead of signifying nonsense the migrant pun indicates a meaning yet to emerge. It is the figurative possibility inherent in language itself that makes the future possible, and not any particular *veritas* that the word may represent.

From a conventional historical point of view, migrant Australian writer Lolo Houbein's discovery of an Asian tribe that shares her name can only be regarded as a mere coincidence. Any meaning she accords it must be regarded as pure autobiographical fantasy. But neither is the case. The fact that 'The Lolo live in the borderlands of Eastern Tibet and Yunnan. They are mountain people. Lolo women are tall, independent and pursue small business ventures. All descriptions of Lolo women tally with what I was and have become' is not simply a nominal coincidence: it is a pun whose full meaning remains to be disclosed. As she says, 'I haven't been there . . . yet.'[29]

Nor can the meaning Houbein attributes to this pun be regarded as merely of biographical significance. It is intrinsic to her migrant mode of being in the world, to her ability to improvise meanings as she goes along: 'Always ready to criticise the home situation . . . and think the fields greener on the other side, I carry an image of Utopia and will not give it up.'[30] The difference between her *figura* of Paradise and the one Auerbach attributes to Dante is that hers is *only* a figure of speech, a promise *in* language, not beyond it. But in sensing this she acknowledges her historical situation, her destiny as a 'typical migrant'. And, what is more, the mere coincidence of sounds becomes a motive for travel, a direction, a destiny.

7

The emergence of meaning in a migrant situation is not the result of a marriage between an old language and a new reality. The empirical resistance of the novel surroundings does not inspire a spontaneous modification and adaptation of the migrant tongue. The crisis of language felt in the migrant environment is not referential but self-referential. Terms that elsewhere seemed 'natural' here appear provisional, even arbitrary. The unspoken cultural, linguistic and social consensus that fixes the sound's semantic value, giving it an air of naming reality directly (when we say *bread* we mean bread), is here revealed as *merely* a convention of meanings. *This* may be bread; it looks and tastes like bread. Nevertheless, it is not *bread* (with all its familiar connotations) in any deep sense. 'Bread' is only the word we use to name it in the absence of its proper name – the name that would conjure up what the word, bread, means to us.

Yet, as we have seen, the ghostly aspect that words assume in migrant discourse is not necessarily a *loss* of expressive power; it reveals the rhetorical and contextual conventions governing *all* expression. The language used in the country of origin was not necessarily richer than the language spoken here, even if it was a great deal more unified: its superior semantic sophistication, its greater power to make subtle logical and descriptive discriminations, contributed greatly to the smoothness of cultural exchange, but it concealed the phonetic and dialogical origins of meaning – the fact that communication is always in the beginning a give and take between two people, always an act of figural interpretation, and that words (or sounds) have no intrinsic meaning apart from the context of their utterance.

The argument *against* a contextual theory of meaning is trenchantly put by Terence Langendoen in his Chomskyan critique of Malinowski's theory of language. Noting how difficult it was to make sense of Trobriand Islander speech simply by translating and transcribing it according to lexical and grammatical rules, Malinowski argued that an understanding of what was being said depended on being privy to its living context: 'a word without *linguistic context* is a mere figment and stands for nothing by itself, so in the reality of a living tongue, the utterance has no meaning except in the context of a situation'.[31] In one later refinement of his contextual thesis Malinowski drew attention to the 'range of meaning' of given words in the native vocabulary: 'Meaning is not something which abides within a sound; it exists in the sound's relation to context. Hence if a word is used in a different context it cannot have the same meaning; it ceases to be one word and becomes two or more semantically distinguishable units.'[32]

Not surprisingly, Langendoen treats these arguments with disbelief. He is committed to the existence of a universal deep grammar, without whose intuitive linguistic capacity verbal communication would be impossible. He attacks the reductive behaviourism of a view that seems to argue that meaning is inseparable from bodily actions, as if a speaker is at the mercy of physical situations and never expresses intentions of his own or refers to invisible or past situations. And if, as Malinowski appears to claim, a word becomes a new word when it is uttered in a new verbal context, it follows absurdly, according to Langendoen, that two words like 'cat' and 'dog', 'occurring as utterance tokens in the same context . . . must be considered synonymous in these contexts'.[33]

But absurd as Malinowski's claims may seem when extrapolated logically, they nevertheless embody an authentic migrant experience of language. Malinowski may have been mistaken in thinking his outsider's perception of linguistic meaning in the Trobriand Islands represented a general condition of communication in an oral culture, but he was not mistaken in thinking his personal difficulties in getting the language had a more general significance. Malinowski's generalizations on the basis of his experience were vitiated by his ethnographic (and ethnocentric) ambition, by a determination to give his personal destiny a literary and historical significance, but they contained an authentic migrant insight, accurately describing 'the long and painful experience of learning a native language'.

The problems of meaning Malinowski encountered are not confined to 'primitive' oral societies: they arise in any social situation where the medium of communication is speech – that is, in *any* day-to-day situation the migrant meets. In such situations, where there is no linguistic or even cultural framework in common, the newcomer is utterly dependent on the speaker's physical gestures and the context of action for an understanding of what is meant; he completes the act of communication, not by answering back, representing his own point of view, but by miming sounds and actions. The word that the migrant repeats has no meaning apart from its context; or, more accurately, it is not a 'word' at all with a fixed semantic core. It is simply a sound, which in another context may mean something else.

The synonymity of 'dog' and 'cat' when used in the same context is not as absurd as it may appear. Although hard to prove empirically, it is easy to imagine instances where the migrant listener, carefully following the extra-linguistic signs, may come to believe that an object formerly designated 'a' actually has another name, 'b'. Perhaps the error that Langendoen makes is to think that ambiguities of this kind are fatal for the efficient operation of language. They *are* no doubt fatal as soon as one begins to consider language as a system whose interlocking parts are by definition distinguishable from one another. But this is not the perception of the migrant, whose view of language is necessarily context-oriented. If what was a 'cat' in yesterday's situation is miraculously reincarnated as a 'dog' today, it merely emphasizes the provisional nature of the migrant's knowledge. However, from a migrant perspective, the apparent synonymity reinforces the point that, *pace* Langendoen, no two living contexts, however they may resemble each other on paper, are historically identical.

Malinowksi, as we noted, absented the father from any biological function in holding primitive society together and giving its structures meaning. Nevertheless this did not prevent the islanders from recognizing a physical resemblance between child and father; this physical resemblance was, paradoxically, a means of 'inserting patrilineal elements into a matrilineal society'. The child may look like the father, but must not look like the mother: 'maternal kinsmen are the same flesh, but similar faces they have not'.[34] One sees that Malinowski here described not only a social structure but a theory of meaning. Physical sounds may sound like other sounds, but they have no meaning apart from their specific incarnation in a social situation. The semantic core of language, its power to engender meaning, resides with the mother tongue, but its physical presence, its phonetic face, belongs to the father. It is their curiously disjunctive dialogue – the variability of the relationship between sound and sense – that defines the meaning of meaning in the migrant context.

8

In his essay 'Traveling Theory', Edward Said draws a distinction between theory and criticism. Taking Lukács's concept of reification as an example of a theory arising originally out of a critical stance towards a concrete historical situation, Said shows how, when Lukács's ideas were divorced from their original context, they suffered one of two fates. Either they lost their critical power and were turned into a totalizing theory by means of which 'disparate, apparently disconnected things are brought together in perfect correspondence', or they retained their critical value, stimulating the emergence of critical consciousness, but forfeited their theoretical, universalizing pretensions.[35] There is no doubt which trajectory Said favours: 'I am arguing . . . that we distinguish theory from critical consciousness by saying that the latter is a sort of spatial sense, a sort of measuring faculty for locating or situating theory.'[36]

Said's account of the vicissitudes of ideas as they travel in time and space is of obvious relevance in understanding, say, the contrasting intellectual journeys of Auerbach and Malinowski: if the philologist seems to have cultivated a critical consciousness and, even in his efforts to demonstrate the unity of European culture, to have avoided a totalizing vision, the ethnographer, despite his empirical rigour and sensitivity, was always drawn towards theory, towards a description of society that ironed out apparent contradictions, tending to reduce them to a self-fulfilling pattern. It does not immediately appear from Said's paradigm, however, that one can expect the emergence of a critical theory at the end, as it were, of the theoretical shift. The best

1 *Top Chambers Pillar*, lithograph, from *The Journals of John McDouall Stuart*, 1862.

2 *Chambers Pillar*, gelatin silver photograph, from Sir Walter Baldwin Spencer, *Wanderings in Wild Australia*, 1928.

3 Figure drawn on roof of cave,
colourprint, from George Grey,
Expeditions into Western Australia, 1841.

4 Figure drawn on roof of cave,
colourprint, from George Grey,
Expeditions into Western Australia, 1841.

5 *Top A View on the Darling*, engraving, from T. L. Mitchell, *Three Expeditions into the Interior of Eastern Australia*, 1838.

6 Eugen von Guerard, *Lake Gnotuk, near Camperdown*, oil on canvas, 1858.

7 *Top* Eugen von Guerard, *From the Verandah of Purrumbete*, oil on canvas, 1858.

8 Eugen von Guerard, *Purrumbete from across the Lake*, oil on canvas, 1858.

9 *Top* Russell Drysdale, *Sofala*, oil on canvas on hardboard, 1947.

10 Russell Drysdale, *Cloncurry, July 1956*, Cibachrome, 1985.

11   *Right* Russell Drysdale,
Mangula, oil on canvas, 1961.

12   Albert Namatjira, *Palm Valley*,
watercolour on paper, no date.

13 *Left* Sketch map of Western
Port District by Asst. Protector
William Thomas, pen and ink,
1841 or earlier.

14 Lake Eyre South and
Environs, detail of *Gazetteer Map
of South Australia*, 1867.

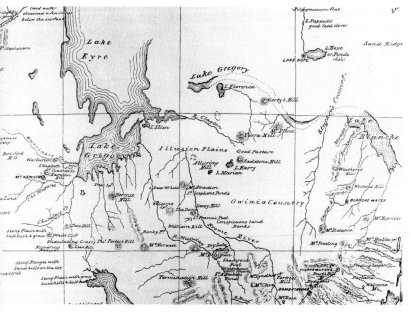

A CORROBBOREE.

15 *Top* W. F. E. Liardet, *The First Punt, Yarra Yarra River*, watercolour, *c.* 1840.

16 *A Corrobboree* [*sic*], engraving, from R. Brough Smyth, *The Aborigines of Victoria*, 1876.

one can hope for is that theory will become the object of critical reflection – by this means continuing to contribute to the process of defining and redefining the world we live in, a process that Said regards as criticism's chief and liberating function.

Perhaps it is not going too far to say, though, that the theory of migrant meaning whose outline is sketched here offers a counter-example to those discussed by Said. Although arising remote from the traditional centres of critical theory, it springs from a situation that resembles the conditions in which Lukács felt impelled to theorize his circumstances: the migrant search for meaning begins in an immediate physical and intellectual perception that the cultural system in which migrants move and act and speak does not speak *for them*; rather, it treats them as 'nature', raw material to be turned into objects (submissive citizens) whose worth can be calculated in terms of the stability of the status quo. Migrants who are struck by the contrast between this social and cultural world view and their own sense of being ungrounded, unreal, unlanguaged, are in the position of Lukács's proletariat – which represents, says Said, 'consciousness claiming its theoretical right to posit a better world outside the world of simple objects'.[37]

The theory of the transmission of cultural forms that I have sketched arises dialectically out of a felt need to oppose the world view that characterizes those who command the resources, and circulation, of discourse. But it is clearly not a totalizing theory, if only because it arises empirically from the *absence* of a theory capable of describing the migrant's ontological angst. Nor, on the other hand, can it be described simply as an exercise in critical consciousness-raising, for quite clearly the attempt to invert the conventional genealogical bias of historical and cultural description, and to lay stress on the provisional, accretive life of cultural forms, is speculative. It attempts to rationalize the 'variable meaning' that characterizes the migrant's experience of a social environment. It aims to establish as a legitimate position the migrant construction of meaning – so foreign to the theoretical assumptions of a cultural orthodoxy that denies to the migrant condition a historical, let alone a critical, value; for the possibility of a critical consciousness hardly arises without improvising, if only temporarily, this theoretical, third position.

The Australian settler G. F. Moore, whom I quoted at the beginning of these reflections, claimed that, to begin with, 'On the part of the settlers generally, there existed the most friendly disposition towards the aborigines, which was evinced on every suitable opportunity, by the offer of bread, accompanied by the imitation of eating, with an assurance that it was "*very good*". And thus this term, "*very good*", was almost the first English phrase used, and became the name by which bread was, for a long time, generally known amongst the natives of Western Australia.'[38]

This anecdote may be interpreted as a perfect illustration of the way in which a migrant culture in which no group of people 'is acquainted with one word of the language of the other' improvises a situational argot that represents, in effect, a distinctive theory of meaning. It strongly reinforces Malinowksi's view that meaning resides, not in the sound of a word, but in the active context where it is used, and that the meaning of any phrase is accordingly unstable; it suggests, furthermore, how, against the Chomskyan argument, two semantically distinct words or phrases like 'very good' and 'bread' might mean the same thing when employed in the same verbal context. Moore's anecdote suggests, too, how in a new situation language recovers something of its figural quality, not simply in the sense that 'very good' is a more expressive signifier than 'bread', capturing exactly the fragile nature of communication in a new country, but also because it shows how an event – in this case, a commonly used phrase – can acquire a deeper meaning in the future.

But Moore's anecdote is also a parable about the *failure* of a third position to emerge. His story is replicated wherever migrants have gone and have sought to speak: the pidginization and creolization of languages – which Moore's tale to some extent reproduces *in parvo* – does not represent their degradation but a creative, migrant impulse to construct meaning out of the ruins of reference. But Moore turns his back on this option: in his *Descriptive Vocabulary*, 'very good' and 'bread' are not cross-referenced. 'Very good' is rendered by an Aboriginal term; 'bread' is not mentioned at all. Implicitly the cross-cultural improvisation is regarded as an amusing misunderstanding, and certainly not as a mechanism for improvising meaning that contains within it the seed of a linguistic third position – a hybrid tongue arising, like Lukács's critical theory, in reaction to a deep and immediate social crisis and capable of transcending it.

It is beyond the scope of this essay to explore the historical reasons for our society's refusal to accord its own oral culture semantic authority or critical significance. It can be attributed to the *literary* nature of our culture, with its consequent need to standardize the representation of speech; it can even be linked to the imperialism of the European project, its desire to forge a travelling theory, a language immune to local conditions. But here we might draw attention to a prejudice of a different kind.

As has frequently been pointed out, mimesis, in the context of European art and literature, does not mean naïve imitation. Auerbach's *Mimesis* is a history of *representation*, not mimicry, and generally in our culture the art of mimetic reproduction, the power to reproduce exactly physical gestures or verbal idiosyncrasies, has been accorded a very low prestige.

> *Mimicry* . . . never fails of yielding a high degree of pleasure. But since this pleasure chiefly results from the principle of *imitation* respecting manner, and not from the purport of the *matter*; since comparatively speaking, it is only attainable by few persons and practised only on particular occasions, – on these accounts it must be refused a place among the modes of useful delivery taught us by general nature, and esteemed a qualification purely anomalous.[39]

So writes one W. Cockin, in *The Art of Delivering Speech*. Cockin upholds a general view, that mimicry is amusing but anomalous. He does not recognize the fact that, wherever people have met and been unable to communicate, mimicry has been the means of initiating friendly relations, however temporarily. For mimicry, however reductive as a theatrical trick, is the means of opening up a dialogue in the migrant situation; and the value of this dialogue does not consist in the matter communicated, but in the manner itself. For while nothing may be exchanged between the two people mirroring each other's voices and gestures, the very act of mimicry opens up a space between them, a place that they agree to share. Mimicry opens up the possibility of dialogue in a situation where, otherwise, dialogue would be impossible. In rejecting this, and the implication that there can be a third position of a spatially contingent history, it may be that our culture suppresses the *other*, not because it is too different from us, but because it fears it is too alike.

6 Crossing the Yarra

A Local History

'. . . Twenty Pair of Blankets, Thirty Tomahawks, One Hundred Knives, Fifty Pair of Scissors, Thirty Looking Glasses . . .'

(items to be given by John Batman and the Port Phillip Association to the 'Dutigalla' tribe in exchange for their land)

Nowhere are the rhetorical foundations of *places* more clearly revealed than in local histories. After all, most local histories are not especially local: they merely reproduce in small the major events in the life of the nation. The dying-out of the Aborigines, the explorers, the pioneer settlers, the laying out of the township and the subsequent development of its public institutions, the Great War and the great depression, and latterly the growing reliance on tourism: these same themes characterize, not only the Centennial Histories, without which no self-respecting rural community can feel its celebrations complete, but also the local histories produced by professional historians. Such histories give a local focus to the national (and nationalist) pageant, but any claim they have as *local* histories is largely rhetorical.

Of course there will be local stories and characters to relate; but even these theatrical events could have been staged elsewhere. In *The Road to Botany Bay* I illustrated what struck me as a particularly local example of human adaptation to the environment: a house made in the stump of a giant blue gum. My identification of it with the pioneer dwelling of one J. Wells of Childers, Gippsland, was based on the assurances of members of the Wells family, and was confirmed by a local historian who provided me with the photograph used in the book. There is no reason to doubt their veracity. Nevertheless I have since discovered the same photograph in G. F. Sydenham's *Notes on the Otways*, where it is confidently asserted that, 'Sam and Bert Miller roofed this burnt out tree in the 1890's and lived in it before their house was built.'[1] Most local events could have happened – and perhaps did happen – elsewhere: the only thing that ties them to *this* place rather than another is the place-name, a purely rhetorical association.

It is hardly exaggerating to say that but for the place-name there would be no place. Certainly as regards local histories this is true; frequently the only thing that holds together the fragmentary collage of milk-production figures, bowling-club presidents and dimly reproduced postcards of ferny dells or the disused railway station is the name – the assumption that, disconnected as these elements may appear to be, both visually and historically, their coherence is guaranteed by the authority of the place where they all occurred. But what is this place except an editorial artefact – a consequence of the decision to solicit and bind together heterogeneous materials, disposed in a roughly chronological order, under the name of a place?

The irony of this is that, by taking the place-name for granted, such histories fail to engage with the one local issue that is not a pale reflection of history elsewhere but is definitively local. The proposition that history occurs within language applies rather literally with regard to the history of places. Places of human significance are the consequence of naming. It is not the topography of a place that qualifies it to circulate in the collective mind, to become a site of economic speculation, a destination for travellers, an address, a home. What matters is its rhetorical identity: its name. Before this town or village became a place, it was an unclear (as well as uncleared) space. But the act of naming changed this: it created a place in the wilderness, a point towards which one might direct one's footsteps; it implied the possibility of reply, a local resonance or, at the very least, a ghostly echo.

In local histories the place serves much the same function as the plot in fiction: it is a means of unifying heterogeneous material, of lending it, rhetorically at least, a unique destiny. But, before they are overcome by this literary enclosure, places begin as *speaking-places*. The first effect of the act of naming is not to separate this place from other places, but rather to open up a space for action. The act of naming is not simply a necessary preliminary to historical progress; it is itself a historical event, representing a *site* of conflicting voices, visions and ambitions. To begin with, any connection between the name and the place it is said to designate is perceived by all parties to be rhetorical; and, as such, it is disputed. For the struggle for a name is also a struggle for power. In this sense the naming of places underlines the point that successful colonization depends not only on the physical exclusion of a former people, but on the suppression of their sounds, the successful reduction of their voices to a background chorus that might be (and frequently was) mistaken for frogs or crickets.

But this rhetorical conclusion is itself open to question. It is at least plausible to speculate that the act of naming did not *merely* signify a power struggle, a contest between competing, mutually exclusive cultural monologues. Perhaps the action it inaugurated resembled a dialogue, and was a means of creating a space in common where the word did not name anything that could be mapped or pegged out, but only a distribution of voices, an arrangement of places rendered memorable by the sounds associated with them. The problem arises, though, of demonstrating this; for by its very nature the distribution of sounds, the immaterial space of dialogue, is not amenable to historical recovery. It goes undocumented – and perhaps one reason for history's linear bias, its blindness to the historical reality of space, is its deafness to sound.

In any case a conventional account of place-naming is unlikely to illuminate its spoken context. To do that it is necessary to evoke its performative nature, the sense in which it and similar rhetorical gestures depend for their effect on the construction of a space shared with an audience and, temporarily at least, on shared mimetic conventions. The notes that follow, on the early history of Melbourne's main river, the Yarra (both the place and the name), outline an approach to such an alternative performative history. This involves a closer attention than is usual in local histories to the conditions of communication in the early years of European settlement, but it may be that the very localness of the inquiry is the key to its more general significance. For the means by which a speaking-place was enunciated only to suppress the specifically local history it might have engendered is a parable of the colonizing process generally, a process that simultaneously seeks out other places and denies them a voice of their own.

I

To begin with, though, and by way of introducing the historical material, it may be useful to substantiate the claim that a conventional historical approach to the phenomenon of place-naming fails to represent its performative context. By a conventional approach, I mean much what Auerbach means when he talks of a history written as an 'unbroken horizontal process', in which the object is to link elements into one unbroken logical chain, to make the facts functional as a narrative. Of course the conceptual framework need not necessarily be a linear, chronological one; the facts may be arranged according to a political, social or even psychoanalytical theory of human behaviour. But the fact remains that all such writing shares a common assumption, that the historical value of phenomena lies in their explanation in terms of a cause-and-effect economy of action. Historical events for them always represent something hidden, whether it is market forces or personal ambition. By contrast I have in mind a description of events that interprets them as phenomena, as open-ended and provisional actions that may, or may not, prefigure the future.

But let us begin, as local histories always do, at the beginning and, for the time being at least, suspend the doubt that the very idea of a 'beginning' may be exactly what vitiates horizontal history's ability to deal with those vertical events that have neither beginning nor end. From this point of view, the story of the naming – or misnaming – of Melbourne's river, the Yarra (see Plate 13), is as follows. On 3 September 1835, during a visit to the camp of pioneer settler John Pascoe Fawkner on the north side of the river, James Helder Wedge of the Port Phillip Association named the 'Yarrow Yarrow' 'from the following circumstance':

> On arriving in sight of the river, the two natives who were with me, pointing to the river at the Falls [illustrated in Liardet's watercolour, Plate 15], called out 'Yarra Yarra!' ['Wedge spelt the name "Yarrow" in his notebook' – editor's footnote] which, at the time, I imagined to be its name; but I afterward learnt that the words were what they used to designate a waterfall, as they afterwards gave the same designation to a small fall in the river Weiribee [Werribee], as we crossed it on our way back to Indented Head.[2]

125

Despite Wedge's candour, his story raises more questions than it answers. Firstly, Wedge already knew the Yarra by another name: on the same day that he made the above entry he wrote to one of the members of the Port Phillip Association, giving his address as 'about six miles up the Eastern River at the head of Port Phillip'.[3] Again, Wedge was quite able to distinguish topographical terms from place-names. He willingly adopted the name 'Barwon' for a river near Geelong, when informed that this was its native name by the ex-convict and honorary Aborigine, William Buckley.[4] Nor can we pretend that Wedge had a romantic interest in preserving the original names: as far as I know, he raised no objection to the replacement (in 1836) of the Aboriginal name 'Werribee' with the English name 'Exe'. Why, *in this instance alone*, did Wedge interpret the Aboriginal words as a proper name? And why, when he afterwards discovered his mistake, did he retain a name that he knew was not *the* name at all?

Taking the evidence at face value, it is hard to avoid concluding that Wedge had a motive. Beneath the appearance of simply reporting a fact, Wedge had a personal reason for singling out this utterance from others and treating it as a name. Wedge considered that Fawkner was trespassing on land belonging to the Port Phillip Association, land that the Aborigines had, he said, signed over to John Batman just three months earlier. Fawkner, needless to say, disagreed.[5] In this context of disputing prior claims, the ownership of the river's name was potentially of considerable rhetorical, not to say legal, importance.

But here we encounter a second difficulty: if Wedge wished to advance the cause of the Port Phillip Association, why did he not go back to the river's original name. Fawkner had already named the disputed stream 'Hunter's River',[6] and Wedge may well have wanted to efface this; but on the map he had himself prepared to accompany Batman's 'treaty' with the Dutigalla people the Yarra was already called 'R. Batman'. The simplest way of asserting the Association's prior claim would have been to resurrect the name of its leader.

To account for this it is necessary to invent a rather subtler explanation, to attribute to both Fawkner and Wedge a certain sense of their own self-importance and the historical significance of their actions. This is not implausible, but it certainly goes beyond the facts. For instance, it could be claimed that Fawkner's name had a certain authority that 'R. Batman' lacked: the connection between Hunter's River and Port Phillip replicated the nature of the relationship between the First Fleet's Surgeon-General and its Commander. In this sense Fawkner aligned his own land claims to those of the colonial government (which was decidedly suspicious of Batman's privatizing schemes).

But still, if we want to preserve its status as a founding act, we have to explain Wedge's choice of a pseudo-Aboriginal name in preference to one with imperial associations. Our best, but somewhat speculative, surmise is that the new name, Yarra Yarra, replaced the earlier, European names because it *disguised* any usurping claims of the newcomers. Its role was diplomatic. Non-associative, evidently meaningless to English ears except in reference to a unique geographical object, it had the prestige of a founding myth; it was as if the Port Phillip Association based its claim on time-honoured fact; as if, in adopting the Aboriginal name, it identified itself with the interests of the indigenous inhabitants.[7]

So much for trying to put the act of naming into some sort of horizontal historical framework. We hardly fare better when we try to place the word-sound 'Yarra' in a linguistic context. Assuming the sound *was* a word, did it mean, as Wedge claimed, a 'waterfall'; or, as Assistant Aboriginal Protector, William Thomas, claimed, 'hair or nap, man or animal'[8] or as Daniel Bunce, Batman's son-in-law, preferred, 'every substance of a flowing character'?[9]

Was 'Yarra Yarra' in any case an Aboriginal phrase? Eleven years earlier, on 16 December 1824, in the course of his overland expedition with Hamilton Hume from Sydney to Port Phillip Bay, William Hovell had noted – apparently in reference to a river sighted from Bald Hill[10] – that water south of the Alps 'is carried off by the Yar through Western Port'.[11] A few days later, Hovell enlarged on this choice of name:

> The great advantage this Country [which Hume and Hovell's modern editor, Alan Andrews, identifies as 'all the country which became Melbourne, from the Maribyrnong River to and around the Yarra'] will derive, will be the Communication, with the Interior as also with the Country East of the alps, along the river Yar, through the Gap, I gave it that Name from the great resemblance

of this Country to the County of Norfolk, and the Yar being the principal river in it . . . [12]

Andrews takes the view that despite 'the thought that it is too neat a coincidence', Hovell's Yar and the Yarra are one and the same.[13] He further notes, 'That Hovell elsewhere also spells both rivers as Yarr only increases our wonderment.'[14]

Could it be that eleven years later Wedge's Aboriginal companions were saying back to him what they took to be the *white* man's word for the river? The two Aborigines who accompanied Wedge came from more or less the same place on Corio Bay where, according to Hume, falling in with some natives on 17 December, 'I learnt from them the native names of several places in sight: the harbour they called Geeloong . . .'[15] Perhaps the explorers reciprocated with names of their own. But there is no evidence of this, any more than, for example, there is proof that 'Yarra' is cognate with Major Mitchell's 1836 name for the Victorian river to the north that later became the Loddon – 'The aboriginal name of this river' is the 'Yarrayne'[16] – or for that matter with another, geographically much closer river, the 'Yarrowee'.

In short, horizontal kinds of historical explanation soon peter out in ambiguity and uncertainty: like watercourses of the Australian interior that fan out rather than converging on a single source, attempts to organize the documentary evidence logically into a coherent narrative tend to diverge into a hundred speculative directions, none of them authoritative. The inevitable consequence is that, if the founding event is to retain its aura of uniqueness and not to appear cringingly arbitrary and absurd, it must be translated into more familiar terms. It may be explained as a political stratagem, a psychological ploy or a fortunate linguistic coincidence, or as a combination of all three. But one thing is certain: none of these accounts will consider 'Yarra' as evidence of a speech act, whose historical context is spoken rather than written.

2

It is not that the name 'Yarra' is wholly arbitrary. There is something to be said for the view that its successful adoption owed much to its rhetorical authority, its imitation of an Aboriginal name. Taken out of context, and in any case misunderstood, the ease with which a sound might come to be understood as the unique name of a place was perhaps proportional to its meaninglessness, to the fact that it did not conjure up distracting, politically sensitive verbal associations. After all, so long as a place-name conjured up one association, it could also conjure up another: Fawkner's 'Hunter' may have commemorated the Surgeon-General of the First Fleet or it may have recalled his less famous namesake, 'Hunter, master of the vessel' that, even before Fawkner's arrival, had transported the pioneer settler George Evans from Launceston to the Yarra.[17] But this merely underlines the misguidedness of seeking a single literary genealogy. It was as a word-sound, as a bridgehead, a way of mimicking the other, of appearing to bring it into cultural circulation while preserving something of its novelty, that 'Yarra' worked.

Nor was it by any means the only word-sound invented to legitimate the white invasion. Batman justified his occupation of the district between Geelong and Melbourne by saying he had purchased the land from the 'Dutigalla' people. But, as far as one can tell, no such tribe existed. As Melbourne historian Alastair Campbell writes,

> Dutigalla was to gain temporary currency after Wedge informed the visiting magistrate Stewart in 1836 that it was the name of the Yarra (Woiworung) tribe. Daniel Bunce . . . held that Dutigalla was a corruption of Nuthergalla from 'nuther' meaning 'no'. However, by then Nuthergalla may have been an Aboriginal corruption of Dutigalla. Subsequent investigation has not shown it to be a tribal name used by Aborigines: it was evidently a misinterpretation or an invention by Batman.[18]

None of this, it should be added, prevented the word from acquiring considerable authority among the white settlers. Like the river, the nascent settlement on its bank also underwent a number of name changes: before it was officially christened 'Melbourne', it had been known variously as 'the Settlement', 'Bearbrass' and 'Batmanville'.

But it may be significant that, when some settlers raised objections to the official name, it was because they wanted 'to keep the early aboriginal name of Doutta Galla for the township'.[19] Perhaps they shared the view of William Thomas, that 'Surveyors' names, of all others, are most ridiculous.'[20] Perhaps this was why Batman stripped himself of his own name and began to call himself 'Dutigullar' instead.[21] But whatever their motives, the authority of their preferred name was phonetic, not semantic: it was the sound that founded a place for them and not any meaning it may have had.

However, as Campbell's reflections make graphically clear, sounds were not imposed unilaterally on places: they arose dialogically, from the efforts of people without a language in common to make sense of each other. For in dialogue even a blank denial communicates something. In this context the meaning and authority of Yarra, like 'Dutigalla' does not depend on establishing a unique provenance for it. Quite the reverse: its historical authority will be best indicated by the *frequency* of its usage, by evidence of the fact that it was *spoken* widely. The variety of ways in which the word-sound is written in the early letters and diaries indicates exactly this.

Wedge's own rendering 'Yarrow', for instance, does not necessarily disclose his geographical patriotism: it is more likely that it reflects his attempt to find the word in English that most exactly approximated to the Aboriginal sound. Hence he rendered Buckley's 'Barwon' as 'Byron' and the 'Werribee' as 'Wearibee', in both cases, presumably, seeking to make the Aboriginal sound memorable by dressing it up with an English form.[22] The function of a word like 'Byron' was not associative – there is nothing to suggest that Wedge had in mind the poet – but mnemonic: the English word was a convenient, if arbitrary, means of remembering the Aboriginal sound. But in any case the sound was not fixed. Visiting the nascent Melbourne in December 1836, George Augustus Robinson described a Mr Robson's establishment known as 'Yarro Store', explaining: 'Yarro Yarro name of a river; Yal-le is a river.' A day later, however, he reported that the 'river at the settlement is called the Yar-rer Yar-rer'.[23] Another newcomer, also writing in 1836, transcribed the name as 'Yarre Yarre', with the stress on the final syllable.[24] Yet another early pioneer, Gellibrand, wrote 'Yara Yara' in his journal and, later in the same day's entry 'Yana Yana'.[25] These may have been errors in transcription, as C. E.

Sayers suggests, or they may simply have reflected the instability of a sound which, nevertheless, was distinctive enough to be memorable.

Its rhetorical power may not have depended on its pseudo-Aboriginal reference, but on its pre-referential sonorousness. 'Yarra Yarra', the Assistant Aboriginal Protector, William Thomas, notes: 'However musical this word sounds, and however it is taken to stand for the river, such is not the case.'[26] But, quite as significant as Thomas's disclaimer is the fact that he does not offer us the true name. It is the sound that signifies in a new country, not the sense. And we might take this further. That second father of Romanticism, Herder, agreed with Rousseau that 'the prosody and the song of the oldest languages' expressed emotions, but he disagreed that the expression of emotions was language's mainspring: the origin of language, 'which . . . was what this song was', according to Herder, 'was the naming of every creature after its own language'.[27] In a sense 'Yarra' was the sound by which, in the absence of a common language, the newcomers announced themselves in a manner that was purely expressive, purely musical.

It is possible that poetic considerations influenced its choice. As a phonemic combination, 'Yarra' allowed considerable flexibility of pronunciation. It could be stressed on the first or second syllable. The syllables could be given equal measure or one made shorter than the other. The repeated vowel sound was an encouragement to vary pitch. 'Yarra' was a mirror word: its two halves echoed each other. But there was not a clean break. The guttural 'rr', like water lapping against the shore or like the rainbow caught inside the mirror's glass revealing the materiality of light and its reflection, glues the two halves together, suggesting their unity in difference. The 'r' is a half-echo of the 'y', implying a dialogue, a difference in unity. Such were the sound's poetic qualities that it seemed in some way to *imitate the place* where it was uttered – in this respect obeying Herder's dictum that the form of words was not arbitrary but, however mysteriously, derived from the senses.

But, if we are to avoid lapsing into a kind of *placism*, identifying the sound with the character of a physical place, we need to locate these poetic qualities within their spoken context. For any pleasure the first settlers and the indigenous people found in saying back to each other this word did not take the form of a highly self-conscious

131

tenson: it derived from the mere fact of having a clearly articulated sound in common, a sound unit that was expressive and memorable, that had all the makings of a word but which retained its musical power to signify without signifying anything, to convey a mutual self-presencing, a mirroring of intentions in the absence of anything else in common.

3

Perhaps the form of 'Yarra' was a metaphor for the kind of dialogue the word helped initiate. If it represented anything it was an echoic back and forth of sounds. Combining them into a single phonetically coherent unit, it improvised a meeting place, a common ground where mimicking noises made sense, settled down and acquired a fixed meaning. It is worth stressing this poetic possibility, if only because history remains resolutely deaf to it. But even so the acoustic phenomena, the modes of vocalization represented by the formulation 'Yarra' did not occur in a historical vacuum. They were highly localized and motivated: it was not a matter of calmly negotiating access to the land or of invoking aesthetic preferences in reaching agreement about a choice of wording. Peaceful relations depended on careful and circumspect diplomacy. It was a matter of urgency to communicate, to fill the air with new sounds, to improvise spaces of exchange; these circumstances had quite as much influence on the form that the name of Melbourne's river took as any inherently poetic qualities the word may have had.

To recover the Yarra's sound history it is necessary to replace it within the context of speaking rather than writing. Anthropologists make the point that in an oral culture the success of a song is measured by the distance it has travelled (both physically and formally) from its point of origin; that the search for an original pure form not only runs counter to the oral impulse to improvise, adapt and transform, but also imports an implicitly textual model of cultural transmission. The search for an Ur-text is mistaken on another ground: as anthropologist Tamsin Donaldson has pointed out, no song or dance can be separated from the context of its performance. No metaphysical point of origin, no autonomous literary form, exists to be unearthed and preserved, only a proliferation of physical and social contexts, each influ-encing the form the performance takes.[28]

Something similar applies to the naming of Melbourne's main river. While a textual history rapidly finds itself tangled up in the metaphysical headwaters of hidden motives, an oral history turns in the other direction, focusing on the rhetorical and spatial context in which the name came to be adopted, where it derived its authority, not from any putative etymology (English or Aboriginal), but from its extreme susceptibility to vocal incorporation and variation. The name 'Yarra' began as a repeated sound, an element in a dialogue, a token of communication. But, as the variety of spellings indicates, Yarra was never a fixed sound; it could be heard and said in more than one way. It began by being something else, another sound, another word. Its origins, that is, were never with the speaker, but with the hearer. As a token of oral exchange, the salient feature of 'Yarra' was its dialogical character, its power to improvise a linguistic clearing where different idiolects could overlap and, to the ear at least, be harmonized.

However, this harmony, this air of mutual understanding, was, of course, a stand-in for genuine communication. It was a means of acting out therapeutically the frustration that arose where two parties were thrown together without a language in common. The improvised words were verbal *symbols* in the original sense of the term: each side possessed only half the word and for one to recognize the other it was necessary to put the sounds back together, to make a word out of it that named the place where they met – and had, in imitation at least, perhaps met before. But this meant improvising words and sentences foreign to both sides; it meant creating a new hybrid tongue exclusively for the purpose of communicating here. What such a tongue conveyed was not information about the country, the local customs or the advantages of nineteenth-century technology, but *the desire to communicate*. It was natural in this context that the hybrid discourse improvised would refer, if it referred to anything at all, to the very process of vocalization whereby, in the absence of meaning, language could be made to mimic meaning.

The journals of George Augustus Robinson, Port Phillip's official Aboriginal Protector, contain many examples of the self-reflexive exag-geration to which such language was prone. Take the following: 'My natives were highly amused and passed their jokes on the gibberish used by the white men, as "very good this way", "no good that way", "man him", "bullock tucker", "talk talk, walk, walk," "where you leep leep". And this is what the white people call speaking the native language.'[29] From a grammatical and semantic perspective, the speech patterns jocularly imitated here resemble the 'restricted codings' of the kind of pidgin language employed where speech 'is not perceived as a major means of presenting inner states to the other'.[30] But from an oral point of view their significance is rather different. As far as we can judge from Robinson's reactions, his 'natives' succeed rather well in 'presenting inner states to the other': at any rate, mimicking the pidgin English the settlers improvise to talk to them, they effectively communicate the non-communication that takes place.

But such mimicry occurs at enormous psychic cost: it implies the abandonment of language, the renunciation of dialogue. Robinson's companions do not simply mimic white attempts at dialogue: they parody it. Or more exactly, they mimic what is already a parody. But there is a fatal difference. While the whites' parodic speech presupposes a non-parodic mode of address (that of ordinary conversation), the Aborigines' mimetic reproduction arises from the fact that they are excluded from such non-parodic discourse. And, not having access to a non-parodic form of language, their mimicry is not parody but, in Fredric Jameson's sense of the word, pastiche:

> Pastiche is, like parody, the imitation of a peculiar or unique style, the wearing of a stylistic mask, speech in a dead language: but it is a neutral practice of such mimicry, without parody's ulterior motive, without the satirical impulse, without laughter, without the still latent feeling that there exists something normal compared to which what is being imitated is rather comic.[31]

In this context the laughter of Robinson's Aborigines is *also* pastiche; that is, it laughs at the emptiness of laughter; it echoes the powerlessness of a people not only prevented from entering into dialogue, but even denied a language of their own in which to remain silent.

And, lest this seem unduly sentimental, we might recall the experience of John Bulmer, a Church of England missionary who, fifteen years after the official foundation of Melbourne, was writing down the language spoken at Yelta mission station on the Murray. Bulmer found that, because communication was so difficult, the Marawara people made much use of repetition. They relied on extreme emphasis and resorted to grammatical over-simplification. Trying to make themselves more comprehensible, they said the same thing in more than one way, a device that led Bulmer to remark, 'One thing I have observed with regard to the language – it is a double language. They have two words for everything.' The Marawara made other concessions: they learnt, for example, to speak very slowly, splitting up syllables so that Bulmer could transcribe the sounds more accurately.[32]

The irony of this effort to evolve a common language was that, as a modern scholar notes, Bulmer only misunderstood the language he was studying more comprehensively than ever, frequently splitting words, with the result that the grammar of the Marawara language was missed, and the language therefore characterized as even more primitive, more foreign to reason than anyone could have predicted.[33] Had he paid attention to the context of utterance – entering into dialogue with a living people, rather than regarding them as representatives of a race doomed to disappear – Bulmer might have heard clearly what was being said.

In this context the repetition of the sound 'yarra' acquires a local significance. It *could* be that the duplication of the word had a grammatical, even a semantic value, signifying the pluralization of the noun or an intensive form of it. Certainly early students of Aboriginal languages confidently interpreted duplication in this way. But as we have seen, at the point Wedge wrote down what he had heard, the sound had yet to assume a definite meaning, let alone a form that might exhibit gender and cases. It is more likely that, by repeating the word, Wedge's interlocuters intended, by the most direct verbal mimicry, to lay stress on the sound, to emphasize its meaning. But such was the paradoxical nature of communication that, putting emphasis on it, they changed it into something else. It is possible that, by emphasizing the sound, repeating and simplifying it for white ears, they facilitated its passage from speech into writing. In which case, the more loudly they spoke the more certainly they spelled out the means of their own silencing.

4

The deeper assymetries attributed here to an apparently symmetrical unit of dialogue may seem overly sinister. But we have considered only one aspect of Wedge's anecdote – its vocal element. Yet his guides not only spoke: they pointed. Wedge makes the assumption that, like antipodean landscape gardeners, their outstretched arms indicate the pleasant prospect that lies ahead of them, that they are pointing to an object visible in the distance. But, rather than indicate a picturesque arrangement, it may have been that their gesture was active, a symbolic way of drawing the country ahead towards them. Later they used 'the same designation' ('Yarra Yarra!') to name 'a small fall on the Weiribee, *as we crossed it*' (my italics). Words may have been inseparable from actions; and actions, rather than symbolizing the distance between human beings and their environment, may have signified its incorporation. They may have been performative, rather than inadequate representations of visual perceptions. Wedge's guides may have been reciting something, rather than seeing it through his eyes and naming it for the first time.

In 1803 William Buckley had escaped from the recently established – and, as it turned out, very temporary – settlement at Sullivan Cove on the south-east shore of Port Phillip Bay; until he was discovered by Wedge thirty-two years later, Buckley had lived with the Aboriginal people of the Barwon River district near Geelong. His ghosted and greatly rationalized account of that period describes his first encounter with the local people in this way: 'After seizing both my hands, they struck their breasts, and mine also, making at the same time a noise between singing and crying: a sort of whine which to me sounded very like premeditated mischief.'[34] A second meeting produced similar behaviour: 'seizing me by the hands and arms, [they] began beating their breasts, and mine, in the manner the others had done. After a short time, they lifted me up, and they made the same sign, giving me to understand by it, that I was in want of food.' Buckley continues:

> They called me Murrangurk, which I afterwards learnt was the name of a man formerly belonging to their tribe, who had been buried at the spot where I had found the piece of spear I still carried with me. They have a belief, that when they die, they go to

some place or other, and are there made white men, and that they then return to this world again for another existence ... To this providential superstition, I was indebted for all the kindnesses afterwards shown me.[35]

Although the belief in reincarnation described here was a commonplace of the early ethnographic literature, Buckley's understanding of it may perhaps be questioned: few who met him seem to have credited him with much capacity for abstract thought. Again, the rationalization of the breast-beating as a sign of hunger hardly seems adequate: people witnessing the reincarnation of a relative might be expected to have something other than food on their minds when they touched the seat of the heart and lungs. Still, the account of how Buckley was adopted is *structurally* interesting. It illustrates that, here at least, gestures were inseparable from vocalization; and that both mimetic actions were not simply adventitious imitations, but acted out a belief. Making Buckley *act* like one of them, they made him one of them – a logic that stemmed from the proposition that he was, in any case, originally their countryman. His whiteness justified his forgetfulness but, paradoxically, it was also proof he was of their colour.

No comparable means of incorporating strange people seems to have existed on the European side. Eighteen months before the establishment of the Sullivan Cove settlement, a reconnoitring party had made contact with Aborigines on the north-west shore of Port Phillip adjoining the Werribee plains. On the face of it the little drama played out there employed the same diplomatic mirror language which characterized Buckley's experience: 'I gave one of them a biscuit; he looked at it; I took it again, eat of it, when he did the same; whatever we said they said it after us.'[36] Here, too, communication is initiated by way of a mime: just as Buckley is encouraged to reciprocate the gesture of breast-beating, so the Aborigines are invited to imitate the Europeans. The difference is that, while the former represents a rite of passage, enabling Buckley to be reborn an Aborigine, the latter represents nothing except a desire to avoid misunderstanding – that is, to short-circuit any genuine exchange by pre-emptively capturing the Aborigines with the mirror of one's own voice and gesture, both of which are 'put on' for the occasion. From a European point of view, no kinship ties follow from the act of eating. From an Aboriginal point of view, the biscuit fails to bring succour because it is *too* edible, it is never made flesh.

It is this different understanding of gestures that overshadows the apparently innocent exchange of words and introduces a sinister assymmetry into the mimetic strategies improvised at the beginning. The depth of this difference – and its fatal implications for the Aborigines – is clearly illustrated in the plans Batman made for his occupation of Port Phillip in 1835. By then, if not before, the new-comers might want to pass themselves off as white Aborigines, but they had no intention of revealing their true colours. Batman recognized that, in the wake of government concern over the progressive genocide of the Tasmanian people, he would need to make some effort to legitimize his invasion. Hence he made much of the fact that, prior to landing his sheep, he had signed a 'treaty' with the local people, whereby they ceded to him their land (extending from Geelong to the Yarra).

The status of this 'treaty' has been much disputed, but there is little reason to disagree with the recently expressed view that 'the deeds were fraudulent ... and [Batman's] intentions almost certainly devious.'[37] Of interest here, though, is the *means* by which Batman so quickly managed to come into such intimate contact with the (as we saw, non-existent) 'Dutigalla' people that he could persuade their 'chiefs' to sign what amounted to their own death warrant. Batman sailed from Launceston accompanied by seven New South Wales Aborigines. The function of these men was, as he explained in his official report, diplomatic. They were to act as go-betweens. Accordingly, when he first made contact with local Aborigines near Point Wilson, in order to explain to them that 'I was, although a white, a countryman of theirs', Batman had *his* Aborigines put off their European disguise: 'I then made my arrangements for the purpose of opening an intercourse with the natives by means of those under my charge. I equipped them in their native dresses ...'[38]

The rationale for this pantomimic diplomacy is more fully explained by the future Port Phillip Aboriginal Protector, George Augustus Robinson, who, even before Batman's 'treaty', was contemplating a mission to the mainland Aborigines and who, in a letter to the governor of Van Diemen's Land, explained that a contingent of Tasmanian Aborigines would be a valuable asset in bringing the New Holland

Aborigines under his sway. First they would be of service 'by exciting curiosity in the minds of the New Hollanders'; then, 'being Aborigines, they would, although unacquainted with the language of the New Hollanders, sooner detect any preconcerted act of hostility than Europeans, and when familiar with the language, and which they would soon acquire, they would become efficient auxiliaries in promoting the objects of the mission'.[39]

There was nothing novel, of course, about employing an indigenous Fifth Column to facilitate the process of invasion, but the difference here was that the imported Aborigines were as unfamiliar with the language and customs of the local people as were the Europeans; and, while they might learn these, in the first instance their effectiveness depended on their ability to mime *being Aboriginal*. The job of the New South Wales and Tasmanian migrants was to appear no different from the 'New Hollanders', to resemble them exactly. To this end Batman has his men take off their European clothes before approaching the Victorian Aborigines. But what does this undressing signify? Batman wants to pass himself off as their 'countryman' although white. Taking off their clothes, his black avant-garde is revealed as unequivocally black: as if underneath we are all the same. But the fact that blackness can be *put on* in this way, simply by the removal of trousers and shirt, also places the New Hollanders in a new light. Apart from the obvious racism of identifying them by the colour of their skins, it suggests that their appearance is a pretence, a symbolic code, a matter of politics.

In view of the fact that the two parties interpreted each other's sign language differently, the in-between people selected to mediate between them rapidly found themselves in an untenable situation. They could pass from one side to the other but, despite their best intentions, found themselves unable to open up a space between, a language of genuine exchange. In this context Buckley's ghosted account of how he made contact with Wedge not only had pathos but profound implications for the future of race relations. No longer able to speak English, Buckley 'was at a loss what to do for the best' when he first came across Wedge and his men near Indented Head, east of the future Geelong in Port Philip Bay. But then his Aboriginal kin 'pointed me out to one of the white people; and seeing they had done so, I walked away from the well, up to their place'.[40] It is Buckley's

Aboriginal status that enables him to open communication with the Europeans.

But then something happens: mere mimicry gives way to memory and, in the moment of understanding what is being said to him, it is as if a new identity closes over him, drowning out the world he has lived in for thirty-two years:

> At length one of them came up and asked me some questions which I could not understand; but when he offered me bread – calling it by its name – a cloud appeared to pass from over my brain, and I soon repeated that, and other English words after him. Somehow or other I soon made myself understood to them as not being a native-born, and so the white men took me to their tents, and clothed me, giving me biscuit, tea and meat.[41]

A cloud has dispersed to be replaced by the lucidness of the mirror; for what is crucial in this passage is the phrase 'and so': he is one of them and, from this moment forward, any allegiance he might exhibit to his native family must only be diplomatic, a make-believe designed to forward the interests of a people who, Buckley painfully learns, 'intended to remain in the country'. Otherwise, how will this convict avoid further punishment? How will he earn his freedom, unless by betraying one side to the other?

Unable to find a third position of mutual acceptance, Buckley resigned as interpreter for the Port Phillip Association less than two years after accepting the position: 'when I reflected on the suspicion with which I was viewed by the most influential white men, and on the probable doubt the natives would entertain in my sincerity after having left them, I thought it best to retire to Van Diemen's Land [Tasmania].' And he adds, 'Indeed, I could not calculate on one hour's personal safety from either party under such circumstances.'[42]

So brittle was this mirror world, so little was it able to translate mimicry into metaphor, to improvise a verbal and gestural language symbolizing a new and common space of dialogue, that it could not accommodate the smallest revelation of difference. So fragile was it that any unreciprocated gesture could only be construed as an 'act of hostility' spelling imminent destruction. The people in-between upset this barren symmetry. In the interests of both parties, it was better to remove them, to turn the sounding space into a glassy barrier keeping both sides apart.

5

From one point of view the naming of the Yarra was a small, not very significant cog in the huge machine driving the juggernaut of colonization. Historically, it was only another minute step in implementing the strategy of planned invasion whereby Europe's imperial powers inscribed themselves over the late eighteenth- and nineteenth-century world. Just as the machines of the first industrial revolution were conceptualized as 'closed systems and linear relationships in which small inputs yield small results', so the local history of the Yarra was a small event yielding small results. But from another, non-linear point of view, the naming of the Yarra threatened the machine-like model of invasion. Here was a sound that was not immediately an English word; here was a term that resisted Enlightenment philosophy's ambition to reduce the world to equivalence. Here, potentially, was a chaotic element, one that brought into question the whole cultural rationale for subsuming difference to universal rules.

Recent proponents of chaos theory have explained how under certain circumstances apparently linear systems can give rise to 'disorder, instability, diversity, disequilibrium, non-linear relationships (in which small inputs can trigger massive consequences), and temporality'.[43] As certain boundary conditions are approached and transgressed, order gives way to chaos. Something similar may be true in history. There are situations where certain physical and psychological boundary conditions are transgressed, where the normal predictive laws governing human behaviour break down and phenomena assume a chaotic appearance. In a spatial historical sense, the comprehensive transgression of metaphysical as well as physical boundaries represented by the act of colonization is just such a moment: the Enlightenment rhetoric of progress breaks down, to be replaced by apparently chaotic phenomena – proliferating sounds, mimes empty of meaning, paths leading in all directions nowhere.

The analogy between physical and historical events is fertile in another way. For, as Ilya Prigogine and others have shown, the chaotic appearance of non-linear reactions is apparent only and is, in fact, evidence of the existence of a higher, more integrated order of physical reality. Something similar was also true on the Yarra. In its naming history bifurcated, revealing the possibility of two markedly different futures. One of these was the higher integration of Aborigines and Europeans in the forging of a creole culture. The other was the suppression of this anomalous, unpredictable possibility, by way of retreat into the former linear hypothesis of cultural transmission and colonization. But such was the power of the non-linear possibility that it could not be ignored completely: its anomalous sounds and signs were already powerfully in circulation.

In this situation the machine of colonization had little choice but to rationalize the irrational, to make it as far as possible a mirror to its own closed system. This mirroring process, whereby the colonists retreated from the possibility of chaotic, creative dialogue with their surroundings, became, in fact, the primary means whereby, rhetorically and spatially, the newcomers grounded themselves in the new country. But because this grounding was mechanistic, and for all its talk of progress rigorously suppressed the experience of temporality, the contingency of time, it could not escape from the mirror world of its own construction. The world across the river – for very rapidly the south bank of the Yarra came to be an ironic image of life on the north bank – might *coincide* at every point with developments on the other side; but at no point did the mirror image indicate mutual understanding or the existence of a higher, inclusive order that made sense of their mimicry. On the contrary, it merely indicated the fate of imitation when the mimetic behaviour characteristic of boundary transgressions failed to transmute itself into communication of a higher order.

6

The naming of the Yarra made possible two histories. One, amply documented in early histories of Melbourne and the fate of the local Aborigines, is the linear one, withdrawal from the chaos of a sounding space into the silence of picturesque distance. Here 'Yarra' did not name a 'river'; rather it brought a river into existence, licensing the construction of a (linear) place that would carry forward a certain kind of history. To begin with, Wedge's 'Falls' served neither as a means of navigating the interior nor as a reliable means of transport. All these riverine properties had to be imposed, in the process turning a meeting place into a one-way flow, a rounded basin into a pair of mirroring banks.

Indicative of the ambiguity surrounding the water was the debate about the future of the 'Falls' themselves. Both Hoddle and Lonsdale favoured using the natural barrier as the foundation of a dam. This would protect Melbourne's fresh water supply, but it would also see the river's arrest. The future movement of water below the dam would have been inward and upward on the rising tide. The reversal of the river's direction, its promotion as a mode of arrival and disembarcation, implied other physical modifications: the lower river needed to be dredged and staked and its banks needed to be defined and wharved. Further, the natural 'pool' below the Falls had to be widened to accommodate ships turning. The apotheosis of this process was perhaps Lonsdale's suggestion that, to facilitate the discharge of cargoes, 'the banks of the basin [should be] cut so as to make the sides of it at right angles to the town'.[44]

By all these modifications the Falls were progressively reduced to reason: the clatter of water was reduced to a smooth curtain, soundlessly emptying into the harbour. The ill-defined edges of the water were streamlined and wharved, permitting the disembarcation of men and cargo to go ahead with a minimum of chance, as if the water already had the stability of land. The centre of the water was dredged and staked to allow access to vessels of deeper draught. The dam wall, although it looked like a bridge, was not any longer construed as a means of communication across the water, but as a barrier dividing the flowing water into two mirroring pools. To make up for the arrest, a stone bridge was constructed downstream.

Later still, the rhetorical basis of settlement was made explicit when the reef which caused the Falls was blasted away, to allow ships to pass further upstream, to make even smoother the passage from one place to another, one element to another. The mirror glass of water which followed the destruction of the reef perfectly reflected the culture now established there, a culture which believed in closed systems, whose machine-like functioning was independent of local conditions. The fact that the unified surface of the stream now reflected nothing except the sky perfectly embodied the colonists' own claim to be 'countrymen', as invisible as the Aborigines.

A comparable mirroring logic filters out the chaos of the Aboriginal presence. From the earliest days when, thwarting an Aboriginal attack, 'Fawkner and his men, aided by Henry Batman, then herded the blacks into their bark canoes and had them towed across the river; they burned the canoes and returned to the settlement',[45] the south bank came to be associated with those who, by a reversal of natural vision and logic characteristic of the mirror, could now be regarded as occupying the country illegitimately. But the Aborigines did not go away. Instead there grew up across the water a ghostly canvas town mirroring the makeshift dwellings built by the Europeans on the north side.

If Batman's first house on the north side was 'a sod hut to house hay, stores and tools. The roof was of interlaced branches, roughly thatched with reeds and long grass', on the south side they were building 'mia-mias [which Robinson intriguingly refers to on one occasion as 'mira miras'], rough huts of tree branches covered with the tough bark of gum trees'.[46] One pioneer, David Fisher, writes of Fawkner's first hotel that 'This building was of turf or sods, with a portion of wood, and comprised six apartments of a very primitive order'[47] – a description that loosely recalls Robinson's account of native huts 'large enough to contain seven or eight persons (adults). They were made in form of a cupola with bark and sods over them with a doorway.'[48] The forms may have differed but not, apparently, the building techniques and functions. And, to judge from another passage in Robinson where, in reference to 'a black man's house', his 'native companions' gloss it as 'a large one like white man's house',[49] on one side at least the similarities may have seemed not only obvious, but worth imitating.

But to a people bent on self-definition these mirror buildings on the south bank could only seem chaotic. They created the same feeling of unease as the Aboriginal habit of adopting European names. In the streets of Melbourne after dark there walked 'Lonsdale' – 'called himself my brother'[50] – and, even though the settler Gellibrand was dead, possibly murdered, his Aboriginal double, 'Gellibrand', paraded as large as life, shaking hands, begging a twist of tobacco. These were joined by other European *doppelgängers*: Tyers, King and Gipps. This

Aboriginal attempt to pass beyond mimicry to kinship could only inspire in the newcomers a superstitious fear of being haunted and mocked to their faces. It made them all the more anxious to put the water between them.

The zoning of the races was made official in June 1836 when the government established its Aboriginal mission about two miles from the settlement on the banks of the Yarra. Here, on the river's south bank, the process of civilizing the natives was to be carried forward through the establishment of a village along Owenite lines. The model village lapsed for lack of Aborigines willing to inhabit it but, rather than draw the conclusion that the local people had no wish to be confined apart, George Langhorne, the mission's administrator, attributed the failure to *insufficient* separation of the races: 'I considered that unless there was almost complete isolation for such an institution it could not succeed, as the contaminating influence arising from close proximity to the settlement must necessarily ruin any effort made for the visual improvement of the Aborigines in the neighbourhood.'[51]

Langhorne's phrase 'visual improvement' implies that the Aborigines were features in a landscape, something to be seen and disposed picturesquely, rather than people who might speak expecting to be heard. It is significant that, in contrast with most missionaries, who acknowledged the need to learn the Aborigines' own tongue, Langhorne proposed to teach exclusively in English: if the Aborigines were to enter into dialogue with the British, it would be entirely on British terms. Similarly, if they were to enter their new world, it would be by way of abandoning their own dwelling places and coming to live in a *Utopian* village, a city of the future.

The sequel was predictable: in May 1840, the land on which the government mission stood was sold as allotments. The Aborigines, by now greatly reduced in number, were forbidden to enter 'North Melbourne' (i.e. the settlement north of the river). In future, religious and government Aboriginal missions were to be located far away from the city – well out of sight.

7

This was one future, according to which the smooth mirror of history, temporarily ruffled by a wind scudding upstream, resumed its implacable horizontal shift. It was a future in which, as soon as the mirror symmetry of first meetings was shattered, one side or the other was bound to disappear for ever. It is said that the first Europeans to be killed by Aborigines in the Port Phillip area were two shipwrecked sailors. At first 'kindly treated', they were 'savagely murdered, whilst crossing the Yarra River'.[52] This might be a parable of life and death in a mirror state: so long as both sides were content to reciprocate gestures, all was well. But the moment they turned their backs and sought to escape to a world of their own, they exposed themselves to death.

But crossing the Yarra might symbolize rebirth, not death. The same historical breath of air that made the surface grow tremulous, chaotic, also outlined another vocal and spatial history. It could not be represented, as in a photograph or engraving. It was best thought of as shivering light or the vibration of the air. In this other history people without a language in common managed to get through to each other, to cross the Yarra without being killed. Shattering the mirror of their own culture, they found that they had not drowned. A cloud had passed from their brains and they could communicate.

What is the evidence for this alternative history? Borrowing again the analogy from chaos theory, we can make the point that the higher social and spiritual integration that 'Yarra', the speech act, made possible did not exclude the mechanist model of historical progress: rather it was higher order already immanent in the cause-and-effect linear configuration of ordinary history. In this sense, the failure, say, of a creole culture to emerge in early nineteenth-century Australia is not a missed historical opportunity, a once and only chance of metaphysical grounding in a new country that was passed up. On the contrary, it remains immanent within our own historical myth, our Western culture's persistent dream of self-transcendence in the return to an Eden from which, but for our wrong use of language in naming what had already been named, we might never have been exiled.

But this is not to say that such a history is merely a Utopian dream. There is the mundane fact that the first magistrate of Port Phillip, William Lonsdale, imagined creating a hybrid Australian race through the interbreeding of Aborigines and the British lower orders. Less imperialistically – although also precipitated by the act of colonization – there occurred in the early years within the increasingly rigid mirror culture many events that, while historically insignificant, might have had an effect out of all proportion to their 'input' into the cultural system. Consider the following touching scene narrated by William Thomas, which took place in January 1839:

> This morning early while sitting at my tent door, my little boy Jemmy called out, 'Look at those blacks' (pointing to the other side of the river). I called out as loud as my lungs would permit. Some made a stand. I hastened to the brink of the river, holding up a fourpound loaf as high as I could. I ordered my men to get the boat, and went over. There were thirteen blacks. Six of them returned with me after shaking hands and we ascended the rise where the tents were. I made them sit down. I sat down with them, little Jemmy bringing my tea. Mrs T. made each a pint of good warm milk, water and sugar and divided a four-pound loaf between them ... [Later] I accompanied them to the yonder side, when after walking half a mile I left them highly delighted with my breakfast.[53]

Without sentimentalizing this episode, it is clear that here at least the Yarra became a means of people meeting, not dividing. The distance did not frame visually; it created a speaking and signifying space large enough to accommodate difference, to entertain rapprochement. The mimetic actions did not mimic each other, but followed one after the other, as events leading to further events.

There were other occasions where performance broke through into lived life and, briefly at least, the civilizing process did not rule out reciprocal arrangements. The pioneer David Mercer describes an incident thematically and structurally replete with mirror symbolism:

> being occupied in shaving, which operation being observed by some of the natives afforded them much amusement, and one of them signifying a desire to be trimmed, I undertook the task, which I accomplished amidst the yells, shouts, and laughter of some fifty savages with their lubras, who enjoyed the affair very much; and thus I believe myself to be the first that shaved an aboriginal in New Holland.[54]

Their amusement seems hollow if we recall Buckley's fate: no sooner had Batman and his companions got him in their power than they set about washing him, shaving him and cutting his hair.[55] Buckley's new, civilized face disguised him. It facilitated his physical as well as emotional separation from the Barwon people (who would now hardly recognize him). Perhaps a similar unease informed the laughter that surrounded Mercer as he wielded scissors and blade. Nevertheless, where such performances became absorbed into everyday life they could empower both parties. Again it is William Thomas who casually notes in his journal: 'A black lent me a looking glass, I got a shave and was clean and comfortable before his Honor came.'[56]

In such moments of simple, intimate exchange, 'Yarra' ceased to signify a mirror place and became instead somewhere where a genuine give and take occurred. It is easy to write off such moments, to see through their sign language, treating them as nothing more than illustrations of cultural and technological imprisonment. But all human exchange is mediated culturally and symbolically; what matters is the uses to which those symbols are put. When, in 1838, Mr George Hollins's bay mare Mrs Dutigalla won the Town Plate at the Melbourne Race Club's first meeting,[57] one historical course was trivialized by backing another. When, instead of employing him, they tried to exhibit Buckley on stage, billing him as 'the huge Anglo-Australian giant',[58] an important future was put behind not only him but us. In this context, even the small acts of tentative dialogue had the power to precipitate a revolutionary change.

Gradually a consensus grew up among early writers that 'yarra' was an Aboriginal word whose primary meaning was 'hair' or 'flowing hair'. In this context one might ponder the symbolic meaning the local people attributed to having their hair cut. From our point of view, the symbolic coincidence lies elsewhere – in the thought that the word-sound signified an alternative history in which time was not fixed cartographically or with the help of dams, but flowed; and flowed, not like the stream of history, but like light hovering along the irregular rim of a natural weir, like the sound of words tripping off the tongue and eternally being returned in different forms.

7 Grass Houses

Vincenzo Volentieri, A Bicentennial Memoir

> *Here I lie, clock-a-clay,*
> *Waiting for the time of day . . .*
>
> John Clare

Who has not as a child lain down in a field of wheat or meadow grass and, like Gulliver in Brobdingnag, discovered a buzzing city, a migrant host, a world of slender, towering stems, and imagined himself an insect atop the highest grass head or curled in its drooping fan? And thought this delicious elevation and disappearance the highest form of happiness?

Some such experience surely lay behind Vincenzo Volentieri's finest public building, his migrant accommodation, *Gondwanaland*. Now that his floating estates have become so familiar, it is hard to imagine the childish delight with which the public first greeted them. Strung out along our arterial roads at heights of two to three hundred feet, attached to the earth by hawsers, his aerial dwellings resembled nothing so much as a giant grass field. At a distance, they appeared like tiny rain clouds, appetizing, full of promise. But to be inside them was, and is, to experience permanently what, for most migrants, is but a first, brief, unique and poignant glimpse of their future home as they come into land: Australia like a carpet, spreading out in every direction towards the flat horizon.

As Volentieri explained when local critics accused him of perpetuating havens of homesickness, these vessels did not signify an Odyssean nostalgia to sail back to Ithaca. They commemorated the migrant's life-long desire to *reach* Australia. Their state of suspended animation corresponded to the migrant's transitional condition. 'It is my heartfelt wish,' he once wrote, 'that these gondolas may one day be hauled down and land.'

Volentieri's sky houses did not come out of the blue. They arose from half a lifetime of consistently original design experimentation. For all their flights of fantasy, they were firmly rooted in Volentieri's own experience and background. Volentieri's origins were clear enough in his face: despite the permanent dark glasses, a swarthy, almost Aboriginal complexion could not mask the finely chiselled Sicilian features. But Volentieri inherited more from his father than good looks and his at times notorious bisexuality: as far back as anyone could remember, his family had been stonemasons. True, Vincenzo never visited his native land, but it can hardly be coincidence that his family was, I find, associated with the construction of that urban Utopia and synonym for public space, New Noto.

In a sense, it was fully to be expected that our first great architect should derive not from England but from Sicily. The parallels between our two cultures are too obvious to be overlooked. Both are products of translation and renovation, both the outcomes of events (earthquake and transportation) that were disasters for those involved. And what is more like the early Australian squatting runs than the Sicilian *latifundiae*? Who, approaching the mythical Enna by way of that endlessly slow *locale* (a veritable camel train, if ever there was one), can fail to notice the extraordinary likeness between the Sicilian and Australian interiors?

In a sense, had Volentieri not come along, architectural history might well have had to invent him. And now that 1988 is upon us – a year in which, we are told, the greatest gift we can solicit for ourselves is a truly great, truly Australian creative genius – it seems timely to revive Volentieri's name.

Volentieri's student space works (1941–3) have not survived, but we do have a brief account of his Palladian phase (1943–4) in that antipodean Pevsner, *The Plains*, by Gerald Murnane. Already, in Murnane's account, we discern preoccupations that were to become the signature of Volentieri's mature work. There is the complete absence of what might be called 'outside'. Walls are dissolved to create a diffused sense of extended presence. Murnane grasped this perfectly when, looking through the library window towards sunset, he 'would have taken all the pale markings for remote shreds of cloud, except that as I walked away one of them remained fixed in the glass while the image of the sky around it changed with every step I took'.

As this passage suggests, from the beginning the perception of

Volentieri's work was dependent on movement. The dweller's sense of architectural stability was a product of his willingness to engage in what Volentieri called 'inner migration'. No wonder, then, that Volentieri found himself out of sympathy with the post-war cult of *placism*, which held that every place had its own individual *spirit*, which it was the artist's task to paint, describe or, in the jargon of the time, 'capture'. The effects of this doctrine were catastrophic. Artistic debate was reduced to little more than a swapping of invitations to come and stay, a comparing of bird lists, and apparently inexhaustible inventories of 'views from my window'. But how much has changed? It is unfortunately true that Volentieri's neglected manifesto, *The Unspeakability of Places* (1951), is more relevant today than ever.

Volentieri's first post-manifesto commission was the logical consequence of his rejection of placism. *The Moving Journey* (1953–5) arose out of a commission to design a suitable memorial to one of Victoria's most illustrious explorers, Sir Thomas Mitchell (1792–1855). The Victorian government was anxious to commemorate this most important, if cantankerous, of founding figures on the centenary of his death. It was proposed to trace the explorer's outward path, a rough diagonal from Swan Hill on the Murray to Portland in the extreme south-west, perhaps with a bicycle track or a special tourist route. Whatever Vincenzo's motives – the project lay well outside his earlier interests – he successfully tendered for the job.

All went smoothly at first. The Transport Minister declared himself delighted when, within a few months, Volentieri proposed a scheme that would (in the architect's words) 'preserve for all time a unique historical experience' while providing the people of Victoria with a monument of 'enduring interest and value in the future'. Imagine, then, the Premier's horror when, less than a week before the official opening, it was drawn to his attention that Volentieri's new work was *not* a triumphal procession but a network of existing *alternative* routes. An official inquiry was set up; the project was cancelled.

Volentieri's career may have been in ruins, his personal life in tatters; it is true he suffered many months of disabling depression. Still, all was not lost. At the official inquiry, he was obliged to explain his ideas, and as a result posterity is able to gain a glimpse into the creative world of one of this country's greatest minds.

Volentieri explained how the exploratory charge of Mitchell's journey was best kept alive by *diverting* travellers into other roads (as he said, 'The Surveyor did not take a camera with him'). The pious, and too easy, retracing of Sir Thomas's footsteps would, he argued, turn the explorer's route into another road. By contrast, his design restored, to some of Victoria's thoroughfares at least, their explorational interest (he also advocated the removal of signposts) *and* kept Mitchell's achievement intact for future generations. As Volentieri later wrote, 'My network of routes, with its permanently changing spectacle of buses, cars and motorcycles criss-crossing each other's (invisible) tracks is, as it were, a mass-kinetic image of exploration. Not only is it truly representative of Mitchell's experience, it is a thoroughly democratic form of memorial.'

If a civilized climate maintains the rivers of tradition, respects and regularly replenishes the reservoirs of intellectual achievement, then ours cannot be said to be civilized. We have been, historically speaking, prone to periodic droughts. Our poets have gone unread, even unpublished; our early artists have been derided for their colonial vision, when in reality the faulty perspective has been ours. For, as regularly as a kind of amnesia has gripped us, so we have looked overseas for ideas with which to populate the desert of our forgetfulness. And, all too often, these fashions, released into our pastures like flocks of sheep, have wandered over the fragile surface of our culture, destroying its delicate equilibrium, effacing every trace of earlier occupation and alternative routes.

It was in this context that Volentieri set about constructing his now-celebrated *Originarium*, the 'history machine' as he later referred to it. The *Originarium* was developed in response to a growing need for conference centres, and was conceived as an authentically *acoustic* public space. As he pointed out, speaking places conceived geometrically and visually failed to take account of how Australia first came into the orbit of civilized discourse, and therefore rendered truly Australian speaking out of the question. Volentieri was in the habit of quoting 'typical' passages from the early travel literature to support his contention that any building that laid claim to historical accuracy was, first and foremost, a sound house, and not necessarily visible.

The *Originarium*'s dimensions were to be determined by the carrying distance of the human voice. It was intended to exploit the sum of echoes arising from any given congregation of voices and to reflect them back into the field of debate. The idea was to set up a constant dialectical exchange between the twin 'origins' of meaning – the voice and the ear. At the time, some complained that such an environment made it impossible to hear what anyone else was saying. As one politician remarked, 'One might as well be talking to oneself'. However, history has more than vindicated Volentieri's vision. *Originaria* have been constructed in all the capital cities and, as a result, the festival and conference industry has flourished. I doubt if there are any conveners, organizers or participants today who would claim – or indeed would want to claim – that the activities they promote any longer refer to anything except themselves.

The *Originarium* was the first building in which Volentieri exploited *grass*. There has been much speculation about the origins of his interest in this most original of building materials. In an obvious, empirical sense, grass was very much to hand. But it also expressed the architectural complementarity of the four elements in an authentically *historical* way: if wind in grass is a dream of sea-borne passage, columns of grass smoke recall arrival and settlement, the desire to bind breezes into substantial shapes – precincts where voices can come and go. In this sense, grass was an authentically Australian material. As I wrote at the time, 'What, after all, is more attractive to the imagination than a smoking chimney?'

Other explanations than my own strike me as absurd. The recent suggestion that Volentieri was familiar with an Aranda tradition that described a mountain springing up 'like a young blade of grass', and aimed to achieve a comparable 'petrifaction', is kitsch indigenization of the worst kind. And I may say that the broken ridge at Mbala, said to be the remains of a grass weir mysteriously compacted into stone, bears no resemblance to any building of Vincenzo's I have ever seen. Nor do I find more convincing the proposition that Volentieri's use of grass resulted from a mere linguistic mistake: a migrant inability to distinguish 'grass' from 'glass'. As if national identities are founded on nothing more than such shibboleths!

Unlike the *Originarium*, Volentieri's next innovation, his *Meteor Lodge*, was designed as a private dwelling place. But, rejecting the conventional house as unsuited to Australian conditions, Volentieri set about devising a house that would preserve the experience of travelling. He wanted his houses to burst on to the landscape like

153

meteors falling out of the sky. They should be unpredictable, like the weather. They might appear cloudy now, opaque as rainforest. Another day, the sun might shine right through them.

In effect, it was necessary to abandon the 'house'. Houses solidified the sky, cheated the seasons, nullified the scent of flowers, creating an altogether artificial climate or, rather, an absence of weather. With their corridors, doorways, cellars, stairs and lofts, they seemed to enclose life itself. Their dark recesses were fantasies of birth; their windows looked through death to 'that brighter country beyond'. They were, in this sense, lives *foretold*. To live in their routine of rooms was to live with no more purpose than a clock pendulum, beating out the minutes towards one's own extinction.

For a culture on the move, one in which new arrivals were being born by the hour (at widely different ages), something else was needed. Taking his cue from the phenomenon of migration itself, Volentieri insisted that the essential feature of 'home' was the sense of direction it created. Birds in flight were not *between* places: they carried their places with them. Sensitive to the earth's invisible roads, its geo-magnetic lines of attraction, they travelled by listening. They sang out to one another in the night, not for solace, but because they were on the road. As a consequence, when they arrived they were as at home as if they had never departed. By analogy, Volentieri argued, a travelling culture could dispense with images of 'home'.

If, like the birds, we could recover the lost community of sound, that bustle of talk that is the sign of places being announced for the first time, we might succeed in creating harmonious environments, not only free from nostalgia but immune to the graveyard rhetoric of stone walls and name plates. In effect, Volentieri's idea was to make places where people could speak *as if for the first time*, environments in which speech would not lapse into routine, where silence would be the counterpart of speech, not merely the absence of chatter. 'Is it fair,' he asked, 'that a society that prides itself on free speech should condemn new arrivals to a generation of self-censorship?'

To some degree, the *Meteor Lodge* was a reaction to what Volentieri saw as the misguided application of his own theories during the early 1960s. It will be remembered that his classic 1958 paper, 'Walking Room Only', pioneered the concept of the DVQ (Domestic Velocity Quotient). The DVQ arose from the observation that no house remained tidy, no matter how many hours were spent in tidying up. To maintain a house in perfect condition, in fact, the house-dweller needed to be constantly on the move. Even then, in houses of conventional design, the domestic velocity quotient (i.e. the average daily velocity required to keep a house spick and span) far exceeded human attainment. It was calculated, for example, that while a mother with one pre-schooler might get away with a steady jog-trot, those caring for two or more would have an average DVQ of approximately 74.2 k.p.h.

The object, then, was to design dwellings that brought the DVQ down to below walking pace. But, rather than recognize this as a challenge to the very idea of the house, architects saw the achievement of realizable DVQs purely in terms of interior design. The property pages no longer spoke in terms of 'room for spa bath' or 'renovator's paradise', but of a building's potential DVQ (or PDVQ). Architects themselves ceased talking in terms of creating 'magic places'; like golfing pros, they simply advertised their DVQ handicaps. Major government building contracts went to the firm that tendered the lowest DVQ, even when this was clearly undesirable, as in the case of the Bicentennial Commemorative Sports Stadium. Who will ever forget that slow-motion sprint for gold?

Vincenzo's *Meteor Lodge* was a reaction to this acronymic madness and, given his deepening interest in flight, it was appropriate that his (literally) revolutionary building should be modelled on that classic instrument of migration studies: the Heligoland Trap. This device consists of three progressively smaller wire-walled cones, laid on their sides, one within the other. Migrating birds entered the largest cone and, pushing along its narrowing interior, found they could not escape except by way of a small hole into the second cone; again, funnelling down that smaller passage, their only means of escape was via the smaller cone beyond. There, they were easily caught to be measured, ringed and weighed.

Here was a device that recognized home as a direction, a beckoning signal, rather than a point of arrival. And Volentieri took the transmitter–receiver analogy seriously: he was fond of saying that the trap's chicken-wire lattices resembled nothing so much as the coiled-up dishes of a radio telescope. At any rate, he conceived the idea of creating a sound house, the dimensions of whose interior space were determined sonically. Hearing and speaking, he said, were conventionally thought of as static activities. But this was a mistake: the reception and transmission of sound was, in reality, a highly dynamic process. Two people engaged in dialogue, for example, might have a mental DVQ equal to, or even in excess of, the speed of sound, yet remain totally unaware of their own speed.

Volentieri used to cite Tolstoy's observation that 'when you fly in a balloon . . . you only feel the wind when you come to a stop'. In conversation it was the same: carried along by it, one did not notice the drift of sound or the migration of meaning. The nightmare of never being able to catch up was nothing more than the effect of silence: clearly, the quietness of conventional houses and the mania for physical tidying up were one and the same. Long before Volentieri, Moholy-Nagy described houses where sound was produced by walking about. But Volentieri's innovation was to envisage a house in which the sound itself did the walking, an environment shaped like talk. Mounted on spindles, breathing in and out like windsocks, revolving all night through our dreams, the *Meteor Lodges* are perhaps the finest testimony to the ethical integrity of his architectural vision. For here movement became a principle of speech and voice a permanent shelter.

Coming to Volentieri's greatest achievement is a painful pleasure. In its realization, our greatest master of space lost his life. But he approached his task with no sense of foreboding. On the contrary, he was ebulliently optimistic, even flippant. *Gondwanaland* was in any case the logical outcome of his two earlier successes. Conceived as a travelling estate, it combined the *Originarium*'s sense of national community with the *Meteor Lodge*'s respect for individual privacy.

In creating the *Meteor Lodges*, Vincenzo had begun to think seriously about the role the telephone plays in our lives. He had observed that, in the conventional house, the telephone is often the only place where real conversation occurs. The reconstituted sound of telephonic communication seemed capable of stimulating a remarkable richness of fantasy, not to mention a variety of tonal and rhythmic skills, almost Shakespearian in their way. It was as if the speaker was *with* his or her interlocutor in a way that was impossible when the voice was *there*, embodied beside him. Volentieri could not help feeling that the smoothness of this communication might have implications for his own work. He coined perhaps his best-known saying: 'A man is not elected without a telephone'.

Telephone wires, he argued, could be thought of as an extended, horizontal ski-lift. With certain safety modifications, tramlets, little groups of mobile houses, could be suspended from the wires. Travelling backwards and forwards, these aerial communities, hanging like Christmas bells between pylons, would not only enhance the visual amenity of the countryside, but immeasurably reduce telephone bills. And, as Volentieri said, 'We are used to aeroplanes and trains. Why not, then, aerial trains offering the delicious intimacy of telephonic communication?'

It was, of course, only a small step from these little fleets of clouds, piloting their private weathers from place to place, in constant communication with everywhere and therefore constantly at home, to *Gondwanaland*. Here was a vortex of shrilling swifts, a community of voices that reminded one of nothing so much as a scene from Alighieri's Paradiso; here was a harmony of heights, as if Vincenzo had sought the architectural form of a Bach fugue trembling through the mighty organ's pipes. Though anchored, how easily these lofty interiors grouped and dispersed, dipped down and rose up! Only by travelling could one remain within their domain; only by speaking could one be at home.

Employing that Fifth Force, long known to the builders of Findhorn, but only recently recognized by science, Volentieri created an aerial community that, merely by the force of its own attraction, resisted the earth's pull. Yet it was a community constantly in evolution, breaking up to form new continents of discourse, new emotional configurations. Like cumulus clouds that in summer days tower up, clench their fists, then mysteriously collapse, *Gondwanaland* was a possibility, a transformation, not a fact. Only those who yielded to its lure heard the 'harmony of the spheres'. And yet great visions, obscure at first, at length filter down, filling the thirsty conduits of our dreams: who now would advertise either telephone or radio without a backdrop of clouds, an appeal to the Gondwanaland of disembodied speech?

Did Volentieri foresee his own electrocution? Strange to think that, in a million households of his own invention, his passing was marked by nothing more than a momentary crackle in the sound environment

– as when lightning interferes with a radio broadcast. Veritably, with his death, a light went out. And yet no obituaries appeared. The media carried on as if he had never lived at all. Even our architectural histories hardly accord him a place. Is this symptomatic of that amnesia to which I have already alluded? Or is there another reason for this extraordinary neglect? Perhaps the calculated invisibility of his work has told against him. Volentieri wanted to create living spaces, places where words rebounded, where space itself stood up and spoke. Like his beloved telephone, like the air itself, Volentieri envisaged a total environment of communication: one in which the charge of difference implied the desire to explore, not the stress of ungovernable fear.

But perhaps we owe this disappearance to our critics. Delighted as I was to find one of our best-known ex-gallery directors hoping that 1988 would bring us 'a decent art critic' (of all things), I cannot help feeling that a decent architectural critic is more urgently needed. Here was an architect apparently *made* for our Bicentenary, a man who had engaged with Australian space as no other; yet we find him forgotten, his work unsung. Of course his buildings are not 'visible' in the empirical sense – can you 'see' space? But for all that, they are not impalpable. Every time we hear sounds that make sense, words addressed to us, we walk in one of Volentieri's buildings. Every time we set out on a journey conscious of its beginning in a word, its ending in the experience of a road truly travelled, as if for the first time, we owe our sensation of being at home on the move to Volentieri's vision.

For Volentieri – and this is a message that we might take to heart at this historic time – there was no such thing as displacement, only a growing sense of the world's insideness. Against the cynics' depreciation of the physical world as a façade of appearances, he celebrated the sensation of the world appearing. As he often pointed out, for the true traveller the act of speaking was the supreme reality – to conjure up the world as the loved one, the one with whom one could 'live together'. The architect's task was not to silence this moment, but to echo it. This is what Volentieri meant when he said, 'My task is simple: it is to preserve the spaces of reality'.

8 Making Contact

History and Performance

> Theater takes place all the time, wherever one is, and art simply
> facilitates persuading one this is the case.
>
> John Cage, Silence

History's formal resemblance to fiction has led some historians to feel
that they must eschew narrative and seek more self-conscious, holistic
modes of explanation – although, as Paul Veyne remarks, 'to explain
more is to narrate better'. But, although the generic devices of fiction
common to a good deal of historical writing has generated some
professional soul-searching, rather less attention has been paid to
another generic resemblance that threatens history's claim to provide
a distinctive kind of knowledge. The Shakespearian metaphor of the
world as a theatre, its great historical figures actors strutting the
boards, may not be taken seriously by historians; nevertheless the
way of conceptualizing events it implies and the assumption that the
historian's task is to restage the past continue to supply the implicit
point of view from which much history is written.

As modes of representation fiction and drama have much in
common, not least their attachment to narrative and plot, but in their
modes of presentation they sharply differ. A piece of fiction may
describe a specific time and place in great detail, but it does not
specify the time and place of reading. Reading is not a performance
and the characters of fiction generally behave as if unconscious of
being observed. But the psychological time and space of the play is
physically contiguous with the location and duration of the action on
the stage. Further, the actors on the stage are conscious of being
seen: they may pretend to be characters in a book, acting as if the
audience were not there, but it is a pretence. If fiction indulges in the
illusion of the unseen spectator, then theatre cultivates a double

illusion: that of the actor acting naturally. If fiction licenses the reader as voyeur, drama demands the spectator's collusion: without a willingness to act his part, to become part of the staged ritual, seeing as he is meant to see, the theatrical experience evaporates.

These differences have a direct bearing on the historical representation of the past. It is one thing for historical writing to fall into the mimetic fallacy of fiction, creating a world bound to the real world 'in the same way,' as Paul Valéry puts it, 'that the *trompe l'oeil* blends into the tangible objects among which the spectator moves',[1] but what if the historical writer is confronted with situations where the tangible objects are themselves illusions, theatrical tricks of perspective corresponding to nothing in reality? What mode of interpretation is appropriate? A mimetic word-painting is clearly out of order, for it will simply reinforce the original theatrical deception. To uncover their historical meaning, it will be necessary to rid historical writing of its own implicit theatricality, its tendency to stage events as if these events were not already staged, already performances.

These apparently esoteric considerations take on an immediate practical value when we try to understand the history of contact between culturally diverse societies. We can go further and say that, without a recognition of the theatrical nature of cross-cultural relations in these situations, the very existence of a contact history may be hard to establish. In Australia, for example, a considerable body of historical writing is now devoted to telling the story of colonization from the other side. This is commendable, but bringing to bear on the Aboriginal material the same empirical criteria used to establish and interpret white Australian history often results in a narrative not of contact but of non-contact.

In consequence, the persistent, frequently melodramatic efforts of both Aborigines and whites to improvise pidginized forms of communication (both linguistic and gestural) are overlooked or treated as the stuff of anthropology. Both indigenes and newcomers are subjected to a form of cultural determinism, according to which they can only view each other naïvely, reductively, in terms of their own rigid, and mutually exclusive cultural expectations. The possibility is never entertained that, on occasion at least, both sides saw themselves *through the eyes of the other* and acted their parts self-consciously, hoping by their performance to initiate a form of communication that might modify the course of colonization and mitigate its trauma.

But first let me illustrate the kind of theatrical event I have in mind.

I

In December 1801 Matthew Flinders and the crew of the *Investigator* spent three weeks in King George's Sound. His visit 'coincided with the traditional summer regrouping of the Nyungar family units' and, unlike George Vancouver who had visited the Sound in September 1791 during the wet season when the local people were away inland, Flinders 'was able to report that the area appeared to be well populated'.[2] After some initial awkwardness – the Nyungar made it clear that they did not want the sailors to enter their camp – gifts were exchanged and both parties went about their business careful to respect each other's space. The Aborigines came to watch the sailors and scientists at work; the scientists took cranial measurements from the men and obtained items of Nyungar vocabulary.

Then, shortly before sailing away, Flinders decided to put on a show for the natives:

> Our friends, the natives, continued to visit us; and the old man, with several others being at the tents this morning, I ordered the party of marines on shore, to be exercised in their presence. The red coats and white crossed belts were greatly admired, having some resemblance to their own manner of ornamenting themselves; and the drum, but particularly the fife, excited their astonishment; but when they saw these beautiful red-and-white men, with their bright muskets, drawn up in a line, they absolutely screamed with delight; nor were their wild gestures and vociferation to be silenced, but by commencing the exercise, to which they paid the most earnest and silent attention. Several of them moved their hands, involuntarily, according to the motions; and the old man placed himself at the end of the rank, with a short staff in his hand, which he shouldered, presented, grounded, as did the marines their muskets, without, I believe, knowing what he did.[3]

Flinders's description makes clear that the Aboriginal spectators did not look on passively. As anthropologist Sylvia Hallam points out, in Aboriginal society meetings between different tribes were governed by elaborate social protocols, including the performance of dances: 'the entire proceedings are formalised, ritualised, ceremonious – a staged drama. The strangers advance in formation, with choreographed motions. And both visitors and hosts join in the movement.'[4] It is reasonable to suppose that the Nyungar interpreted the military drill of the strangers as an appropriate contact ritual. The exchange of new dances was an important means of regulating relations between neighbouring peoples. In this context the meaning of the marines' antics was obvious: Flinders's splendid spectacle was 'a suitable gift bequeathed in exchange for their hospitality – they were being taught a new ceremony'.[5]

The Aboriginal significance of the marines' exercise can be taken a step further. In 1908 the anthropologist Daisy Bates met near Albany a very old man named Nebinyan. As Isobel White reports, 'She said Nebinyan had told her that the Aborigines of King George's Sound believed that Flinders and his men were the ghosts of their own dead ancestors, come back from Koorannup, the home of the dead across the sea. They thought the full dress parade of the Marines was a Kooranup ceremony.'[6] And White comments, 'It is understandable that the ritual they performed was regarded as sacred, to be repeated by the men to whom it was revealed, and by their sons and grandsons.'[7] In other words, by sheer coincidence the Europeans manifested a mode of social behaviour with which the Aborigines could identify. They understood its symbolic value; they could make it their own. Somewhat exceptionally in the history of Australian colonization the Europeans responded to the Aboriginal presence in terms the Aborigines could understand.

But, although the story of the ceremonial drill's incorporation into Nyungar ritual throws a fascinating light on Aboriginal culture, it sidesteps the historical moment Flinders's performance embodied. Retrospectively the Nyungar may have rationalized what they saw, but the fact remains that at the time the military drill was a performance put on *in the absence* of a common language. The ritual meaning the Nyungar attributed to the drill was not the meaning the marines intended. Let us suppose that, for the Nyungar, the ritual implications of the drill were not metaphysical but physical; let us suppose that, for them, the meaning resided in the choreography, and that possession of the white man's knowledge consisted precisely in the accurate imitation of his steps: even so, the Nyungar's imitation was necessarily provisional, open-ended. Whatever the ultimate form of the dance, it was the process, the successful initiation of an imitative ritual contemporaneous with the performance, that constituted the occasion's historical significance.

Besides, what *was* the meaning of the military drill? In putting it on as an entertainment, Flinders subtly altered its significance. The drill was no longer an esoteric military exercise, designed to reinforce group loyalty and discipline: it had been turned into a tourist attraction. The presence of an audience altered the marines' perception of what they were doing. There was the subliminal self-consciousness induced by the awareness that the red coats and white crossed belts had some resemblance to Aboriginal modes of decoration. Instead of straining to behave like automata, the sailors must have been tempted to act their parts, to exaggerate gestures and, as the Aborigines began to imitate them, to parody their own movements. The marines' drill was not simply the repetition of an exercise carried out elsewhere a hundred times: it was a performance subtly modified to make the greatest impression on the audience.

In this sense the motions of the marines represented a contact event. Egged on by the audience, they put on a spectacle that was perhaps both visually and choreographically more emphatic than usual. A subtle pidginization, or vulgarization, of the drill occurred – not least in the imitative efforts of the Nyungar. The meaning of the event is not to be found, then, in an exhaustive history of discipline and ceremony in the Royal Navy, any more than it resides in its future place in Nyungar ritual. Rather, it consists in its ability to create, albeit briefly, a provisional mode of exchange, a physical and symbolic space inscribed with meaning. But the meaning lay neither in the future nor the past, but in the moment itself when two culturally diverse groups of people without a language in common made contact.

2

The Flinders episode was an unusually elaborate, if coincidental, moment of cultural exchange. But similar, less highly rehearsed, attempts to inaugurate communication occurred wherever Europeans and Aborigines came face to face. I have cited typical instances elsewhere in this book – the pidgin English mocked by Robinson's 'natives', the Aboriginal initiation of William Buckley.[8] These efforts to improvise a gestural and verbal lingua franca clearly belong to a particular phase of colonial history; yet somehow the historians overlook them. They relegate them to anecdotal status, implying that, because they did not lead to any lasting result, they lie outside the mainstream of history. Their theatricality has a certain pathos, suggesting the possibility that the future might have turned out differently. But poetic might-have-beens are not the stuff of history.

There is, though, another, more fundamental reason for this neglect. Historical writing is not well-equipped to describe theatrical events. The drill of the marines and the Aboriginal reaction were both self-conscious rehearsals. There was nothing unpremeditated about the spectacle and the reaction it provoked. They were both conscious performances, and the meaning they generated did not lie elsewhere, but in the form and structure of the event itself. In this sense the parade of the marines was an authentically theatrical event. But the facts of history are, it is assumed, not theatrical; they have their causes and their effects, but these lie in the past and the future and are not fully known to those who precipitate them. The agents of history no doubt have psychological motives, but they cannot be fully conscious of what they do. Unlike actors, they are not performing – which is where the historian comes in, for it is the unselfconsciousness of the past that licenses the historian's efforts to endow it with meaning. Retrospectively, the historian may have the impression that the protagonists of the past were actors on a stage, propelled by a script not of their own writing; but the validity of this metaphor depends on the assumption that *at the time* the actors did not realize they were acting.

The corollary of this is that historical events which are recognizably theatrical may be denied a historical status. By a curious twist of logic their self-consciousness places them *hors de court*; as if in their case, because they display a conscious intention, a formal structure, interpretation can only be aesthetic, not historical. They may have poetic, antiquarian or even ethnological interest, but not historical significance. An obvious instance of this discrimination is the way in which authors have described the Aboriginal corroboree. There is ample evidence to show that the corroboree was an Aboriginal counterpart to Flinders's military spectacle: a contact ritual, put on, not simply to entertain, but to mediate events.

Exceptionally, white observers of the corroboree seem to have recognized this. The Western Australian settler G. F. Moore, for example, describes how in 1835, accompanied and subtly guided by an Aboriginal group, he undertook a journey to look for grazing land. Reaching a suitably fertile area, he found 'the natives all encamped near us . . . at night they entertained us with a corrobberry, which was got up on our account . . . The several figures did not differ materially from those which were familiar to us, but the words which accompanied each change contained strong allusions to passing events . . . these ceremonials . . . serve the purpose of historic records.'[9]

Unlike most Europeans, Moore understood something of the local Aboriginal tongues. He could therefore appreciate that the performance he witnessed, although grafted on to traditional dance and song forms, was not a mere repetition, but a unique *rewriting* of these forms specially designed for the occasion. The power of the performers to modify their actions constituted the corroboree as a historical record, the spatial embodiment of a distinct moment in contact history. And, as Moore realized, the historical record was not a reflection on events but, because of its theatrical nature, the event itself. Properly acted upon, the corroboree might have inaugurated a mode of occupancy acceptable to both sides.

But Moore's insight was not shared by the vast majority of white observers. Although no early nineteenth-century visit to the colonies was complete without a description of the corroboree, the event was invariably treated as pure theatre (see, for example, Plate 16). Considerable energy was put into minute descriptions of the preparations for the dance, its picturesque setting and dramatic execution. Some even speculated as to its mythological meaning. But while the writers fully realized that it had been 'got up on our account', they never drew the inference that the corroboree might have a specific, local meaning. Instead – one is reminded of Johnson's dictum that a man argues most fiercely about things he cares least for – they exhausted their rhetorical ingenuity in drawing elaborate and far-fetched parallels between the balletic mimes of the 'savages' and the latest thing to be seen on the London stage. An ornament to the text, the corroboree was purely ornamental.

Nor was this view confined to relative outsiders. The Port Phillip Assistant Aboriginal Protector William Thomas might maintain that 'They have various kinds [of dances], day and night. Although a stranger, after seeing one, may think the whole alike and merely a monotony of sounds and motion, such is not the case',[10] but the more general view – which Thomas implicitly criticizes – was expressed by the colonial surveyor and explorer, Major Mitchell: 'the "corrobory" is peculiar, and, from its uniformity on every shore, a very striking feature of their character'.[11] Mitchell's comment was widely quoted as authoritative, yet it rests on a remarkable act of cultural distancing. The explorer had had ample opportunity on both his first and second expeditions to witness Aboriginal dances that clearly had a symbolic, diplomatic function, and which premeditated action. Nevertheless, he persisted in describing them picturesquely, locating them within a purely aesthetic frame of reference.

In 1835 on the Darling River, Major Mitchell was in no doubt that the 'hideous crouching postures, measured gestures, and low jumps' precipitated by his pistol shot indicated an imminent attack. But he described the scene in literary and theatrical terms: '[it] seemed a fitter spectacle for Pandemonium, than the light of the bounteous sun. Thus these savages slowly retired along the river bank, all the while dancing in a circle like the witches in Macbeth . . .'[12] Even though the object of the Darling people was to change the course of events, to force the invaders to retreat – an aim in which they temporarily succeeded – this did not stop Mitchell from remarking in another place, 'There can be little doubt that the corrobory is the medium through which the delights of poetry are enjoyed, to a limited degree, even by these primitive savages of New Holland.'[13]

Categorizing the corroboree as an 'amusement', a theatrical entertainment whose interest was purely aesthetic, was more than a rhetorical ploy. Placing the Aborigines outside history, it meant that Mitchell could represent his own colonizing expeditions as literary epics. The convenient collusion between epic narrative and the writing of history meant that, while the theatrical treatment of the Aborigines removed them from the historical stage, confining them to a role as picturesque backdrops, Mitchell's own endeavours were defined ever more clearly as historical, as fictions that bound themselves to the real world in the same way as a *trompe-l'œil* blends into its tangible surroundings.

3

Theatrical metaphors not only suppressed the political meaning of the corroboree: they neutralized Aboriginal behaviour more generally. The Aborigines were skilful mimics. There was a cultural explanation for this. As White notes, 'Early European observers, unaware that adult Aborigines were usually fluent in several dialects or languages, often commented on how accurately they repeated English words and phrases at first hearing.'[14] They also mimicked peculiarities of European dress and behaviour: 'Long before cartoonists ridiculed them, Aboriginal communities across the continent were making fun of European habits in camp entertainments.' But such mimicry was not simply a *traditional*, almost unconscious response to European settlement. It was a mode of communication, an improvised behaviour expressing a desire to find common ground. If only because the mimicry was so accurate, it marked a break with the past, a historical gesture. But how could this emerge so long as the Europeans insisted on relegating such behaviour to the realm of the pantomimic?

Early in 1791 the Sydney Aborigines under the direction of the semi-Anglicized Bennelong and Colby put on a corroboree for a European audience. This was not a casual entertainment, but a diplomatic gesture, part of a complex military and political strategy to limit the incursions of the Europeans *and* to turn their superior fire power to account in Bennelong's campaign against his native enemies, the Camaraigals. As the First Fleet's Surgeon-General remarked:

> there was a great deal of art and cunning in Bennelong: he had lately been at Botany Bay, where, he said, they danced, and that one of his tribe had sung a song, the subject of which was, his house, the governor, and the white men at Sydney: the people of that tribe, he said, would not throw any more spears, as they and the Cammeragals were all friends.[15]

But just a few days earlier Bennelong 'had, as usual, whenever those tribes were mentioned, requested the governor to kill them'.[16]

Yet this tactical subtlety, which would have done credit to any

European military commander, did not earn Bennelong respect or political influence. Unable to escape from the theatrical gaze the colonists turned on him, unable to close the distance their way of seeing opened up, he was transformed into an actor, whose performance, though droll and occasionally moving, was not to be taken seriously. Little wonder if, in these circumstances, Bennelong could only gain attention by mimicking himself, by acting the part, by sending himself up. At any rate the more brilliantly he acted, the more certain he was to slip off the historical stage. Apparently blind to the intentions determining Bennelong's behaviour, one contemporary wrote him off as 'garrulous and engaging; extroverted and theatrical – undoubtedly Australia's first great skite'.[17]

Mimicry, the form of behaviour that on the face of it minimized differences, served in the colonial context to exacerbate them. Holding up a mirror the Aborigines found themselves imprisoned behind it; regarded as actors, not inhabitants of a common, yet to be denominated, historical space, they were rendered invisible by the very act through which they intended to be seen. Or, more exactly, they were reduced to a purely visual spectacle, their spatial history, the contingency of their physical and verbal gestures, and the potential dialogue it implied, suppressed. To recover that contingency, to give back to the contact situation its third and fourth dimensions, seems, then, an urgent necessity, particularly if we are ever to make our differences, and not our ideologically imposed likenesses, the basis of an Australian identity, rather than an excuse for further social fragmentation.

4

One approach to the theatricalization of Aboriginal behaviour is to turn the tables, subjecting the behaviour of the Europeans to a comparably ethnographic interpretation: what cultural assumptions determined the European response to the Aborigines' efforts at negotiating a mode of symbolic exchange, preliminary to regularizing relations? Why did they treat the corroboree as theatre – and what did they understand by theatre? This approach is certainly enlightening. It underlines, for instance, that the corroboree, like the 'Aborigine', was a European invention, a cultural generalization reflective of difficulties of communication in the contact situation.

This is true in the weak sense that Europeans *saw* the Aboriginal dances generically as theatrical performances, and therefore failed to understand their significance as means of regulating social relations, treating them instead as entertainments put on *for them*. However, the corroboree was a European construction in the much stronger sense that it was improvised and institutionalized *in response to the white invasion*. As the Victorian squatter John Cotton realized, the native performances were a form of barter. He observed. how, shortly after he gave one of the Devil's River tribe a suit of European clothes, 'One of the tribes performed a corroboree or native dance.' He also noted that 'At the conclusion of the performance some of them came up to me and asked for tobacco . . .'[18] Corroborees like these had the same symbolic function as the 'war implements' and the 'opussum rug' that Cotton obtained in return for supplying the local people with rice, sugar and bread.[19] These items, it seems, were manufactured specifically as tokens of exchange. Whether or not their design was traditional, their symbolic function was to normalize an extraordinary state of affairs – the appropriation of their land – and to inaugurate and stabilize a new system of trading and reciprocal obligations.

Culturally speaking the corroboree was, like the Aboriginal arte-facts, a transitional object, a specially manufactured symbolic event that, quite literally, attempted to articulate the disputed space occupied by Aborigines and Europeans. Some Europeans intuitively understood this and manipulated the corroboree to their own political ends. The Aboriginal Protector, William Thomas, for example, took advantage of the ease with which the dances could be assimilated to a theatrical performance to use them diplomatically to impress and flatter important visitors. Thomas notes in his journal for 18 November 1839, 'His Honor and Lady, Chief Protector and several fashionables visit the encampment and see the corroboree.'[20] As the Chief Protector and his fellow Protectors were struggling to raise funds for their activities, the arrangement of appropriate entertainment clearly had a political motive.

Implicit in Thomas's diplomatic ploy was the assumption that the theatre was a place where people met to entertain *each other*. The performance on stage was, here as in London, a form of personal flattery, a measure of one's esteem for one's guest. The stage show was, in this context, little more than a catalyst, a recognized means of smoothing the way for otherwise difficult extra-theatrical negotiations, whether of a personal or political nature. In any case, while Thomas grasped the exchange value of the Aboriginal dance, he did not step outside the theatrical frame of reference and the ensuing negotiations excluded the dancers.

The corroboree was a kind of spatial pidgin improvised to meet the difficulties of communication in a contact situation where neither side could represent their intentions to the other. But generally it was treated, even by ethnographers like James Dawson – who took a particular interest in the Aborigines' political and social organization – as an 'amusement, which somewhat resembles pantomime, and consists of music, dancing, and acting'.[21] The ubiquitous treatment of the corroboree as a species of theatre is, again, not without anthropological interest. The parallels that writers drew between Aboriginal performances and the latest developments on the London stage throw light on changing European theatrical fashions.

The growing *taste* for native performances in the 1840s and 1850s probably reflects changes in the standard repertory, as well as the technical resources, of the English theatre. The timing of corroborees to coincide with the full moon was picturesque: but to colonial visitors who had recently witnessed the introduction of gas-lighting into theatres it was also intensely theatrical. Gas-lighting could be turned up or down to signify the start of the play, a change of scene or even to create the illusion of sunrise or moonrise: but here the spectator lucky enough to 'contemplate the picture [with] the moon shooting from behind a cloud and showing her bright face' and to find 'the Corrobbaree was announced as about to begin' enjoyed the same effects *au naturel*.[22]

Perhaps Darwin might have been less dismissive of the corroboree he witnessed at King George's Sound in 1836 – 'It was a most rude barbarous scene & to our ideas without any sort of meaning'[23] – if he had had the advantage of Isaac Nathan who, fresh from London in the early 1840s, indulgently referred to a dance in which 'the limbs quivered nervously, and their knees clashed together in a singularly forcible and energetic manner – their voices bearing chorus, as, in rapid transition, they performed a species of saltatory movement'.[24]

Nathan, unlike Darwin, was up to date with the new taste for the melodramatic and spectacular:

> Legitimate drama, the repertory of proven plays which with occasional additions had served the Georgian theatre, yielded to the demand for spectacle and sensation. Pantomime and ballad-opera were already firmly established at the two patent theatres [Drury Lane and Covent Garden]; now melodrama, equestrian drama, aquatic drama, and every kind of 'show' conquered even these sanctuaries of English drama.[25]

In this context the Aborigines' dance made a good deal of sense: 'we cannot better describe [it]', wrote Nathan, 'than by comparing it with some of the peculiar gambols of the grotesque *artistes* of Saddler's Wells, and Astley's Amphitheatre.'[26]

One may even speculate that the political passivity attributed to the Aboriginal performances reflected the newly passive role assigned to the Victorian theatre-goer. Developments such as the removal of the apron stage, the plunging of the audience into darkness during the performance and the insistence on silence served to distance the actor from his audience, to diminish any possibility of live exchange. Similarly it is striking how often contemporary depictions of the corroboree represent the European spectators – the invited guests – as silhouettes located outside the firelit circle of Aboriginal onlookers in the darkness of the night. Hovering on the outskirts, the Europeans remained aloof from any invitation the Aborigines might extend to join the dance; and, refusing to enter that symbolic space, they implicitly declined to enter into negotiations over ownership of the land.

5

Turning the tables in this way certainly highlights the cultural and historical assumptions that determined the European response to the Aboriginal corroboree and associated mimetic modes of behaviour, but it still avoids any recognition of these events as characteristic phenomena of contact history. The dumb shows, the mimetic speech, the resort to elaborate parody: these features of Aboriginal–European intercourse may have been culturally determined. But to imply that these improvised modes of communication were employed mechanically, that they merely reflected traditional practices or were simply interpreted according to theatrical conventions, by no means exhausts their meaning. In particular, it fails to acknowledge the originality of such events, the sense in which such performances were not merely repetitions, but uniquely improvised in a particular time and place.

Such attempts to make contact not only occurred in history, but were historically contingent: they tried to inaugurate a dialogue, that was necessarily open-ended and unpredictable. They implied the possibility of escaping from the two-dimensional world of the mirror into a third and fourth dimension of mutual and mobile recognition. But to recognize this means abandoning history's rather naïve view of historical events. We need a vocabulary able to describe self-conscious events, capable of revealing the subjective significance of perform-ances. It is not enough to describe what they represented or how they were seen; we also need to ask what was intended and how (quite literally) the intention was embodied.

It is a peculiarity of contact events that the dynamic they generate is internal: cause and effect are two aspects of a single event and, feeding back into each other, serve to reinforce its dynamic structure, in the process isolating the moment from what comes before and after. What defines the episode in King George's Sound as a contact event is the sympathetic mimicry the marines' performance induced and, in return, the possibly parodic exaggeration the Aboriginal antics encouraged in the marines. This self-constituting dynamic did not lead to anything: on the contrary, like a theatrical performance, it seemed to stand apart from the everyday intercourse that preceded and succeeded it. Nevertheless it marked a unique and distinctive moment of cross-cultural communication. But in what did the com-munication consist?

Any answer to this question has to begin with a recognition of the *poetic* structure of contact events. To return to an incident mentioned in an earlier chapter, on 18 February 1802 sailors from the survey ship the *Cumberland* encountered a group of Aboriginal men on the Werribee plains south-west of present-day Melbourne. The form the meeting took is preserved in one of their diaries: 'I gave one of them a biscuit; he looked at it; I took it again, eat of it, when he did the same; whatever we said they said it after us.'[27] Even this brief account makes it clear that communication was not a matter of one side naïvely and mechanically imitating the other. It was a question of actively initiating reciprocal actions: so the sailor is not content that the Aborigine should merely look at the biscuit; he wants him to behave as he would and to this end mimes the appropriate action. Yet the object is not to sustain the Aborigine, but to sustain the dialogue, to improvise an internally coherent repertoire of actions and counter-actions that both parties can agree upon. Exchange was not by way of symbolic objects – the biscuit might as easily have been beads or a looking glass – but through the creation of a mutually intelligible symbolic form. What ensured the meeting's diplomatic success was the internal symmetry of the interplay between physical organisms, their voices and gestures: in short, the *poetic* coherence of the meeting.

This distinction between poetic events and merely historical – or fictional – ones is well brought out by the poet Paul Valéry when he writes, in a passage partly quoted earlier:

> While a poem brings our physical organism directly into play and has as its final term song, which is an exercise in precise and continuous liaison between the sense of hearing, the form of the voice, and articulate expression, the novel aims at awakening the general and intermittent sense of expectation which is the same as that aroused in us by real events . . . while the world of the poem is essentially closed and complete in itself, being a pure system composed of the ornaments and happy accidents of language, the world of the novel, even the fantastic novel, is bound to the real world in the same way that the *trompe-l'oeil* blends into the tangible objects among which the spectator moves.[28]

Like a poem, whose meaning is generated internally through the formal interplay of parts, the contact event achieves its meaning internally, through the creation of a verbal and spatial interplay between the different human elements. The dance-like to-and-fro that results is composed of 'ornaments and happy accidents' – gestures and sounds improvised for the occasion – that have no reference to the external world of history or fiction nor any expectation of finding a place there.

The parallel between the performative nature of the contact event and the active self-generating character of the poem is made even more explicit where Valéry writes, 'Lyric poetry is the development of the exclamation'; it 'is the kind of poetry that thinks of the *voice in action* – the voice as direct issue of, or provoked by – things that one sees or feels *present*.[29] The corollary of this view is that a narrative of the Werribee Plains meeting will fail to convey the voice (and the body) 'in action'. Even a direct transcript of the sounds – the repetition of simple words like 'bread' – would not convey the subjective quality of the event, the sense in which sailors and Aborigines responded to things they saw and felt present. A more adequate description of such a scene involves representing its *spatial* dimension; for the essential function of the contact rituals was to open up a symbolic space where communication might occur. The meaning of the event lay not in what was exchanged, but in the improvisation of a space bounded by a distinct verbal and gestural grammar.

If we substitute balletic poses for words, their orderly arrangement for syntax, then the exercise that Flinders's marines undertook is formally little different from a poem by Mallarmé, which, Valéry tells us, 'has no *subject* distinct from itself, but a sort of *program* consisting of a collection of words, among which certain conjunctions [are] *as important as* nouns and types of *syntactical moments* (that is, components of forms) and above all, a table of the tonalities of words . . .'[30] It was not the subject the drill represented that counted, but the internal organization of parts. What signified was not the static pose, the striking image that arrested the eye, but the continuous dialogue between stasis and motion, the balletic progress from pose to pose. If this prefigured Mallarmé's stress on conjunctions rather than nouns, his table of verbal tonalities had its intuitive predecessor in the colour of the marines' costumes, the tone of the fife, the beat of the drum.

6

Recognizing their poetic structure, we begin to see why contact events are impervious to conventional historical interpretation. History is about the past, but contact events seem to lack both a past and a future; the meaning of the performance is conterminous with its location and duration. Again, because its business is the past, history is an interpretative discourse; it assumes a gap between historical event and historical account, a distance between past and present. However, the contact event begins with a distance (a physical and psychological abyss between two peoples) and proceeds to dissolve it; further, the poetic means it uses not only bridges a physical gap but renders it immune to the distant, retrospective rationalizations of the historian.

The contrast between a poetic event and the events of history is trenchantly made by Valéry: 'what we learn from history is not changed into types of action or into functions and operations of the mind'.[31] Thinking of the poem, he adds, 'When the mind is wide awake it needs only the present and itself.' The past of the historians is a myth: 'it is made up of accounts given by witnesses, generally in writing, and these undergo a double selection: one by the witness, which is partial if not tendentious, and the other by the historian. The first is a source of incoherence, a collection of lifeless things. The second is always arbitrary.'[32] The philosopher Paul Ricoeur alludes to the same difficulty when he describes the interpretation of a piece of writing as a special case of 'the dialectic of distanciation' that characterizes all language when considered as discourse.[33]

According to Ricoeur the problem of understanding begins in the act of speech, which implies from the beginning another person, and hence a distance between self and interlocutor. From this original, irreducible distance, which is not only the condition of communication but the source of partial understanding and incoherence, all other problems of interpretation can be derived. The vexed relations between speaking and writing and between writing and reading are only variations on the original 'distanciation' that brings language into the realm of discourse. It follows from this account that what historians need, no less than other students of language, is a method of interpretation, a textual hermeneutics that will lend their readings of primary material some semblance of consistency and plausibility; it was exactly this that F. H. Bradley attempted to provide a hundred years ago in his essay 'The Presuppositions of Critical History'.

But even this brief account is sufficient to show why a textual hermeneutics, however sensitively employed, is unlikely to penetrate the meaning of those self-conscious performances associated with migration, colonization and first meeting. While, for Ricoeur, distance is a source of misunderstanding, for the people who meet for the first time without a language in common, distance is the condition of communication. Ricoeur conceives of discourse as a vehicle for the transfer of meaning. In principle, he writes, a historical text reflects 'a meaningful intention . . . precisely by virtue of the surpassing of the event by the meaning'.[34] But the intercourse the newcomers and natives initiate is, potentially at least, imitative, reciprocal and self-contained. Its discursive model is not the monologue but the dialogue: the distance, the space between self and interlocutor, is not an irritating reminder of the limitations to knowledge imposed upon us by the enigma of intersubjectivity, but the indispensable ground of two-way communication. But for the existence of the other, there would be nothing to do or say, no event, no song and dance.

In effect an understanding of the distinctively theatrical behaviour characteristic of contact events seems to demand a historical poetics – an approach that not only recognizes these events' self-consciously poetic or theatrical nature but also defincs the difference between them and merely theatrical occasions, that difference that defines them as historical events. On the face of it a historical poetics seems a contradiction in terms: however much we may admire the clarity of Flinders's prose, no one would mistake it for a poem. Flinders may describe a poetic event, but he does so as a fiction writer would, by inviting us to see the external world through his eyes. There is no question of his conjuring up his meaning actively, through the internal organization of sounds and sense. The physical organisms he describes implicitly invoke a representational space outside, not inside, the text.

And what is true of Flinders is generally true of the historical sources on which historians draw and of their own writing. Such writings may describe performances but, unlike a poem, they are not themselves performative. A poem may be activated simply by reading it. A historical text, on the other hand, requires interpretation. The point is, though, that, in analysing the events of contact history, the interpretative method has to be matched to the text's poetic content, the poetic structure of the events represented there.

7

One obvious way to elucidate the theatrical nature of certain kinds of historical event is through the analogy of play. It is an analogy that has been explored in some detail by the philosopher Hans-Georg Gadamer. For Gadamer the dialogue that occurs whenever a text is subjected to interpretation is a kind of play. He sees in play a solution to the false 'subjectivism' of Western scientific thinking, that accords the self a sovereign position outside history (Valéry's aesthetics no less than Ricoeur's hermeneutics is guilty of this one-sidedness). As he writes, 'the basic constitution of the game, to be filled with its spirit – the spirit of buoyancy, freedom and the joy of success – and to fulfil him who is playing, is structurally related to the constitution of the dialogue in which language is a reality'.[35] In this sense those inter-cultural moments of mutual accommodation are 'language games' in a very literal, physical sense.

Gadamer's model has a further attraction, in that it seems to overcome the issue of self-consciousness. The spatial dialogue associated with contact events resembles theatre because it provokes theatrical behaviour but, according to Gadamer, all dialogue is playful, theatrical. Further, in play, he says, the false subjectivism of the cogito is transcended: 'even for human subjectivity the real experience of the game consists in the fact that something that obeys its own set laws gains ascendancy in the game'.[36] In play Gadamer's subjectivism yields to a sort of self-forgetfulness, an integration of self and world that transcends the Cartesian split between the thinker and what is thought.

But it is just here perhaps that Gadamer's thesis fails us. For in the contact situation the historical actors are not merely playing: they have no alternative but to play, to enter into a game that will differentiate the future from the past. In such situations there is no distinction between playing and being. That is, 'playing' is not simply a metaphor to describe a cognitive process: in a historical context, play remains irreducibly physical and spatial. The playful back and forth of a tennis ball, the complete absorption of the players in the game, may be a fertile metaphor to describe the dialogical nature of all knowledge, but it ignores the fact that the absorption of the tennis players, their self-forgetfulness, depends on a prior agreement to stay within the court demarcated for play and to obey the rules of the game. But in a historical situation, where the game is being played for the first time, it is precisely the space that has to be demarcated, the rules that have to be agreed. In reaching this prior agreement the historical actors must necessarily reflect on what they are doing and become conscious of themselves as actors who cannot be anything else.

Gadamer's model of dialogue, whether with the past or with one's neighbours, depends on *an understanding of the rules*: play is possible only because the players tacitly accept a distinction between play and non-play. As Gadamer's translator David Linge puts it, Gadamer believes that:

> the game cannot be taken as an action of subjectivity. Instead it is precisely a release from subjectivity and self-possession. The real subject of playing is the game itself. This observation is not contradicted by the fact that one must know the rules of the game and stick to them, or by the fact that the players undergo training and excel in the requisite physical methods of the game. All these things are valuable and 'come into play' only for the one who enters the game and gives herself to it. The movement of playing has no goal in which it ceases but constantly renews itself . . . Thus the game has its own place or space (its *Spielraum*), and its movement and aims are cut off from direct involvement in the world stretching beyond it.[37]

Evidently Gadamer has aestheticized textual hermeneutics to the point where, once again, understanding is placed outside history; and, as a result, subjectivity remains idealized, the exclusive domain of those whose culture and background provides sufficient room to reflect, to play . . . But our events cannot be treated as self-sufficient systems of this kind. They make no distinction between play and non-play. Their playfulness, their theatre, does not stand outside the historical world. It is saturated with the tension of historical contingency. The antics of Flinders's sailors and the Aboriginal response are distinguished by the fact that, as yet, the rules of the game *are not known*. As yet the play is something more, possibly the difference between life and death. It is precisely this that lends the event its historical contingency *and* its power to set the historical actors' minds to work, making them divine the meaning little by little, sharing in a creative process that is not only dialogical but actively self-conscious.

When the explorer Colonel Warburton describes a diplomatic interlude in the native camp – 'We passed our hands over each other's beards, for what purpose I cannot exactly say, unless it was to assure ourselves that they were not tied on; and after this little formality we were good friends'[38] – he certainly evokes a moment of deliberate playfulness. But the playfulness, the incipient comedy, consists in *not* knowing what the gestures mean – whether they are playful or not.

Contact depends, not on playing the game, but on setting up the *rules* of the game. It consists in improvising, and not merely rehearsing, the means of dialogue, the gestures, the sounds. But the very fact of treating these gestures theatrically in order to inaugurate a dialogue changes them. A previously unconscious movement – stroking the beard – is suddenly invested with a symbolic, playful meaning. Mimetic behaviour may have no other goal than 'playing the game'; but the very constitution of this goal – the elaboration of a repertoire of shared gestures – involves an access of historical self-consciousness. The conscious mimicry of voice and hand creates a spatial dialogue historical and poetic.

8

Contact history is spatial history. The meaningless gestures and sounds that criss-cross the meeting space, briefly bringing strangers into contact, serve to delineate a symbolic zone, to inscribe a space historically. The exchanges, whether of sounds, gestures or objects, are like surveyors' lines connecting horizon points: their thickening network of sightlines, orienting this person to that person, this face to that face, help to map a common space, to characterize its behavioural and symbolic topography. Their value lies, not only in bringing people without a language in common together, but in opening up a space between and around them, a dynamic space that, unlike the proscenium stage of later nineteenth-century theatre, kept all the views open; that, unlike the monocular perspective of the ideal theatre-goer, preserved the intervals of difference.

This may be eloquent, but what does it mean to inscribe a space historically? The significance of the King George's Sound episode did not reside in its precise physical location. The sailors' theatrical performance did not sanctify a place. It would be a mistake to think the meaning of the event could be adequately commemorated with an obelisk and plaque erected 'on the spot'. Similarly, although the space it opened up was obviously social, the dance did not teach people to find their places: it did not lay the spatial groundwork for any future social organization. Historical space is not a kind of archaeological site *manqué*, a place of previous occupation that has unfortunately failed to leave behind material remains.

Historical space is immaterial. In this sense it is not historical but poetic in nature. The drama of the space people improvise between themselves resides, as Gadamer recognizes, in its essentially dialogical nature; that is, in the dynamic back and forth of gestures, sounds, counter-gestures and counter-sounds. But even this description needs to be modified. For in a group of people or even between two human beings striving to communicate, the 'back and forth' does not occur like a telephone conversation, one speaking while the other remains silent, and so on. Rather the exchanges are simultaneous, the back and forth being temporal as much as spatial. There is a continual harking back to earlier unfinished gestures and sounds, an endless recapitulation with variations of half-begun utterances, a dance-like circling of ambiguous word-sounds that may, just may, conjure up a common tongue, a point of meeting.

The logic of this playful dialogue is not determined semantically: the aim is not to translate or interpret, not to find a common meaning – if the meaning of this dance could be written down, there would be no need to go on playing – but to find a system of communication where the greatest differences can be expressed simultaneously and, instead of cancelling each other out, be instantaneously transferred from one side to the other. The apparently reductive mimicry characteristic of contact behaviour is a device for rendering expressible the most extreme differences. Although it resembles the figure of speech known as simile, the real ambition of mimicry is metaphorical, in the primary sense of seeking to reveal the meaning of a sign by physically displacing it from its accustomed surroundings. The ultimate goal of such a mimetic system is not dialectical but musical or poetic: to render even the greatest deformations of sense harmonious, to act out complete misunderstandings in perfect unison.

The challenge for early telegraphy was to design wires capable of carrying messages simultaneously both ways. In a sense this was also the goal of those theatrical contact performances: to render the intervals, the spaces between, dense with criss-crossing messages – messages that might be mutually incomprehensible but which nevertheless sustained the space, rendering it ever more vibrant and sociable the more closely its lines of communication were occupied. Describing the transformational power of the poetic mind, Valéry uses a spatial metaphor:

A flower, a proposition, and a sound can be imagined almost simultaneously; the intervals between them can be made as short as we choose; and each of these objects of thought can also change, be deformed, lose its initial qualities one after another at the will of the mind that conceived it, but it is in one's consciousness of this power that all its value resides.[39]

Similarly the historical space of the contact event is a poetic space defined by its capacity to transform meanings, to render opposite meanings equally significant.

Such a space is historical, as well as poetic, because, unlike Valéry's poem, it is experienced existentially as a space between people, and not simply as an imaginary, or geometrical space. It is the intersubjective nature of historical space that lends it its contingency, its drama. Where people of different cultures meet (whether on a nineteenth-century mission station or in the interview room of the migrants' hostel of Bonegilla), and try to interpret each other, 'A flower, a proposition, and a sound can be imagined almost simultaneously' – where there is no or little language in common this is the rule rather than the exception. But the semantic chaos is not perceived as part of a higher imaginative logic; rather, the very forces of comprehension brought to bear on the discourse of the other breaks it up, until sounds and gestures stream through one's eyes and ears like subatomic particles scintillating against a screen, patternless, unpredictable.

Unlike Gadamer's discursive space, where there is ideally a perfect match between player and play, and the communication effected resembles a closed system, the playful dialogue of historical space is fraught with ambiguities, with gestures that miss their mark, with lines that the other side does not catch or fails to respond to. In addition to what is picked up and mimicked there is a supplement of energetic signs that are lost. From Ricoeur's point of view, this is the inevitable consequence of the primary distanciation that characterizes dialogue. But from our position this overcharge of potential meanings that remain uninscribed defines the space of dialogue as distinctively historical.

However theatrical the performance, however mechanical the imitation, there is no way of knowing what is significant, what has been missed. It is this uncertainty that marks the space out, and continually remarks it. One recalls Leonardo's famous anti-perspectival vision: 'The air,' he says, 'is full of infinite lines, straight and radiating, intercrossing and interweaving without ever coinciding one with another; and they *represent* for every object the true FORM of their reason (or their explanation).'[40] Valéry finds in this a model of the poem, but in its spatial conception of meaning, its recognition that identity is not only defined geometrically but dynamically, as a never-ending improvisation of sightlines necessarily at cross-purposes with one another, it might equally be a description of historical space.

9

Historical space is performance space but, unlike the action in a theatre, the historical performance that defines it is always occurring for the first time. Because, unlike a theatrical performance, it represents nothing, it is always under a necessity to reconstitute itself, to renegotiate the rules of exchange. A theatrical performance is perceived by the audience as a repetition. When colonial observers categorized Aboriginal behaviour as theatrical they aimed to deny its historicity, the possibility that something was being communicated here and now for the first time. By contrast, the contact event internalizes repetition: the saying back of words, the imitation of gestures, dissolves the difference between performers and spectators. The resulting symmetry represents the event to itself so completely that any later historical representation must be necessarily one-sided, and lacking its self-referential dynamic.

How, then, are such spatial events to be represented, introduced into history and made part of our contemporary consciousness, without destroying their poetic self-sufficiency? An obvious, if radical, answer is that historians should abandon their word-processors and take to the stage. The appropriate way to represent the characteristic events of contact history is theatrically, by interpreting the written and visual sources spatially and thus representing their essentially performative nature. The difficulty is, though, to conceive of a kind of performance that is not implicitly the representation of an earlier state of mind and body.

Richard Schechner of the Performance Group defines performance as 'restored behaviour': 'Performance means: never for the first time. It means for the second to the nth time. Performance is "twice-behaved behaviour".' He argues that the function of rehearsal is 'to build a score, and this score is a "ritual by contract": fixed behaviour that everyone participating agrees to.'[41] This reminds us of the common origins of nineteenth-century theatre and Aboriginal dances, but it also begs the question of representing a performance *for the first time*. Contact events were not so much performances as rehearsals which, although theatrically improvised, were not intended to lead to other performances. Even as performances, they were never merely repetitions. The past they enacted existed only in performance; that is, it existed only in the present. Repetition was always for the first time.

These points are clearly made by Australian anthropologist John von Sturmer in a recent article on the role of song and dance among the Aurukan people of the Edward and Holroyd Rivers in the Northern Territory. He notes that, whereas songs can be sung without particular significance attaching to them, dances or performances are not mere mimicry but define historical continuity: 'These performances mark out moments in time which stand in memory and which people strive to reproduce from time to time through a combination of bodily and group techniques.' But the stress here is on the originality of these reproductions, which derives from the physical nature of the performance and the context in which it occurs: 'Here the body speaks – directly and in its totality.' And von Sturmer argues that, without a proper definition of performance, we 'invite Aborigines to participate in illegitimate – from their point of view – performance contexts; make the spirit subservient to the [recording] machine; and deny ourselves the possibility of ever understanding how . . . the techniques and content of dance come together for the creation of such intense meaning, overflowing with conviction.'[42]

In other words the power of such performances resides as much in the difference as in the resemblance between them and previous events. It is the difference that makes the repetition possible and desirable; and if we ignore this aspect of the performance, we miss not only its spiritual meaning but its profoundly historical significance. *Mutatis mutandis*, the same would apply to the spatial representation of contact events: a slavish imitation might succeed in reproducing every aspect of costume, movement and sound with complete historical accuracy. It might even succeed in creating a spectacle visually indistinguishable from the event it was based on, but this very attention to detail, this suppression of difference, would mean that the performance was merely a historical enactment and failed to make the original event present as if for the first time.

The point is that any performance that does not make the physical body, and the space contingent on the body's gestures and voice, the central event merely represents the past, and, as such, has no greater claim to authority than the literary description on which it is based. The early Victorian composer Isaac Nathan, who arranged a number of Aboriginal 'songs' for pianoforte, ingenuously illustrates this point when he writes: 'One of them who alternately laughed and wept from excessive joy, at hearing his own native melody, sung and accompanied by us on our Piano Forte, most positively affirmed that "Koorinda-braia" [a phrase repeated over and over in Nathan's setting] meant nothing more or less than the red and white chalk with which they paint their faces on days of festivity.'[43] Nothing could demonstrate more clearly the fallacy of dissociating any element of the dance from its physical and ceremonial context.

Although Nathan's report is enigmatic, it suggests that, as in a contact event, the various elements of the Aboriginal performance were self-referential rather than representational. The marks on the body could be construed as a kind of score; or, more exactly, the body itself was an instrument scored to move and sing. But none of this spatial meaning would be preserved merely by recording the song. And again, by extension, any historical performance must not simply be 'twice behaved behaviour', but must reveal its own scoring, the steps by which the dance was generated. In the context of representing primarily spatial events, such a performance would not focus on the dancers but on the choreography of space as such. For it is precisely space, the invisible medium of communication, that such events score. But that score exists nowhere except in the unique configuration of bodies and voices that inscribes it with historical significance. Consequently every later interpretation of the event must begin and end in the recovery of history as space.

In his 'Conversation on History', Valéry reports a 'quip of Henri Poincaré's on Carlyle': 'The Scottish historian was walking past the bridge at Montereau. "To think," he said with deep feeling, "that

John the Fearless, Duke of Burgundy, once crossed this very bridge, just before he was murdered." And Poincaré added, as a physicist: "Cheer up! He won't do it again." '[44] Valéry tells the story to reinforce his argument that history's claim to provide useful precedents, bringing the past to bear practically on our present actions, is illusory. History never repeats itself: a truism that, for Valéry, reflects not so much on the nature of time as on the character of the *language* in which history is written.

But perhaps Poincaré (and Valéry) missed the point. Carlyle's thrill at walking in the footsteps of the great may have been naïve, but it was, maybe, the frisson of difference that moved him, not his power of identification. Here was the place, and yet it was not the place, for it was empty now, merely a stage: what survived, what linked him historically to the unhappy duke, was the architecturally inscribed physical and existential space that, as he strode out, billowed around him and closed behind. It was the spontaneous identification of his memory with his footsteps that moved Carlyle, the intuition that spaces were scores and historians the instruments tuned to play them. Briefly the historian embodied his thought. He had the sensation of history occurring now, again for the first time.

9 Post-Colonial Collage

Aspects of a Migrant Aesthetic

> The experience of my reader shall be between the phrases, in the silence, communicated by the intervals, not the terms, of the statement . . .
>
> Samuel Beckett, *Disjecta*

In my radio and performance scripts an impression of many voices criss-crossing each other, an illusion of dialogue, is created, not by multiplying characters, but by cutting up lines that a less *cubist* author might have assigned to one actor, disposing them instead over time and interleaving them with other similarly fragmented utterances.[1] The effect is to introduce noise into the system: previously unrelated statements are brought into apparently meaningless conjunction and, cut up and rearranged, made to yield a new and (one hopes) poetic sense. The new meaning resides less in a fresh intellectual synthesis than in the discovery within the patterns of interference of a musical order, a grammar of sounds that is usually sublimated or suppressed.

This collaging of 'found objects' (historical sources, literary texts, my own earlier writings) is hardly an original compositional method, but the particular qualities of the colonial materials on which these scripts largely draw and the post-colonial context in which they are written creates an effect remote from that intended by a Max Ernst or an Ezra Pound. For the Modernists collage was a disruptive device, a mechanism for undermining bourgeois notions of representation and tradition. It existed in a dialectical relationship with these notions. Ernst, for example, described collage in frankly Hegelian terms as a mechanism whereby an image could 'pass from its false absolute, through a series of relative values, into a new absolute value, true and poetic'. The resulting synthesis, 'the coupling of two realities', resembled, he thought, the act of love.[2]

But in a post-colonial society (which means in Australia a migrant society), it is quite different. Here collage is the *normal* mode of constructing meaning. Everyday speech does not flower out of any deeply held and mutually shared unconscious grammar but is patched together from heterogeneous lexical, syntactic and grammatical sources that are generally reproduced imitatively, without any sense of context. Visually, one need only think of our major suburban streets, with their eclectic mix of commercial signs, advertising hoardings and historically parodic architectural styles. In this context to use collage as a compositional technique is no longer to borrow a radically disruptive tool: it is merely to imitate things as they are and, what's more, to mirror them without any obvious addition of meaning.

To reinvigorate collage it is necessary to place the emphasis, not (as Ernst does) on its synthetic power, but on the logic of its fragmentation. Stylistically, post-colonial collage fragments the semiotic field exactly as a commercial radio station does or the front page of a newspaper or a car journey downtown. The difference lies in its attention to the fissures, its interest in mapping the gaps, the interzones where discontinuities are suppressed, but where possibly the resulting silences may speak more eloquently of our condition than the Martian images flashing on and off round what Ernst calls 'the planes of non-agreement'. Rather than recompose disparate realities, the goal of this collage is to decompose them further, to relocate and sound the spaces in-between.

Modernist collage takes to its logical, or illogical, conclusion the rhetorical device of quotation. The historian or orator sets his quotations like jewels in the crown of his discourse. They enliven his remarks; they lend his argument literary and historical authority. But, as Walter Benjamin understood, quotations also signify the passage of memory from the oral to the written: they revive a historical event, but they also bear witness to the fact that the event has passed out of living memory.[3] Seizing on this paradox, the Modernists aimed to prise quotations from their historical matrix, to display the jewels without the rhetorical crown. The very absence of a linear discourse linking them would revitalize these texts, revealing their metonymic potential so that they resonated with intimations of the whole in a way that was impossible when they were buried beneath later layers of language. As Mandelstam observed, a 'quotation is not an excerpt. A

187

quotation is a cicada. Its natural state is that of unceasing sound. Having once seized hold of the air, it will not let it go.'[4]

But our situation is different because the historical and literary material is different. Many of the colonial sources for our history *begin* as quotations. This is true in the simple sense that some of the most poetic, if also absurd, records of the early contact period are contained in the Aboriginal grammars and vocabularies compiled by nineteenth-century missionaries. Aboriginal phrases, literally translated to illustrate a grammatical point, yield expressions so incongruous that their meaning must be assumed to lie somewhere else, in a contact history that has not been reproduced. Sentences such as 'He was between kangaroos' or 'Give him a stone' are already quotations out of context;[5] their absurd interference of lexical and grammatical elements is already a kind of collage.

Larger, narrative units are often no more self-explanatory. The following anecdote stands by itself in parenthesis in an appendix to a well-researched study of the Wotjabaluk people who originally inhabited north-western Victoria: 'Jowley did not like to be called "Jowley", but if one called him it, he'd call you Jowley. If you called him Mr. McGuinness, he'd call you Mr. Hatcher, and if you called him his most preferred name "Mac" he'd call you Mac.'[6] This reads like a fragment taken out of context. But there is no context. We can identify both Mr Hatcher and Mr McGuinness as former employers of Jowley. And perhaps Jowley disliked reference being made to his double chin. But the meaning of the anecdote remains obscure: the grammatical form looks logical, but the content renders it illogical or at least incongruous. Again two linguistic elements brought into arbitrary conjunction create an absurdity resembling the effect of collage.

When pressed to justify his apparently chaotic collaging of voices, languages and historical sources, Pound compared the effect he intended to that of listening to radio: 'there ain't no key. Simplest parallel I can give is radio where you tell who is talking by the noise they make'.[7] Perhaps Pound anticipated its technical meaning in information theory when he used the term 'noise', perhaps he simply referred to such vocal qualities as accent, pitch and timbre. But the ambiguity is convenient and underlines the difference between his sources and the motivation of his fragmentation of them and our own situation.

Pound, Joyce and Eliot could afford to introduce 'noise' into their writing, through the device of elaborate quotation and cross-reference, because they embraced a poetics of *eloquence*. Eloquence was the criterion that determined their choice of texts: Homer, Virgil, Dante and Shakespeare, even the Troubadour poets and quattrocento humanists like Sigismondo and Valla. These writers had been taken over and entombed by history. The resurrection of their words depended on isolating their intrinsically poetic qualities. The non-linear logic of collage was a means of liberating them from the 'false absolute' of history and replacing them in a context, where they achieved a 'new absolute value, poetic and true'.

But the materials for a post-colonial collage cannot be treated in this way: the stilted exchanges between two migrants, the enigmatic Aboriginal vocabularies compiled by nineteenth-century missionaries, the post-modern newspeak of TV and radio commentators – these sources *begin* as noise, as utterances whose original eloquence has already been lost. It is even misleading to attribute to them a lost eloquence, as if a judicious writing up of them – whether in the form of history or drama – can translate them back into their original tongue. Unlike Pound's quotations, quoted words like 'Mac' or 'Mr. Hatcher', do not allude metonymically to a lost, but presumably more eloquent, context of understanding. Beneath and behind them spreads a widening cone of silence, of hostility and mutual incomprehension. And this is true of the anecdote as a whole: it is a quotation without a source; its eloquence resides in its self-parody, in the disjunction between its internal parts, in its isolation on the page.

The inspiration of the *Cantos* may have come, as Eliot said, from Pound's 'knowledge of history'[8] but, as those who heard him read attest, the arrangement of material was always driven by a desire to clarify a contemporary (and perhaps universal) poetics, a mode of phrasing analogous to what in music Pound called 'absolute rhythm'. Now in the end this is our goal as well, to find a rhythm or repertoire of rhythms that may provide the ground of true exchange between people (or voices) who in our history have not had a language in common. But to approach this goal we have, amongst other things, to abandon the Modernist distinction between poetry and history.

For Valéry, as for Eliot, history was anti-poetic: the transcendental qualities they attributed to poetry were a means of overcoming the alienation modern, and sensitive, men felt in contemplating a historical past at once stupidly remote and oppressively influential. 'There are occasions', says Sir Claude, just one of the frustrated artists in Eliot's *The Confidential Clerk*,

> When I am transported – a different person,
> Transfigured in the vision of some marvellous creation,
> And I feel what the man must have felt when he made it.
> . . . when I am alone, and look at one thing long enough,
> I sometimes have that sense of identification
> With the maker, of which I spoke – an agonising ecstasy
> Which makes life bearable.[9]

On occasions like these poetry and the poetic sensibility resonate in sympathy and succeed in transcending the interference patterns of a history that normally renders us deaf to our deepest desires.

But our situation is different: without a language in common, we can have no certainty that the sensation of becoming 'a different person' in the presence of a work of art is synonymous with a 'sense of identification/ With the maker'. Sir George Grey was impressed by the Wandjina figures, but it did not enable him to identify with their makers. Eliot's emotional transport assumes a common language, a shared tradition of artistic expression, but it is precisely these that our post-colonial society lacks – or possesses only eclectically, pre-collaged, as accidental products of our history.

In a suddenly emotional passage in 'The Presuppositions of Critical History', F. H. Bradley (the subject of Eliot's Harvard thesis) explained the historian's motivation: 'it is ourselves that we seek in the perished (and is there anything else which we seek?); if the object of our endeavour is to breathe the life of the present into the death of the past, and re-collect·this into the pantheon of the mind the temporal existences which once seemed mortal; – then, where we encounter an alien element which we cannot recognise as akin to ourselves, the interest fails, the hope and purpose which inspired us dies, and the endeavour is thwarted.'[10] But in a society that lodges a multiplicity of traditions and which, rather than espousing a single language, lives *between* languages, the transcendental simplicity of Bradley's vision fails.

We begin where he stops: with the 'alien element', the incongruous expression that fails to speak to us in our own language. It is the resistance of the past that attracts us to it, its lack of eloquence; and, if it is ourselves we recognize there, then it is a migrant self aware it does not speak the language of the country. There is no question of making the past present to ourselves through the transcendental medium of poetry; for our past (and our present) lacks the eloquence essential to that mode of recovery. Any recovery will be historical, dwelling on the difference of the source material, the distance that isolates it from its textual surroundings and which prevents us from entering into easy dialogue with it.

But what kind of historical recovery is envisaged here? Not the poetic history of Bradley, which assimilates the voices of the past to the educated tones and accents of the present. But not, on the other hand, the prosaic monologue of the master historian, carefully contextualizing, ingeniously ironing out differences in the interests of his grand narrative. The poetic history of Bradley, the collaged treatment of sources by Eliot and Pound, are implicitly dramatic. They make the past present by dramatizing it as an arrangement of voices; they create an imaginary theatre where previously isolated monological texts are brought into dialogue with one another; and where, as a result, superficial differences yield deeper likenesses, profound vibrations uniting them. By this poetic synthesis historical differences are transformed into a pattern of equivalences.

In a migrant context, though, the assumption of ultimate equivalence has to be dramatized and dethroned; the meaning of our writing will not be recovered simply by setting it for voices, by recovering the lost context of meaning dialogically. Coleridge, it may be remembered, distinguished between the lower unity of history 'resulting from succession' and historic drama's 'unity of a higher order . . . which presents men in their causative character'.[11] But the assumption that human behaviour is causative, that its manifestations can therefore be translated and represented, may be the very means of obscuring further its obscurity.

To dramatize, say, the Jowley anecdote, turning the writer and 'Jowley' into two characters taking part in a dialogue is already to take sides with the ideology of equivalence. It may look as if Jowley is given a voice of his own, but this is not so: he is simply allowed *to speak English*. This may endow him with a theatrical eloquence, but it also serves to disguise the fact that Jowley's English parodied English. The true character whose behaviour is subjected to scrutiny in the Jowley story is neither the narrator nor Jowley: it is the language of power. What is the characteristic mode of communication in the contact situation if not the interrogation? Jowley's responses mock its pseudo-scientific solemnity. Jowley refuses to speak as he is asked to do. Although they go through the motions, he and his interlocutor avoid entering into dialogue.

Yet a kind of communication occurs: the very refusal to introduce difference – Jowley's resolve to say back whatever word is said to him – dramatizes difference. The closed circuit of a dialogue that is not dialectical but imitative or echoic draws attention to an assumption that, in our historical and discursive circumstances, is unwarranted. The dialogical space of Bradley's exchange with the dead or Pound's 'radio' where, however differently they may sound, all the voices broadcast on related frequencies, cannot be taken for granted. For Jowley and the narrator the rules of the dialogue game are yet to be found. In this context, it is the gap between them that the anecdote reveals, the paradoxical phenomenon of a verbal exchange that serves only to communicate the absence of a language in common.

It appears that to recover the unspoken meanings of such incidents a mode of re-presentation is required that is both historical and poetic. The eloquence of such events lies in the silences; and the silences are historical, even if the means of *sounding* and articulating them is poetic.

But apart from the presumption of discussing certain preoccupations of mine in the same breath as the great masterpieces of literary Modernism, it may be objected that the difference between Modernist collage and my own version of it is rather less portentous than I have made out. Isn't it simply that post-colonial collage perversely focuses on marginal events, extraordinary textual moments that are hardly representative of colonial or post-colonial experience generally? After all, despite their differences, people get on and eventually understand one another. Isn't this interest in the background noise, the interference between stations, just another instance of literary decadence, characterized, according to Nietszche, by the fact that life no longer dwells within the whole? The word becomes sovereign and leaps out of the sentence, the sentence spreads out and obscures the sense of the page, the page gains life at the expense of the whole.

The difference is that *we* seize on these fragments not 'at the expense of the whole' but in its absence. The fragmentation of discourse, the clinging to words amid the shipwreck of grammar on a sea that offers no contextual landmarks, is not a rare or paranoic condition. It characterizes everyday contact, not just in the remote colonial past, but in the post-colonial present where even those who claim English as their first language do not live *in* language, but speak reluctantly, falteringly, as if speech were foreign to them and did not prophesy their personal fate. They do not speak as if words rose within them, eloquently, poetically, according to an unconscious metre; rather you see them watching your lips, silently rehearsing phrases as if they stood there before their eyes, as difficult as the writing on Belshazzar's wall, and as threatening. Here the book has had most of its pages excised; the pages that survive have had the key sentences underlined; the chief words in those sentences have all been glossed in the margins.

Of course there is a certain guilt attached to this linguistic withdrawal. The lexicon with its Byzantine pursuit of semantic distinctions, the analytical grammar, with its insistence on the logical organization of the parts of speech, retain a certain patriarchal authority. It is hard to admit that words no longer represent meanings, but are a smokescreen concealing the dissolution of reference. Yet, if there is any doubt of this, it is enough to glance at any bureaucratic document. A major limitation of pidgin languages is said to be their inability to generate abstract terms. Yet in the policy statements of our social services, planning and education departments it is precisely the pidginization of abstract nouns that we witness. Synonyms are collaged (for no intervening sentence structure serves to reveal the tautologous nature of their lists of goals and priorities) in a way that shows they are for the writer utterly opaque – pure abstractions that have no meaning in everyday speech or experience.

But this sensation that language no longer functions non-contextually, but is become a gestural, almost physical device – the piling up of words and lists (a feature of the baroque style favoured by our novelists as well as our policy-makers) being intended to convey an emotion rather than any definite proposition – a development akin to that which, according to Herder, marked the *beginning* of language – 'These sighs, these sounds are language. There is ... a language of feeling . . .'[12] – this substitution of sound for meaning is hardly acknowledged. Officially at least we cling to the idea that every sound represents a single word, an unequivocal meaning. Sounds may burst on the ear punningly like a meteorite breaking up but, denying this everyday aural and oral experience, we explain our difficulties in literary terms.

Take the following migrant tale. Its linguistically incompetent subject gets into trouble at work because he fails to understand the carpenter's request for a 'nell'. His wife (the book's author) describes how she pondered the problem: ' "Nell – Nell – of course it's a girl's name – or a word used in poetry which means the sound of a bell at a funeral – he couldn't have meant that . . ." ' She then proceeds to make a deduction worthy of Pycroft Holmes: 'The man must be a Scot and what he asked for was a "nail" – Scots people don't talk like Australians and when they mean to say *nail*, it sounds like *nell* or *nil* . . .'[13] This semantic and phonetic reverie is hardly believable. It assumes an exactness of pronunciation and oral transmission that the context makes extremely unlikely. Still, the author's desire to give the episode a fictionally satisfying form and resolution underlines how strong the urge is to reduce the noise of discourse to the silence of univocal meaning, to impose upon the polysemous potential of speech a literary economy.

It is here perhaps in articulating the difference between our oral/ aural experience and the conventions of writing and reading that a post-colonial collage finds its dialectical role. For in dramatizing the gap between hearing and reading, in refusing to rationalize sounds, recognizing their cubist potential to signify many meanings at once (and to intend none of them), collage reveals a non-linear, phonic logic which the unreflective collage of everyday communication fails to recognize. The culture of collage takes for granted the singular meaning and identity of each of its parts. Ernst's conjunction of a vacuum cleaner and a canoe is 'absurd' because distinct connotations attach to both. They are assumed to belong to the real world of bourgeois interiors and bourgeois weekends.

In our world, though, the origins of the vacuum cleaner and the canoe are no longer in the experiential world. They are advertising icons, metonymic fantasies for home and leisure. They are encountered as signs, as gigantic hoarding images riveted to rooftops, as five-second grabs on television. The challenge is not to transform them into something else, but to dismember them in such a way that their structural integrity is uncovered and their deep connection with the world re-established.

The nature of this logic is partly historical, partly poetic – a fact already evident in the anecdote of the nail where the husband's communication problem arises out of a definably historical circumstance, but the regression of a spoken word to a meaningless sound is an essentially poetic deviation. The poetic turn – a willingness to free associate phonemically – is the means by which a historical moment comes into clear relief. But it is not possible to distinguish the historian's 'intuition of the actual' from the artist's 'intuition of the possible'. The historical significance of his experience lies in its revelation of the baffling possibilities inherent in the actual, the aleatory associations immanent in even the most minimal of utterances.

The aesthetic basis of our collage is not primarily intellectual but phonic or musical. In Modernist collage, a new poetic truth arose out of the synthesis of elements that were, from a historical and cultural point of view, unrelated. The synthesis was rhetorical, even (in *The Wasteland*) metaphysical. The poetry lay in the conspicuous, and continuous, transformation of images; the poem was a meta-poem, a machine for revealing the poetic possibilities in the ordinary – it served to prove that 'A flower, a proposition, and a sound can be imagined almost simultaneously'. But our approach to collage begins from an antithetical position: that a flower, a proposition and a sound *are* the same thing. In our situation the attachment of a signifier to any signified has been so weakened that the signifier is a free-floating sound that attaches itself transiently and punningly to whatever meanings are in the air.

The deductive process that led to the identification of the word-sound 'nell' may be fictionalized, but the logic of that process is accurate. In post-colonial, migrant discourse a sound may signify simultaneously an object, a girl's name or a sound. It may *mean* much more: what Croat associations, for instance, did it have for the husband? Or did he hear in the hint of a Lallans disyllable the command to 'kneel', as if it were not to escape arbitrary execution

195

that he came here. But if it means all this, it also means nothing or, as the book tells us, 'nil'.

Beginning with the sound, aware that its significance is so uncertain that it cannot be treated as an image and brought almost simultaneously into conjunction with an unlike term, we proceed outwards imitatively, echoically, punningly, by way of an infinitely fine gradation of phonic variations. The principle of our collage – for the semantic conjunctions that result from these subtle modifications may be 'absurd' – is not to leap from planet to planet of poetic transformation, but to nose our way into the starless interstices which, because they are ambiguous and may lead punningly in many directions, do not remove us from the ground but rather create an atmosphere, the beginnings of an air we can breathe, in which sounds may begin to map a speaking-place simply by virtue of their internal orchestration, their pattern of echoes – echoes which are never simply echoes but, because of the distance they cross, always something else, a clearing of space, a basis of dialogue.

The value of this phonically based collage is for others to decide, but it seems to me liberatory if only because it acknowledges what is usually suppressed, that ours is a culture of coincidence, where meanings emerge out of misunderstanding rather than understanding. Discourse is constantly short-circuited by an interference pattern of phonic associations that prevents the communication of unambiguous *meanings*. As a consequence, discourse refuses to lie down and become a *semiotic system*, a simulacrum of language, silently transporting meaning from one place to another. Instead it disrupts the linear exchange of ideas, insisting on the confusion of sound, the independent logic or illogic of purely phonetic contrasts and coincidences.

This slippage of speech from its mooring in meaning, this substitution of a form of vocal gesture for a grammatically sound language of propositions, is a form of linguistic pidginization. It seems to curtail severely *what can be said*: where a nail may be a mourning bell or a fiancée, it is hardly possible to express finer shades of meaning. The very idea that language may be a medium of personal expression becomes laughable: a fantasia of puns may convey one's loneliness, the cry of one who inhabits a world without words, but the alienation it expresses will hardly help to initiate a dialogue. Generally pidgins are regarded as 'defective' languages, used where 'speech is not perceived as a major means of presenting inner states to the other'. In this context, to insist on the regression of words to sounds hardly seems a promising solution to the problem of saying what our already pidginized everyday speech seems unable to say.

Nor are the objections to a sound-based logic of communication simply psychological or emotional: they may be political too. The migrant, for example, who cannot escape from the initial confusion of tongues he encounters on arrival, who cannot become a master of the pun, may, in future, not be allowed to stay. At least this is the implication of R. F. Foerster's classic *Italian Emigration of Our Times*. Noting that many Italian migrants to the United States seemed content to speak 'a hybrid tongue which meets the elementary demands of communication but has ordinarily far to to go in accent, grammar, and vocabulary',[14] he concluded that Italians did not make good migrants: 'In many things the Italian has the mind of a child.' As he explained, 'What marks off the mature citizen of the world from the child is a certain fitness for dealing with the world's revolving facets, with the changing demands, contingencies, and conjectures it presents.'[15]

But quite aside from the fact that in the post-colonial situation the official language of colonization no longer has the same authority – and, rather than assimilate to a tongue that now lacks resonance, many migrants will withdraw, reacting like the Italian couple in South Australia who at first 'suffered from not knowing the language' but 'After . . . felt we did not care any more';[16] quite aside from this, the object of our collage is not to mesmerize the ear, to fill it more than ever with a buzz of indistinguishable sounds, but to draw attention to the spaces immanent in the noise and to the poetic possibilities latent there.

Cross-questioned by the teacher, a child finds the sums swimming on the page before her; her gaze narrows until she can see nothing. So with the interrogated newcomer, trying to make sense of the questions: his auditory imagination shrivels until it no more comprehends what is being said than a scratch on the record understands the music. But our aim is wide, to evoke the plurality of meanings potential in any situation, their contingency and the possibility that, plumbed for their musical logic, they might express differences, a future other than this.

Far from making a fetish of the word, post-colonial collage aims to recover the spaces between words, the formative intervals of sound. It opens windows on to natural environments – which are never 'natural' but, associated with our history, belong to our future; it lets languages cross-fertilize, deform and reform each other, not with the object of imposing a new language – some kind of macaronic creole perhaps – but in order to focus interest on the occasions of speech. Within the ritualized performances of language, where it is supposed only outer states are communicated, there is latent a deeper poetics, a suppressed logic of association mediated through sound, cadence, rhythm, pitch and stress. To become aware of this bird-like dimension of language is to become the subject of language, not its object, the actor not the acted upon, the singer not the silence.

Not being able to speak a language induces depression; the strain of trying to interpret sounds makes one prey to paranoia. But the strain of speaking a language *perfectly* is even more acute, its psychological consequences even more extreme. It may be disorienting to feel sounds swirling around one's head like a flock of swifts screaming over a belfry, but how much worse to inhabit a crystalline world in which everything speaks, everything has a name and where the slightest movement, the smallest shadow of silence risks collapsing the whole edifice. This is the nightmare of Freud's celebrated patient, Schreber. As Elias Canetti writes, 'To him all sounds were voices, the universe was full of words: railways, birds and paddle-steamers *spoke*. When he was not uttering words himself they immediately came from others. *Between* words there was nothing . . .'[17] But if Schreber's collage of words, his inability to contemplate intervals and causal relations, leads him to seize the world through language, 'as though language were a fist and the world lay in it', our aim is to relax the grip, to open the eyes, to intimate the artefactual nature of our reality and the possibility of reconsidering it.

Notes

Introduction

1 Adrian Stokes, 'Inside Out', in *The Critical Writings of Adrian Stokes*, ed. Lawrence Gowing (London: Thames & Hudson, 1978), vol. 2, p. 156.
2 Susana Walton, *William Walton: Behind the Façade* (Oxford: Oxford University Press, 1988), pp. 48–9.
3 The Sitwell brothers and sister shepherded both Stokes and Walton on their first trips to Italy.
4 Marcus Clarke, 'Waterpool near Coleraine', in *Documents on Art and Taste in Australia, The Colonial Period 1770–1914*, ed. Bernard Smith (Melbourne: Oxford University Press, 1975), p. 135.
5 See 'The Quattro Cento', in *The Critical Writings of Adrian Stokes*, vol. 1, especially Part 2.
6 See Johannes Friedrich, *Extinct Languages*, trans. F. Gaynor (New York: Philosophical Library, 1957), p. 156.
8 Adrian Stokes, *With All The Views*, ed. Peter Robinson (Manchester: Carcanet New Press, 1981), p. 95.

1 Plotting – *Australia's Explorer Narratives as 'Spatial History'*

1 Both remarks appear in an Advertisement in Charles Sturt, *Narrative of an Expedition into Central Australia* (London: T. & W. Boone, 1849), vol. 1, p. 417.
2 For a fuller discussion, see my *The Road to Botany Bay* (London: Faber & Faber, 1987), pp. 122–34.
3 Charles Sturt, *Two Expeditions into the Interior of Southern Australia* (London: Smith, Elder, 1833), vol. 2, p. 134.
4 George Grey, *Expeditions into Western Australia, 1837–1839* (London: T. & W. Boone, 1841), vol. 1, p. 104.
5 Edward J. Eyre, *Journals of Expeditions of Discovery . . . in the Years 1840–1* (London: T. & W. Boone, 1845), vol. 2, p. 113.
6 Ibid. p. 114.
7 Sturt, *Two Expeditions*, vol. 1, p. 86.
8 Ibid., p. 87.
9 Ibid., p. 76.

10 Peter E. Warburton, *Journey across the Western Interior of Australia* (London: Sampson, Low, Marston, Low & Searle, 1875), p. 254.

11 Sturt, *Narrative*, vol. 1, p. 88.

12 Eyre, *Journals*, vol. 1, p. 327.

13 Peter Brooks, *Reading for the Plot* (Oxford: Oxford University Press, 1984), p. 21.

14 Grey, *Expeditions*, vol. 1, p. 401.

15 Brooks, *Reading for the Plot*, p. 139.

16 Ibid.

17 Ibid., p. 125.

18 Ibid.

19 John L. Stokes, *Discoveries in Australia* (London: T. & W. Boone, 1846), vol. 2, p. 317.

20 Ibid., p. 316.

21 Eyre, *Journals*, vol. 2, p. 113.

22 Ibid., vol. 1, p. 265.

23 Sigmund Freud, *Beyond the Pleasure Principle*, in *The Complete Psychological Works of Sigmund Freud*, ed. J. Strachey (London: Hogarth Press, 1955), vol. 18, p. 39.

24 Ibid., p. 12.

25 Thomas L. Mitchell, *Field Books*, C26, Mitchell Library, Sydney.

26 See Brooks, *Reading for the Plot*, p. 92.

27 Cited by Brooks, ibid., p. 338, n. 9.

28 See Donald P. Spence, *Narrative Truth and Historical Meaning* (New York: W. W. Norton, 1982), esp. Chapter 7.

29 William W. Hovell, *Journal*, in *Hume and Hovell, 1824*, ed. A. E. J. Andrews (Hobart: Blubberhead Press, 1981), p. 159. I have standardized spelling, but left punctuation unaltered. Until recently Hovell's *Journal* was only available as *Journey of Discovery to Port Phillip*, ed. W. Bland (Sydney, 1831). Bland by name, the editor was bland by nature, and his written-up version of Hovell's rough narrative loses much of the flavour of the original.

30 See David Carr, 'Narrative and the Real World: An Argument for Continuity', *History and Theory* (May 1986), pp. 117–31.

31 Hayden White, 'The Historical Text as Literary Artefact', *Clio* 3, no. 3 (1974), p. 278.

32 Paul Veyne, *Writing History* (Middletown, Conn.: Wesleyan University Press, 1984), p. 93.

33 Carr, 'Narrative and the Real World', p. 124.

2 Invisible Journeys – *Exploration and Photography in Australia, 1839–1889*

1   Dr Pole, 'Photography for Travellers and Tourists', *Proceedings of the Royal Geographical Society*, vol. XVI (1871–2), p. 47.
2   John Thomson, 'Photography and Exploration', *Proceedings of the Royal Geographical Society*, vol. XIII, new series (1891), p. 669.
3   Ibid.
4   See Gael Newton, *Shades of Light: Photography and Australia, 1839–1988* (Sydney: William Collins in association with the Australian National Gallery, 1988), Chapter 5, for information in this paragraph.
5   *Australasian Chronicle* (13 April 1841); cited by Newton, *Shades of Light*, p. 5.
6   Ibid., p. 62.
7   Ibid., p. 19.
8   Ibid., p. 49.
9   Ibid., p. 40.
10 'The Application of the Talbotype', *Art Union* (1 July 1846), p. 195.
11 Thomson, 'Photography and Exploration', p. 670.
12 D. R. Stoddart, *On Geography and Its History* (Oxford: Clarendon Press, 1986), p. 61.
13 General R. Strachey, 'On the Scope of Scientific Geography', *Proceedings of the Royal Geographical Society*, vol. XVI (1871–2), p. 443.
14 Stoddart, *On Geography and Its History*, p. 75.
15 Strachey, 'On the Scope of Scientific Geography', p. 443.
16 Major Wilson, 'Address to the Geographical Section of the British Association for the Advancement of Science', *Proceedings of the Royal Geographical Society*, vol. XIX, p. 69.
17 For further discussion of this point, see my *The Road to Botany Bay* (London: Faber & Faber, 1987), pp. 99–102.
18 E. M. Curr, *Recollections of Squatting in Victoria* (Melbourne: Melbourne University Press, 1883), p. 116.
19 Newton, *Shades of Light*, p. xii.
20 *Art Union*, p. 195.
21 Cited by S. Wiencke, *When The Wattles Bloom Again* (Melbourne: privately published, 1984), p. viii.
22 A. E. J. Andrews (ed.), *Hume and Hovell, 1824* (Hobart: Blubberhead Press, 1981), p. 147.
23 Ibid., p. 146.
24 Ibid., pp. 158–9.
25 *Art Union*, p. 195.
26 For a discussion of the relation between mapmaking and discovery in the Australian context, see Paul Foss, 'Theatrum Nondum Cognitorum', *The Foreign Bodies Papers, Local Consumption Series 1* (Sydney, 1981), pp. 15–38.

27 See my *The Road to Botany Bay*, Chapter 3 *passim*.

28 J. M. Stuart, *The Journals of John McDouall Stuart during the years 1858–1862*, (London: Boone & Sons, 1865), pp. 150–52.

29 Ibid., p. 150.

30 Sir Walter Baldwin Spencer, *Wanderings in Wild Australia* (London: Macmillan, 1928), vol. 1, p. 54.

31 Andrews (ed.), *Hume and Hovell, 1824*, p. 235 (punctuation modified).

32 Thomas L. Mitchell, *Field Books*, C52, Mitchell Library, Sydney, unnumbered.

33 F. W. L. Leichhardt, *Journal of an Overland Expedition in Australia ... in 1844–45*, (London: Boone & Sons, 1847), p. 118.

34 J. Macgillivray, *Narrative of the Voyage of H.M.S. Rattlesnake ... 1846–50* (London: Boone & Sons, 1852), vol. 2, pp. 267–8.

35 Ibid., p. 242.

3   Culture of Coincidence – *An Alternative Australian Visual Tradition*

1 Salman Rushdie, Introduction to Günter Grass, *On Writing and Politics, 1967–1983* (London: Secker and Warburg, 1985), p. xiii.

2 F. W. and J. M. Nicholas, *Charles Darwin in Australia* (Cambridge: Cambridge University Press, 1989), p. 51.

3 Rudolf Arnheim, 'Space as an Image of Time', in *Images of Romanticism and Visual Affinities*, ed. K. Kroeber and W. Walling (New Haven: Yale University Press, 1978), p. 6.

4 George Grey, *Expeditions into Western Australia, 1837–1839* (London: T. & W. Boone, 1841), vol. 1, p. 201.

5 Ibid., p. 203.

6 Ibid., pp. 214–15.

7 See I. M. Crawford, *The Art of the Wandjina* (London: Oxford University Press, 1968), p. 66.

8 Grey, *Expeditions*, vol. 2, p. 210.

9 Crawford, *The Art of the Wandjina*, pp. 64–8.

10 I. M. Crawford, 'The Relationship of Bradshaw and Wandjina Art in North-West Kimberley', in *Form in Indigenous Art*, ed. P. Ucko (Canberra: Duckworth, 1977), p. 369.

11 I. Tillers, 'Fear of Texture', in *Art & Text* (Winter, 1983), p. 18.

12 Grey, *Expeditions*, vol. 1, p. 205.

13 Ibid., p. 215.

14 Ibid., p. 207.

15 Ibid., p. 216.

16 For this and previous paragraph, see my *The Road to Botany Bay* (London: Faber & Faber, 1987), p. 128, and T. L. Mitchell, Field Books, C52, 9 August 1835, Mitchell Library, Sydney.

17 Sir T. L. Mitchell, *Journal of an Expedition into the Interior of Tropical Australia* (London: T. & W. Boone, 1848), p. 123.

18 Ibid., p. 81.

19 James Smith in the *Argus*, Melbourne, 13 July 1870, cited by Candice Bruce in *Eugen von Guerard* (Canberra: Australian Gallery Directors Council, 1980), p. 133.

20 Daniel Thomas, Introduction to Bruce, *Eugen von Guerard*, p. 11.

21 Alison Carroll, *Eugen von Guerard's South Australia* (Adelaide: Art Gallery Board of South Australia, 1986), p. 6.

22 John Tregenza in ibid., p. 64.

23 Critic in the *Argus*, Melbourne, 5 August 1858, quoted in ibid., p. 8.

24 Gael Newton, *Shades of Light: Photography and Australia, 1839–1988* (Canberra: William Collins in association with the Australian National Gallery, 1988), p. 48.

25 Mary Turner Shaw, *On Mount Emu Creek* (Melbourne: Robertson & Mullens, 1969), p. 158.

26 Bruce, *Eugen von Guerard*, p. 47.

27 Ibid., p. 59.

28 H. Hodge, quoted in Peter C. Nicholls, 'The Golden Hill', *Walkabout* (June, 1966), p. 32.

29 W. Howitt, *Land, Labour and Gold* (Sydney: Sydney University Press, 1972), Letter XIII, p. 205.

30 Douglas Lockwood, *I, the Aboriginal* (Adelaide: Rigby, 1962), p. 9.

31 See for example Rex Battarbee, *Modern Australian Aboriginal Art* (Sydney: Angus & Robertson, 1951), pp. 10–11, and Joyce D. Batty, *Namatjira: Wanderer between Two Worlds* (Melbourne: Hodder & Stoughton, 1963), pp. 39–40.

32 Battarbee, *Modern Australian Aboriginal Art*, p. 12.

33 Batty, *Namatjira*, p. 39.

34 In Batty, *Namatjira*, pp. 39–40.

35 T. G. H. Strehlow, *Rex Battarbee* (Sydney: Legend Press, 1956), p. 21.

36 Ian Burn and Ann Stephen, 'Traditional Painter: The Transfiguration of Albert Namatjira', *Age Monthly Review*, vol. 6, no. 7 (Nov. 1986), p. 10.

37 Daniel Thomas, 'Albert Namatjira and the Worlds of Art', in *Albert Namatjira*, ed. Nadine Amadio (Melbourne: Macmillan, 1986), p. 26; Brackenreg's comment is quoted in the same publication, p. 12.

38 Charles Mountford, *The Art of Albert Namatjira* (Melbourne: Bread & Cheese Club, 1944), pp. 78–9.

39 Salman Rushdie in Günter Grass, *On Writing and Politics*, p. xiv.

40 Charles Darwin, *The Expression of the Emotions in Man and Animals* (London: John Murray, 1873), p. 382.

41 Ibid., p. 239.

42 F. W. and J. M. Nicholas, *Charles Darwin in Australia*, p. 136.

5   Living in a New Country – *Reflections on Travelling Theory*

1   G. F. Moore, *Descriptive Vocabulary . . . of the Aborigines of Western Australia* (Nedlands: University of Western Australia Press, 1978), p. i.

2   Lolo Houbein, *Wrong Face in the Mirror* (St Lucia: University of Queensland Press, 1990), pp. 259–60.

3   G. F. Moore, *Diary of Ten Years Eventful Life of an Early Settler in Western Australia* (Nedlands: University of Western Australia Press, 1978), p. 177.

4   B. Malinowski, *Diary in the Strict Sense of the Term*, trans. N. Guterman (London: Routledge & Kegan Paul, 1967), p. 236.

5   B. Malinowski, *Crime and Custom in Savage Society* (London: Routledge & Kegan Paul, 1926), p. 42.

6   See D. T. Langendoen, *The London School of Linguistics* (Cambridge, Mass.: MIT Press, 1968), p. 13.

7   E. Said, 'Secular Criticism', in *The World, the Text, and the Critic* (London: Faber & Faber, 1984), p. 6.

8   Ibid., p. 8.

9   E. Auerbach, *Literary Language and its Public in Late Antiquity and in the Middle Ages*, trans. R. Manheim (London: Routledge & Kegan Paul, 1965), p. 6.

10 Ibid.

11 L. Nelson, 'Erich Auerbach: Memoir of a Scholar', *Yale Review*, vol. LXIX, no. 1, p. 319.

12 Auerbach, *Literary Language*, p. 7.

13 Langendoen, *The London School of Linguistics*, p. 14, quoting Malinowski, *Argonauts of the Western Pacific* (London: Routledge & Kegan Paul, 1922), pp. 21–2.

14 Malinowski, *Diary*, p. 186.

15 Ibid., p. 175.

16 Ibid., p. 219.

17 Ibid., p. 31.

18 Ibid., p. 113.

19 E. Husserl, in J. Derrida, *Edmund Husserl's Origin of Geometry*, trans. P. Leavey (New York, 1978), p. 163.

20 B. Malinowski, *The Father in Primitive Psychology* (London: Kegan Paul, Trench, Trübner & Co., 1927), p. 81.

21 D. Wetherell and C. Carr-Gregg, *Camilla* (Sydney: University of NSW Press, 1990), p. 50.

22 *Encyclopaedia Britannica*, Micropaedia vol. 7, entry on Malinowski.

23 Said, 'Swift's Tory Anarchy', in *The World, the Text, and the Critic*, p. 58.

24 R. Barthes, *Roland Barthes by Roland Barthes*, trans. R. Howard (New York: Hill & Wang, 1977), p. 151.

25 P. Ricoeur, *The Rule of Metaphor* (London: Routledge & Kegan Paul, 1978), especially Chapter 7, 'Metaphor and Reference'.

26 E. Auerbach, 'Figura', in P. Valesio (ed.), *Scenes from the Drama of European Literature* (Manchester: Manchester University Press, 1984), p. 53.

27 Ibid.

28 Ibid., p. 59.

29 Houbein, *Wrong Face in the Mirror*, p. 54.

30 Ibid., p. 271.

31 Quoted by Langendoen, *The London School of Linguistics*, p. 16.

32 Ibid., p. 31.

33 Ibid.

34 Malinowski, *The Father in Primitive Psychology*, pp. 90–91.

35 Said, 'Traveling Theory', in *The World, the Text, and the Critic*, p. 235.

36 Ibid., p. 241.

37 Ibid., p. 234.

38 Moore, Preface to *A Descriptive Vocabulary*, pp. iii–iv.

39 W. Cockin, *The Art of Delivering Written Speech* (Menston: Scolar Press, 1969, orig. published 1775), p. 5.

6 Crossing the Yarra – *A Local History*

1 G. F. Sydenham, *Notes on the Otways*, annotated by Jack Loney (privately published: 1987), p. 21. The same photograph is reproduced in my *The Road to Botany Bay* (London: Faber & Faber, 1987), Plate 20.

2 R. D. Boys, *First Years at Port Phillip* (Melbourne: Robertson & Mullens, 1959), p. 44.

3 See T. F. Bride (ed.), *Letters from Victorian Pioneers*, ed. C. E. Sayers (Melbourne: Currey O'Neil, 1983), p. 84.

4 J. Morgan, *The Life and Adventures of William Buckley*, ed. C. Sayers (Melbourne: Heinemann, 1967), p. 29.

5 C. P. Billot, *The Life and Times of John Pascoe Fawkner* (Melbourne: Hyland House, 1985), Chapter 11 *passim*.

6 C. P. Billot (ed.) *Melbourne's Missing Chronicle* (Melbourne: Quartet Books, 1982), p. 4.

7 As for the real Aboriginal name (or names) of the river, G. A. Robinson claims that 'the Yarra Yarra at Melbourne is a misnomer, Parahan being the original name of that River' (*George Augustus Robinson's Journey into South-Eastern Australia – 1844*, ed. G. Mackaness, privately printed: 1941, p. 28), while Robert Brough Smyth gives 'Birr-arrung' as the river's native name (R. Brough Smyth, *The Aborigines of Victoria*, Melbourne: John Currey, O'Neil, 1972, orig. published 1876, vol. 2, p. 88).

8 Sayers (ed.), *Letters from Victorian Pioneers*, p. 404.

9 Daniel Bunce, *Travels with Dr. Leichhardt in Australia* (Melbourne: Oxford University Press, 1979, orig. published 1859), p. 75.

10   A. E. J. Andrews (ed.), *Hume and Hovell, 1824* (Hobart: Blubberhead Press, 1981), p. 203.

11   Ibid., p. 211.

12   Ibid., p. 235.

13   Ibid., p. 25.

14   Ibid. But not the wonderment of Brough Smyth who, taking etymological determinism to its logical conclusion, remarked, 'The names of several British rivers, such as the Yare, the Yarrow, and others, as well as many Australian streams, as the Yarra-yarra (flowing-flowing) seem to have had a common origin' (*The Aborigines of Victoria*, vol. 2, p. 5). But perhaps it was a case of convergent, rather than divergent evolution: well after the river's name had been fixed Batman's widow began referring to the river as 'Yarrow Yarra' (see Alastair Campbell, *John Batman and the Aborigines*, Malmsbury, Victoria: Kibble Books, 1987, p. 227).

15   Ibid., p. 265.

16   A. E. J. Andrews (ed.), *Stapylton, With Major Mitchell's Australia Felix Expedition, 1836* (Hobart: Blubberhead Press, 1986), p. 121.

17   G. Presland (ed.), *Journals of George Augustus Robinson* (Melbourne: Ministry for Conservation, 1977), p. 4.

18   Campbell, *John Batman and the Aborigines*, p. 114.

19   A. P. Bell, *Melbourne, John Batman's Village* (Melbourne: Cassell, 1965), p. 21.

20   See Sayers (ed.), *Letters from Victorian Pioneers*, p. 404.

21   Campbell, *John Batman and the Aborigines*, p. 115.

22   See Morgan, *The Life and Adventures of William Buckley*, p. 29.

23   N. J. B. Plomley, *Weep in Silence* (Hobart: Blubberhead Press, 1987), p. 410.

24   Boys, *First Years at Port Phillip*, p. 63.

25   Sayers (ed.), *Letters from Victorian Pioneers*, p. 27.

26   Ibid., p. 404.

27   Johann Gottfried Herder, 'Essay on the Origin of Language', in *On The Origin of Language*, trans. J. H. Moran (New York: Frederick Ungar, 1966), p. 137.

28   Tamsin Donaldson, 'Making a Song (and Dance) in South-Eastern Australia', in *Songs of Aboriginal Australia*, ed. M. Clunies Ross, T. Donaldson, S. A. Wild (Sydney: University of Sydney, 1987), p. 25ff.

29   G. Presland (ed.), *Journals of G. A. Robinson, May to August 1841* (Melbourne: Ministry for Conservation, 1980), p. 47.

30   D. Hymes (ed.), *Pidginisation and Creolisation of Languages* (Cambridge: Cambridge University Press, 1971), p. 134.

31   F. Jameson, 'Postmodernism and Consumer Society', in *Postmodern Culture*, ed. Hal Foster (London: Pluto Press, 1985), p. 114.

32   Luise Hercus, 'The Marawara Language of Yelta: Interpreting Linguistic Records of the Past', *Aboriginal History*, vol. 8, part 1 (1984), p. 59.

33 Ibid., p. 60.
34 Morgan, *The Life and Adventures of William Buckley*, p. 15.
35 Ibid., p. 21.
36 Shillinglaw papers, Box 83, Port Phillip, First Survey, printed Victoria 1878, p. 16.
37 Campbell, *John Batman and the Aborigines*, p. 106.
38 M. Cannon and I. MacFarlane (eds), *Historical Records of Victoria, Volume 1, Beginnings of Permanent Government* (Melbourne: Victorian Government Printing Office, 1982), p. 6.
39 M. Cannon and I. MacFarlane (eds), *Historical Records of Victoria, Volume 2A, The Aborigines of Port Phillip, 1835–1839* (Melbourne: Victorian Government Printing Office, 1982), p. 11.
40 Morgan, *The Life and Adventures of William Buckley*, p. 86.
41 Ibid., pp. 86–7.
42 Ibid., p. 104.
43 I. Prigogine and I. Stengers, *Order out of Chaos* (Toronto, New York: Bantam Books, 1984).
44 M. Cannon and I. MacFarlane (eds), *Historical Records of Victoria, Volume 4, Communications, Trade and Transport* (Melbourne: Victorian Government Printing Office, 1985), p. 110.
45 Billot, *The Life and Times of John Pascoe Fawkner*, p. 116.
46 Bell, *Melbourne, John Batman's Village*, p. 4.
47 Sayers (ed.), *Letters from Victorian Pioneers*, p. 38.
48 G. Presland (ed.), *Journals of George Augustus Robinson, March-May 1841* (Melbourne: Ministry for Conservation, 1977), p. 36.
49 Ibid., p. 48.
50 M. Cannon and I. MacFarlane (eds), *Historical Records of Melbourne, Volume 2B, Aborigines and Protectors 1838–1839* (Melbourne: Victorian Government Printing Office, 1983), p. 586. Captain William Lonsdale was Melbourne's first Police Magistrate.
51 Cannon and MacFarlane (eds), *Historical Records of Victoria, Volume 2A*, p. 177.
52 Morgan, *The Life and Adventures of William Buckley*, p. 82.
53 Cannon and MacFarlane (eds), *Historical Records of Victoria, Volume 2B*, p. 437.
54 Sayers (ed.), *Letters from Victorian Pioneers*, p. 42.
55 James Dawson, *Australian Aborigines* (Canberra: Australian Institute of Aboriginal Studies, 1981, orig. published 1881), p. 111.
56 Cannon and MacFarlane (eds), *Historical Records of Victoria, Volume 2B*, p. 552.
57 Boys, *First Years at Port Phillip*, p. 64.
58 Morgan, *The Life and Adventures of William Buckley*, p. 112.

8   Making Contact – *History and Performance*

1   Paul Valéry, *Masters and Friends*, vol. 9 of *The Collected Works of Paul Valéry*, ed. Jackson Mathews (Princeton: Princeton University Press, 1955–1970), p. 296.

2   Neville Green, *Broken Spears* (Perth: Focus Education Services, 1984), p. 31.

3   Matthew Flinders, *A Voyage to Terra Australis* (London: G. & W. Nicol, 1814), vol. 1, pp. 60–61.

4   Sylvia Hallam, 'The Other Side of the Western Frontier', *Aboriginal History*, vol. 7, no. 2 (1983), p. 136.

5   Ibid., p. 146–7.

6   Isobel White, 'Birth and Death of a Ceremony', *Aboriginal History*, vol. 4, no. 1 (1980), p. 35.

7   Ibid., p. 40.

8   See Chapter 6.

9   Cited by Hallam, 'The Other Side of the Western Frontier', p. 137.

10   William Thomas, 'Brief Account of the Aborigines of Australia Felix' in T. F. Bride (ed.), *Letters from Victorian Pioneers*, ed. C. E. Sayers (Melbourne: Currey O'Neil, 1983), p. 402.

11   Sir T. L. Mitchell, *Three Expeditions into the Interior of Eastern Australia* (London: T. & W. Boone, 1838), vol. 2, p. 5.

12   Ibid., vol. 1, p. 248.

13   Ibid., vol. 2, p. 6.

14   White, 'Birth and Death of a Ceremony', p. 33.

15   Keith Willey, *When The Sky Fell Down* (Sydney: Collins, 1979), p. 121.

16   Ibid.

17   Ibid., p. 109.

18   *The Correspondence of John Cotton*, ed. G. Mackaness (Dubbo: Review Publications, 1978), Part 1, p. 25.

19   Ibid., Part 2, p. 17.

20   M. Cannon and I. MacFarlane (eds), *Historical Records of Victoria, Volume 2B, Aborigines and Protectors 1838–1839* (Melbourne: Victorian Government Printing Office, 1983), p. 563.

21   James Dawson, *Australian Aborigines* (Canberra: Australian Institute of Aboriginal Studies, 1981, orig. published 1881), p. 80.

22   W. H. Leigh, *Travels and Adventures in South Australia* (London: Smith, Elder and Co., 1839), p. 142.

23   See F. W. and J. M. Nicholas, *Charles Darwin in Australia* (Cambridge: Cambridge University Press, 1989), p. 111.

24   Isaac Nathan, *The Southern Euphrosyne* (London: Whittaker & Co., 1848), p. 98.

25   George Rowell, *The Victorian Theatre 1792–1914* (Cambridge: Cambridge University Press, 1978), p. 11.

26   Nathan, *The Southern Euphrosyne*, p. 98.

27 See Chapter 6, note 36.

28 Valéry, *Masters and Friends*, p. 296.

29 Paul Valéry, *Selected Writings of Paul Valéry* (New York: New Directions, 1964), p. 149.

30 Paul Valéry, *Leonardo, Poe, Mallarmé*, vol. 8 in *The Collected Works of Paul Valéry*, p. 395.

31 Ibid., p. 69, marginal note.

32 Paul Valéry, 'Conversation in History', in *History and Politics*, vol. 10 in *The Collected Works of Paul Valéry*, p. 522.

33 Paul Ricoeur, 'The Hermeneutical Function of Distanciation', in *Hermeneutics and the Human Sciences*, ed. and trans. J. B. Thompson (Cambridge: Cambridge University Press, 1981), p. 131ff.

34 Ibid., p. 134.

35 Hans-Georg Gadamer, *Philosophical Hermeneutics*, trans. and ed. David Linge (Berkeley: University of California Press, 1976), p. 66.

36 Ibid., p. 53.

37 David Linge, Introduction to ibid., p. xxiii.

38 Peter E. Warburton, *Journey across the Western Interior of Australia* (London: Sampson, Low, Marston, Low & Searle, 1875), p. 232.

39 Paul Valéry, *Leonardo, Poe, Mallarmé*, p. 14.

40 Ibid., p. 55.

41 Richard Schechner, *Between Theater and Anthropology* (Philadelphia: University of Pennsylvania Press, 1985), p. 36.

42 John von Sturmer, 'Aboriginal Singing and Notions of Power', in *Songs of Aboriginal Australia*, ed. M. Clunies Ross, T. Donaldson, S. A. Wild (Sydney: University of Sydney, 1987), p. 74.

43 Nathan, *The Southern Euphrosyne*, p. 107.

44 Valéry, *History and Politics*, p. 523.

9 Post-Colonial Collage – *Aspects of a Migrant Aesthetic*

1 'Mirror States' and 'Cooee Song' are printed in Paul Carter, *The Sound In-Between* (Sydney: New Endeavour Press/University of New South Wales Press, 1992).

2 Max Ernst, 'What Is the Mechanism of Collage?' in H. E. Chipp (ed.), *Theories of Modern Art* (Berkeley: University of California Press, 1968), p. 427.

3 Walter Benjamin, *Illuminations*, trans. H. Zohn (London: Fontana Collins, 1982), p. 257.

4 Osip Mandelstam, 'Conversation about Dante' in *The Complete Critical Prose and Letters*, ed. J. G. Harris (Ann Arbor: Ardis, 1979), p. 401.

5 These and many other comparably decontextualized 'specimens of the language' can be found in R. Brough Smyth, *The Aborigines of Victoria* (Melbourne: John Currey O'Neil, 1972, orig. published 1876), vol. 2, p. 440ff.

6   T. G. Allen, *Wotjobaluk* (Hopetoun, Victoria: T. G. Allen, 1976), Appendix IV, p. 1.

7   Humphrey Carpenter, *A Serious Character* (London: Faber & Faber, 1988), p. 446.

8   James Langenbach, *Modernist Poetics of History* (Princeton: Princeton University Press, 1987), p. 11.

9   T. S. Eliot, *The Confidential Clerk* in *Complete Poems and Plays of T. S. Eliot* (London: Faber & Faber, 1969), pp. 465–6.

10 F. H. Bradley, 'The Presuppositions of Critical History', in *Collected Essays* (Oxford: Oxford University Press, 1935), vol. 1, p. 39.

11 S. T. Coleridge, 'Shakespeare's English Historical Plays', in *Essays and Lectures on Shakespeare* (London: Dent, 1951), p. 108.

12 Johannes Gottfried Herder, 'Essay on the Origin of Language', in *On The Origin of Language*, trans. J. H. Moran (New York: Frederick Ungar, 1966), p. 88.

13 I. Milutinovic, *Talk English Carn't Ya* (Melbourne: Hyland House, 1978), p. 6.

14 R. F. Foerster, *The Italian Emigration of Our Times* (Harvard: Harvard University Press, 1919), p. 442.

15 Ibid., p. 437.

16 S. L. Thompson, *Australia Through Italian Eyes* (Melbourne: Oxford University Press, 1980), p. 222.

17 Elias Canetti, *Crowds and Power*, trans. Carol Stewart (London: Gollancz, 1962), p. 452.

Index

Adelaide, 12, 30, 83
Aeneas, 102
Albany, 53, 162
Alice Springs, 29, 69–70
Andrews, A. E. J., 127–8
Aristotle, 106
Arkaroo, 82
Arnheim, Rudolf, 51
Auerbach, Erich: figural interpretation, 112–15; historical approach, 125; Malinowski comparison, 103, 105–7; mimesis, 121; writer in exile, 99, 101–3
AUSTRALIAN ABORIGINES: corroboree as theatre, 165–71; exploration and, 11, 34–7, 46–8, 51–6, 57, 93, 161–4; Malinowski and, 106–7; place-names, interpretation of, 84–5, 124–31; representation of, 67–73, 87–8, 133–5, 180, 190–91; rock art of, 82–3; treatment of, 144–5

Bald Hill, 127
Ballarat, 64–5
Barthes, Roland, 22, 25, 111
Barwon River, 126, 130, 136
Basin Banks, 62
Bates, Daisy, 162
Batman, Henry, 144
Batman, John: Aborigines in disguise, 138–9; Buckley capture, 147; Dutigalla 'treaty', 122, 126–7, 129–30, 138; house, 144; name, 130
Battarbee, Rex, 70
Beckett, Samuel, 186
Beethoven, Ludwig van, 96
Bell, Alexander Melville, 79
Benjamin, Walter, 187
Bennelong, 167–8
Birdsville Track, 85
Bland, William, 36–7
Boswell, James, 28, 90
Botany Bay, 167

Brackenreg, John, 72
Bradley, F. H., 175, 190–2
Braque, Georges, 105
Brooks, Peter, 17–18
Brown (Aboriginal 'guide'), 46–7
Bruce, Candice, 59, 62, 63
Buckley, William: contact with Europeans, 139–40, 147–8; life with Aborigines, 136–7, 164; place naming, 126, 130
Bulmer, John, 134–5
Bunce, Daniel, 127, 129
Burke, Robert O'Hara, 29
Burn, Ian, 72
Burnell, George, 30
Buvelot, Louis, 5

Cage, John, 159
Callitris plains, 81
Camoes, Luis de, 10
Campbell, Alastair, 129, 130
Canetti, Elias, 198
Cape York, 11, 34, 66
Carlyle, Thomas, 184–5
Carnegie, David Wynford, 45
Carr, David, 25, 26
Carroll, Alison, 60
Central Ranges, 42
Chambers, James, 39, 40
Chambers Pillar, 38–44
Charley (Aboriginal 'guide'), 46–7
Charlotte Waters, 42
Childers, Gippsland, 122
Chirico, Giorgio de, 67
Clare, John, 149
Clarke, Marcus, 2, 5
Clayton River, 87
Cloncurry, 67
Cloven Hills, 61
Cockin, W., 121
Coincidence *see* Cultural convergence
Colby, 167
Cole, E. W., 30